FL ASSES THROUGH AFRICA

JACK MITCHELL

Edition: First

E-book ISBN Number: 9781540136091

ISBN   9781520119014

Cover Photocourtesy of: Heather Arnold

Cover Photo Artwork: MarnaJanse Van Rensburg
                                      Maun, Botswana
                                      marna@korudesignsbotswana.com

Stipulation:
As a Non-fiction text many of the names have been changed to satisfy possible litigation issues. The few real names which appear the author has received written permission from these individuals to reproduce their names, images, and stories as part of this text.

People reproducing this text without permission will be doing so without the benefit of said written permission!

Dedicated to the memory of Steven J. Hollingworth (1962-2010) an aviator, a humorist, and a friend.

And, to all pilots who have undertaken or continue to undertake Charter flying, push the positive in the industry; all while dealing with those few very special people who are comics, moron's, or racists.

ALWAYS REMEMBER

THE DIFFERNCE BETWEEN GENIUS AND STUPIDITY IS GENIUS HAS ITS LIMITS
- Albert Einstein

Caution: This book contains personal opinions, political views and strong language – reader discretion is advised! Yes, I'm not kidding.Look, these are stories and not everyone sees the world the way I do, so take them as one point of view!

TABLE OF CONTENTS

STARTING OFF

Welcome and many thanks for selecting such an odd sounding title.

Nobody I know flies Donkeys around, why would you? This book is about People! It was written to make you laugh, principally at other people. Along time ago I was taught this was considered poor manners, nevertheless I still wrote the book.

Much of what I have written centers around Air Charter Companies, and their operations in Botswana, Zambia, and Tanzania, colorfully referred to as Bush Flying. Some tales depart to countries like Congo, DRC, etc. Unlike airlines which operate on a schedule; Charter operations are principally non-scheduled therefore their flights usually involve journeys to more remote destinations. Some of us deal with scores of tourists while other pilots fly equipment, manpower and occasionally medical staff. This is a lesser known section of the aviation community and one most people are not aware of.

I have gone as far as including photos pertaining to a given story; as well as other photos that will give you a general idea of the areas I am describing. From time to time I need to acquaint you with other things, sort of background information. Please accept this as a learning experience for the day you decide to come on Safari or fly to some isolated shanty town on the Continent with your selected Charter operator.

I have worked as a Charter Pilot for almost ten years and during this time I have met quite a few characters and seen some very strange things. To be clear not all of these stories are mine, therefore some have been recountedas they were told to me. Regardless as to what the following may appear to bring for me on an emotional level, I have been very fortunate to have been exposed to *most of the people* I have met during this time. This book is about just a few of them and the more amusing and retarded aspects of flying around Africa.

To get you going I am going to tell you a few stories which I extracted from different Chapters. Only then will I give the books 'Introduction'. It's a bit of 'The Cart before the Horse', I think it works but you decide?

Wheeled away

In 2015 there was a pilot working for XYZ Air Charter Company in East Africa – this very real company has to remain nameless as you will see. They fly the reasonably-sized Cessna 208B Grand Caravan (pilot plus 13 passengers) and today the pilot is scheduled to fly from the lovely, picturesque city of Dar-es-Salaam, home to about 5 million (ok, so I may be exaggerating a fraction on the picturesque bit), over the ocean for 20 minutes to the mystical, romantic island nation of Zanzibar.

Cessna C208B Grand Caravan (example only, not the airline in question)

The pilot, sitting in his small cockpit, awaits his passengers whilst looking at the darkening skies just northwest of Julius Nyerere International Airport, hoping he can leave on time so he can get back on time. Methods for loading aCharter aircraft differ with each company. In some companies the pilot stands at the door to see each person on board but this company has ground staff to assist him. Eight people have boarded the aircraft while the last one is sped across the apron in her wheelchair, lifted up the aircraft stairs, manoeuvred into a seat right at the back of the cabin and buckled in. The doors close and the pilot calls the tower for start and taxi.

The flight was uneventful which meant all aboard arrived safely, disgorged themselves from the aircraft, off to see the sights as tourists do or visit family members which are separated by a short expanse of the Indian Ocean. Only one of the passengers seems not to be in a hurry, still seated, belted in, with their head leaning on the window. 'Oh yes', the pilot recalls the late arrival, 'the wheelchair'.

The pilot was keen to get back to the mainland so he called out to his dozy passenger. No reply – the first thought he had was maybe she's drunk. From his seat he called out to the first member of the ground staff within sight to go and rouse sleepy in the back. When the ground handler attempted to wake the passenger it proved difficult as she seemed to be – well, dead. Needless to say this caused a few moments of panic. The ground handler shot off to get a police officer and hopefully some medical help, leaving the pilot to ponder all the paperwork he was going to have to fill out to satisfy the authorities – damn!

In aviation nothing is simple and they have paperwork for even the tiniest thing, so one can only imagine what a death on a commercial flight might bring. Add to this there would most likely be a police interview with accompanying investigation and possibly a coroner's enquiry all in a country where most inhabitants do their level best to avoid getting involved with anything resembling officialdom.

The police and medics arrived and the woman was pronounced dead. The pilot rolled his eyes as if to say 'you hardly need a fucking medical degree to figure that out'. "But", the doctor went on, "she has been dead for some time, maybe a day". Ah, maybe the degree holder was useful after all. It wasn't until the next day, after a couple of interviews and a few phone calls that it was discovered the woman had indeed died the day before her flight, somewhere near Dar es Salaam. Unfortunately for her she lived in Zanzibar and needed to get home.

There are many excellent reasons for burying people quickly. For many western people it is for *closure,* which to me sounds like double speak for 'it's all done and out of my hands'. For those of us living in the Third World it may involve more pressing problems. It could be a storage issue: there may be no space available at the morgue (people die faster in some of these countries than you may be used to); or it may be no refrigeration exists (no electricity, awaiting a spare part, etc). Either dynamic can cause problems especially in hot, humid African countries. There are also the possible religious customs which need to be adhered to, a time frame for burial and so on. Whatever the reason, most families want the body returned home in a timely fashion.

XYZ Company does provide this transportation service: if you charter the entire aircraft they will remove the seats of the very aircraft typeour lethargic friend ended up flying in. The company is then presented with a shipping coffin for the flight home with all of the accompanying pesky paperwork: authorization to transport a body, outgoing Police clearance to take the body from one country to another, Incoming Police clearance to bring a body into Zanzibar, coroner's or doctor's report, and maybe a Dangerous Goods authorization (a body falls into this category based upon certain personal fluids and the possibility of them leaking in the aircraft). Colourful aye, but in short, it's a major hassle.

On the day in question it is also possible there was no aircraft available to be chartered for such work, but a more plausible explanation is the woman's family simply could not afford to charter the entire aircraft, especially when the probability was the breadwinner had just departed to another world (you will find in Africa it is women who seem to do most of the work). The family may have been worried about their future financial situation, done a bit of research into alternatives to chartering the whole aircraft and discovered a single air ticket (special discount for locals) is much less expensive. The police slowly discovered this through their enquiries and were quite admiring of the whole process, especially the speedy wheelchair journey across the apron.

How did they pull the whole thing off? One of the ticketing ladies remembered a ground handler telling her he needed to collect the ticket as the person in the wheelchair was unwell. She also recalled looking at the womanthrough the glass door a thinking 'yes, she doesn't look well at all.' Yes darling, she's dead. In the ticketing lady's defence you shouldn't have to ask if a passenger is still *functional*. Still it's aviation and always possible this will form some part of a new procedure.

Then there was airport security: to get to the aircraft you need to get through the annoying metal detector, you know the ones these days you are practically naked before you come out the other side, sort of like a birthing process. Wheelchairs tend to set those things off; so along comes a highly cooperative airport security guard. In fact he was as cooperative as the ground handler was – money tends to do this. The machine was turned off and the body pushed through. The only flaw in the plan was no one had thought to send anyone to pick the body up in Zanzibar.

So in the end two wayward individuals, along with a down-and out-family (my condolences by the way) circumvented the entire air travel system, shipped a body economy class, with paying passengers sitting right there in the cabin, the pilot up front, and the airline office behind them, all completely oblivious to the whole thing. Next time you fly you might be tempted to lean over and shake the person sleeping across the aisle - just in case.

PS. We never did find out how she got to the airport in Dar Es Salaam in the first place – by bus, maybe?

Free collection, maybe keep this number – just in case

Situational Awareness

Situational Awareness is the idea of knowing what's happening around you and more importantly how it will affect you. As human beings we *should* be highly attuned to this defence mechanism however in general the bulk of us practice it sparingly. The most understandable analogy would be the concept of Defensive Driving. This is the idea in which an individual driver is on the lookout for someone else (and their car) to make a mistake thereby endangering you and your vehicle. In aviation Situation Awareness is paramount and a subject which gets in-depth instruction. Good pilots hone this skill and should practice it <u>even when they are not flying</u>.

Meet a young man we will call Kirk who is an excellent pilot with a small medical issue. Kirk needs to urinate, we all do, but he needs to pee a little more than the rest of us. He's not incontinent but could be at a push. He needs to go every 20-25 minutes which is perfect as most of the flying where Kirk works is reasonably short sectors so he can steal away between landings for his moment of bush relief.

It's late August 2012 and Kirk has landed at an airstrip call Xarakai (pronounced Care-a-kai) in the northern part of Botswana's Okavango Delta and he is bursting to go. He unloads the guests and quickly moves them and their bags over to the Game Vehicle. The problem is the Guide is taking his time and Kirk is dangerously close to one of those moments most of us have not experienced since childhood – the difference being Mum will not be there to clean up the mess.

The Guests finally in the vehicle, it leaves to drive to the middle of the airstrip and await Kirk's aircraft to depart. Kirk moves quickly, basically he's running, for the nearby scrub, pants down to his thigh he releases and moisture rains over the small dry area. Now, as pilots we have these little moments throughout the day – maybe not as often as Kirk, but we do. For obvious reasons it is important you are not doing it in full view of the clients. So in this spirit Kirk is sort of not looking where he is peeing, he is looking over his shoulder. You could say he is practising one form of Situational Awareness.

For aviation Situational Awareness is more about safety and staying alivethan the social niceties Kirk is currently focused on. As Kirk continues to pee, the clients safely away, he can hearthe buzzing of flies, and not just a few, there are a lot of them near where he is. He is peeing into a large bush, about chest height. But now he sees there is something under the bush, it's a dead Zebra; Kirk is peeing on a dead Zebra. The Zebra seems to be twitching, this is because there are two Lions right there, quietly consuming the carcass. Kirk's bladder which was far from empty is immediately ignored and the peeing stops rather suddenly. He grabs the back of his trousers and holds them up and slowly backs away. He told us one of the Lions was staring him right in the eye while she continued to eat. He backed up 10 meters before running the remaining ten and leaping into the aircraft. The Lions didn't move, possibly they had liked the additional seasoning Kirk had provided the Zebra and they didn't want to upset the SousChef.Kirk then sat in the pilot's seat with the door open and finished his pee. This became his preferred method of urination until his Bush Flying job finished.
PS. After this incident Kirk's Situational Awareness improved tremendously.

Sikh out the racists

A group of twenty Americans were visiting Botswana and due to fly from Khwai River on the eastern edge of the Okavango Delta to Jack's Camp in the Makadikadi Pans, essentially a one-hour flight. However, today, the take-off was being delayed, as all twenty of them wanted to go with a pilot we shall call Alan. The other pilot, a Sikh (you see him later in another story as Pilot B), had no takers for his aircraft. It seems pretty much all of them had got together and had a chat with Alan, the consensus being: "We don't feel comfortable flying with *the Muslim*". Now you will note this is presented in quotations so you can fully grasp the absurdity of the conversation these guests were having with Alan in full view of their Sikh pilot. Now I need to address a few points:

First, let's get something straight - just because someone wears a turban on their head they are not automatically a Muslim. Maybe let Fox News in on this little secret and they can spread the word, this is if they're not too busy winding up the planet for the next terrorism incident – yeah, maybe a conflict of interest there.

Second: even if he were a Muslim this does not mean he would automatically feel tempted to fly into a tall building, of which there are none around here anyway.

Third: Like all of the crew here this pilot has been chosen for his expertise and will use it to get you to your destination safely.

Finally: where the hell do *you people* come from?

The group don't know how lucky they were I was not there as I tend to be very undiplomatic on occasions like this! But my hat was off to Alan as he got stuck in to them in a very direct fashion pointing out not only was this guy *not a Muslim*, but he had actually been involved in some of Alan's training, making him the more experienced pilot of the two. Alan went on to tell them racist remarks are illegal in Botswana and could easily lead to them being charged with an offense before being deported from the country.

He suggested the group immediately reconsider their position and ten people present themselves at the other aircraft. He then told them he was going to have a cigarette while they considered his advice. After about 20 minutes (yes, it took this long) ten of them relented and as promised, they reached Jacks Camp without mishap – although still as socially inept as slugs – idiots!

Don't be a chicken

During some of our off-hours pilots tend to tip back a few beverages and beer is often to blame for a lot of the pranks or ideas with which we come up. It's also responsible for some of our disagreements. Most of this banter takes place in bars - not church - and from time to time certain more serious aerodynamic questions move beyond the confines of the establishment, especially when there is a pressing need to prove the aviation point under discussion.

One such drunken disagreement between three pilots took place in Maun, Botswana back in the late 1990's. The basis of the argument was one of the group saying if given the proper motivation *a chicken could fly*: this was booed down by the other two and so a challenge was laid down by the aspiring aerodynamic engineer. He would put up three cases of beer which, in those days, equated to an evening out in alcohol terms before ones day off. The other two were told to put up or shut up. The two conferred about the size of the bet but the pro-flightindividual was adamant: three cases or the wager was off. "Put your money where your mouth is", he insisted. They finally agreed.

The following day the pro-poultry pilot buys a live chicken at the local market who we'll call Harry. Yes, I named a chicken, get over it, besides think of how much more personally invested you are if *it* has a name. The pilot followed the bagging regulations for carrying livestock on an aircraft and, once at the airport, Harry goes through security, who don't bat an eyelid (though in those days it could have meant the guard was actually asleep). The aircraft calls for taxi for a …*flight test* (technically correct). Then the three (plus Harry) take off for the two-minute flight to their newly-opened testing ground just outside the Okavango Delta.

At roughly 5,000 feet (1,900 above ground level), the aircraft is levelled, slowed, the window is opened and Harry is removed from the bag. It seemed from the way it was

14

described, Harry was not happy with all the noise and I am guessing the open window did not help to diminish the stressful situation. Nevertheless, sacrifices have to be made for scientific research and shortly after this Harry departed the aircraft flapping his wings madly - seemingly he was flying.

"Ha, 3 cases of beer!" reportedly cried the pilot. Sadly, his victory was short-lived as poor Harry gave up after five seconds, folded his wings against his body and plummeted toward greener pastures. To this day Harry is remembered as a true Prince of the scientific cause.

Learning can be fun(ny)

As I have said, we pilots like to have a little fun with our clients and a pilot who we will call Frank decided a year into his flying that this particular week he was bored. He sat in his office awaiting a flight that would only happen later that day. Something occurred to him and he retrieved a blank bit of paper and a red marker pen and got to work. He flew out to Xakanaka airstrip in the Moremi Game Reserve (Botswana) to collect three people that afternoon. The following was stuck to the inside back window of his Cessna 206.

He greeted the clients and eventually one of them asked:

"What's this?"

"What's it look like?"

"It looks like a Leaner's plate."

"Yes it does, there you go, well done! Anyway, is everyone ready to go?"

There was a bit of a stunned silence after which the guests had a rather long and concerned conversation with Frank before hefinally admitted he did it just for a bit of fun and he was not actually a Learner flyer. Yes, not all of our jokes go over the way we hope they will.

Have a seat

As you see we get a number of interesting people here and some have issues. Usually these stem from recent medical problems; hip operations, a broken arm or leg, or they are just elderly. One lady was visiting a lodge in the Khwai River area while I was on leave a few years back had some other problems.

I had managed to get a couple of days in camp by myself, to unwind. There were only four people in the camp: a couple from Britain and two ladies from the United States. I was shown to my room and on the pathway I noticed a chair had been placed every five metres or so. The Manager burst out laughing when I asked what the seats were for and he promised to explain later.

Back in the dining room I introduced myself to three of my fellow guests (the fourth was having a spa session) and then I sat down for lunch which consisted of stuffed chicken breast *or* a Greek salad with sliced sirloin. There was some vegetarian option which my eye skimmed over and immediately forgot, (I'm not Australian - more about this later).

We were all chomping away when this last lady (let's call her Martha) finally made an appearance. From where I was sitting I had a view of the spa building some forty meters away and Martha was being helped down the pathway by a staff member. Either she had some medical affliction or it had been such a serious spa session I needed to consider avoiding the place for fear of losing my mobility. I looked at Martha who was on the big side and compared her to the tiny spa lady and decided it was probably the former.

Martha was now at the main deck and had made it (with continued assistance) up the two small steps. At this point she shrugged off further help assuring her caregiver she would be fine, much like people do when they lose their crutches or wheelchair for the first time. She now needed to make it the 15 metres across the deck to her friend's table, which was in the same line as mine, only nearer to the steps. Martha stood there concentrating on her table but it felt as though her eyes were actually focused on me.

She gripped the banister and started breathing deeply (like a high jumper just before they start their run for gold). At this point she let go: she was off and motoring toward her table. I prayed she knew how to stop or she would be landing at my lap in no time. A few seconds later she had grasped her chair and entered the warm-down period of her pre-lunch exercise routine, which involved lots of breathing and a distinct inability to speak. What crossed my mind was she must be really ill. Now seated, she was ready to order:

"I'll have the Greek salad with sirloin *and* the stuffed chicken. Can I get a triple vodka and Coke no ice? Just bring the Coke separately and I'll mix it myself. I'd also like a large glass of red wine and one of those beers you gave me for breakfast"

Beer, Breakfast WTF? I had finished my lunch but decided to have a cup of tea. Okay, okay, to be truthful, what I really wanted was to see where this lady's meal and bar offensive was going. She consumed both main courses at a speed which would make most mothers proud of their children. No fussing with the vegetables: down the hatch they went as well. The beer was gone in the first three minutes of it hitting the table. The Coke remained untouched and the vodka vanished to be replaced by another. She proved to be a true wine connoisseur as the Merlot they served lasted throughout the meal, its bouquet being thoroughly appreciated in tiny sips.

The wine had its work cut out in cleansing duties, as her palate was getting a serious hammering. After her friend had left Martha looked around the dining room in a furtive way and then ordered another stuffed chicken – she did not seem to notice me or she didn't care. I downed the rest of my tea and made my way to the manager's office.

Of course I took a picture of the chairs – who wouldn't!

"I've got it! The chairs are for the big American woman I just witnessed knocking back half your bar; and I now must assume there is a food shortage in the camp?"

The manager gave no comment, just shook his head and laughed. I started to walk back to my room and there halfway up the path, sitting in one of the chairs, was Martha, with an unopened bottle of Absolute Vodka in her hand. I asked her if she was okay. "Fine, I'm just resting", she replied, breathing heavily. I went to my room to get my swimming trunks and when I came back down the path 10 minutes later she had made it to the last chair and would now need to physically commit to the five steps up to her tent.

At about three o'clock we all appeared for afternoon tea which consisted of a beautiful selection of freshly baked scones with jam and fresh cream, and an assortment of little finger foods, fresh fruit as well as the usual coffee, tea, and homemade lemonade. Martha was having none of the children's stuff: she polished off a third of a bottle of vodka while we meekly dunked our sponge fingers before the four guests finally departed for their game drive. I skipped the game drive and chose to stay in camp as I wanted to chill out a bit. I don't know about you guys, I drink, but if I had gone through this much booze, I would be flat on my back for a day or so.

Dinner-time came and, amazingly, Martha was still standing. She ordered vodka and also asked for a bottle of red wine to be left on the table. Martha's friend didn't look happy about all the drinking an asked if the wine was really necessary. "Yes, it is!" was shot back.

Next morning at breakfast I was chatting with her friend, who had obviously become rather embarrassed about the boozing as she brought it up with me. I assured her I had not noticed a thing - what else was I going to say, 'I think your friend is one drink away from her grave?'

Martha arrives and is offered breakfast: "Would madam like an omelette?"

The suggestion seemed to appeal, but what to have in it?

"We have three kinds of cheese, tomatoes, mushrooms, cilantro, bacon, sausage, avocado, onions..." The choices seemed endless.

"Sounds good: I'll have an omelette".

"And which ingredients would you like?"

The look on her face seemed to indicate she was a little taken aback by the question. "Why, all of them!"

Wow, no wonder we have trouble walking! We consume alcohol like Prohibition is being reinstituted tomorrow and eat everything in sight which has not been nailed down. Martha and her friend left after breakfast to go on to another camp and this is when I found out she was working: yes, she was one of the Agents who book the Lodges. I don't know, maybe Martha was trying the whole bill of fare just to make sure the clients would be satisfied with it. It certainly seemed the vodka would pass muster – if there was any left for the guests!

INTRODUCTION

Those stories will give you an idea of what is coming but now I need to explain the dynamic of the book. We all have different ideas of what makes us laugh and not all of us agree on when it is appropriate to do so. In this respect I may push your personal boundaries. Of course some of the following are my personal views and you may not agree with all of them. That's okay with me, have a different opinion, even voice it – just have a reason for doing so. I have had any number of people voice strong objections to things I have said or done and when I ask them 'why' they cannot give any reason whatsoever – 'just because' is a favorite. I can't accept this as a reply.

We have quite a few nationalities represented throughout this text, with some countries citizens making more appearances than others. Please try to remember these idiots are individuals even though from time to time I represent them in a somewhat xenophobic way. A few words to summarize the following anecdotes:

Funny, sad, politically incorrect, rude, racist, hysterical, ridiculous, opinionated, sardonic, sarcastic, condescending, vulgar, and occasionally philosophic!

I offer this warning - I call them the way I see them; this is probably evident considering the above list of words. In this regard much of my writing is very direct, and I am sure some could even say offensive. If you are sensitive regarding a given story you need to either harden up a little or move on to the next one. These true events are what they are and altering them would be unfair to their moment in history or to the people who created them.

There are subjects in these pages for which I get quite wound up about, so you know my emotions stem from the story and how it affected me. One such subject is Racism – I absolutely hate it. Intolerance or prejudice of any kind is wrong, yet you could accurately say that I am intolerant of stupidity, which for me sums up Racism.

Regardless of some of the things which transpired please understand as pilots we are professionals and no matter how much fun we are having with our passengers, safety is always our main aim. This banter represents how we get through the day, stay sane, to live, laugh and fly another.

But before we get in to the stories, you need to better understand who we are as aviators, as well as get an idea of *some* the people we deal with; so let's look at a few small areas that will help you with this. Who are pilots? Some categories of passengers and Darwin Award nominees?

Perceptions of the job

Society loves labels, especially with jobs which are considered professions. Doctor, Lawyer, Fireman, Police officer, Ship's Captain, and Commercial Pilot fit some of these appointments. So if I asked you what do you think a pilot does what would you say?

It seems like a simple question, but if you put it to a group of people you would get a lot of different answers. The thing many people fail to remember is there are numerous areas in aviation; therefore a diversity to what a pilot does. Of course we all fly an aircraft, that's obvious; but most of us would first picture an Airline pilot; very few of us would immediately consider other areas such as Fighter pilot, Agriculture pilot, or Charter pilot as part of this image. Whatever your idea of our job, many of you might still hold an image of a time of awe around the men who flew aircraft – aviators were special people, idols of a sort. Unfortunately, even today, that mind-set is still being instilled among some new commercial pilots and is summed up in a very old joke:

'What is the difference between a Pilot and God…., God does not think he is a Pilot….'

My personal view is that I hope this pious mentality is diminishing from our industry. Pilots should realize flying is not a calling from the Devine to float into a room behind virgins distributing fresh rose petals to signify an aviator is shortly to grace us with his presence. We don't walk on water and never have, we are just people.

Having said this, I fully agree to the fact that some passengers have taken their view of pilots to the other extreme. A Commercial pilot now fits in with your Waiter, your Style Guru and Life Coach, Yoga Instructor, Hair Stylist and other such trades; yes, for a great many of the public, pilots are wrongly perceived as *service staff**. The truth is we would prefer to be somewhere between the Divine and the Cleaner. This passenger mentality is especially true with Charter Pilots who undertake their duties in an *open cockpit environment.*

* The writer accepts no reader rebukes regarding the use of these professions as examples; if you are offended all I can say is - I think your diaper is showing!

But before we start expanding on some of these *Princes of Ignorance;* I would first like to offer our most sincere thanks to the true Commercial Aviation jocks. The ones who, when they travel with us, get in our aircraft and offer no hint they fly. Normally they sit in the back and the most inkling you might have flown another commercial pilot is when they say 'nice landing' and give you a wink; most say nothing at all which is fine with me. Thanks ladies and gentlemen for not making our work difficult or overly stressful by openly critiquing us; now back to the rest!

Ignorance can be an obsession

It can be said intelligent people understand ignorance and I don't have a problem the subject; what I do have a problem with is people who are absent of the awareness of their condition. I was taught many years ago *if you don't know* - then *don't pretend you do* - as you normally just make yourself out an Ass. Unfortunately there continues to be a growing section of the community which has this want, almost a drive, to tell everyone just how knowledgeable or intelligent they are – these attempts often spawn failure and to me come across as needy. Regrettably smaller commercial aircraft have an open flight deck (no door); so our passengers are sitting in our office (the cockpit) and can see and comment on everything we do – enter the <u>audible ignorance factor</u>. To loosely summarize this behaviour I'll give you a few categories of passengers.

Of course we have the <u>normal everyday passengers</u> who essentially form the bulk of our clientele. These people are great fun to be around and a joy to fly. They say nothing much regarding the aviation side because they either don't want to bother you or have come to the realization they don't know enough to pass judgment on your work. Some ask questions which is absolutely fine; I also like to learn things and asking is the way to do it. I would like to reemphasize these are the majority of the people we fly yet I still have managed to write a book concerning the remainder. Just think about this as you go through these pages - Moving on!

There are <u>mildly irritating passengers</u> who havegarnered their aviation knowledge based upon as little as: a single conversation about flying, their last birthday gift which involved a one hour orientation flight, or what a local news presenter tells them in a three minute segment on an aircraft mishap. They open their mouths (generally only once) as they spout out some fundamentally incorrect aviation detail as *fact* which usually invokes laughter from someone else present; after realizing their mistake, they are tactfully quiet and often regain their dignity quickly.

Then there are the <u>nauseating passengers,</u> who are significantly more qualified than their above mentioned cousins. They have gleaned their awareness of aviation from hours of watching TV shows like Bush Pilots or Air Crash Investigation; or they might have seen the movie Air America six times which, by the way, was complete rubbish – read the book by Christopher Robbins, much better. Sorry Mel and Robert – I love your other work, hugs and kisses. These passengers, even after making more than a couple of important mistakes, will just keep talking, secure no one has noticed when clearly a few of us have. They seem oblivious to the fact they are making a complete Tit out of themselves and embarrassing the people they are travelling with. We fly a lot of couples and this is about the time the woman is normally either shaking her head or is attempting to disassociate herself from the whole moment by looking for something in a bag or starting a pointless conversation with their guide.

Finally, we have every Charter Pilot's favourite, <u>an actual private pilot,</u> a license holder with an amazing 380 odd hours of flying. The same pilot whose experience must be announced either by them or a helpful spouse, which conversation starts, "I have my pilot's license" or "my husband is a pilot can he sit up front with you"? This question is normally accompanied with a reassurance to the remainder of the passengers of what a help they would be sitting in the co-pilots seat should something go wrong! So this little demographic is scaring the shit out of my passengers before we even get in the aircraft –

yeah thanks for the help but I can scare them myself! An analysis of all of the above traits – positive or not - is based upon the passenger's questions and/or actions around any aircraft within three minutes of arrival.

Darwinian nominees

For those of you who do not understand this reference; essentially the Darwin Awards is a darkly humorous honour. Unlike the Academy Awards there is no limit to the annual nominees but the winners are truly special. "And the award goes to…" the person who had the most trouble rationalizing the outcome of their decision which then resulted in a cataclysmic event – in short the biggest idiot on the planet. Please understand the winning recipient is usually dead, which a few of us think is great as it strengthens the gene pool (sorry if this offends - but be aware you may see a few of these comments throughout this text and most of them do not accompany an apology, so accept this one).

The reason for mentioning this is I have observed that Charter flying seems to attract these types of Darwinian people. They can be passengers, ground staff, camp staff, even the occasional pilot. This book has a lot of these sort of situations; it also has other amusing stories of people who just weren't seeing the finished product of either their conversation or their actions. Put another way, their 15 minutes of fame worked out less than flatteringly for them than they would have liked, leaving us shaking our heads or howling with laughter.

The 5% Crowd

In additional to our Darwinian passengers we have people I call the 5% simply because, in my view, five percent of the planet seems to behave this way.

Conversations with people from this group will always include phrases such as: "But why…", "How come….", "Do I have to…", "It's not fair…"; yes, five percenters are the adult version of a six year old child; you know, when kids want to question everything. Regrettably you are dealing with someone who usually drinks alcohol and is in a position to vote. This is the group for which *any* introduction of Instructions or Rules brings an automatic right of challenge or refusal; no matter how reasonable or legal the request is. Go on, I know you know one as they live everywhere.

Name changes

Only 1% of the names in this book are real; so when you see Mick (not real, or let's call him) this is what I mean. To be honest, the remaining 99% would not appreciate the very unflattering light in which they are about to be painted no matter how funny their story is. In all cases I like to avoid being sued; so this book abounds with pseudonyms; it also allows those who participated in making these moments to laugh at themselves without direct embarrassment, so if you see yourself in these pages keep quiet as it is our little secret. If you choose not to keep quiet – then don't blame me if the breadcrumbs lead to you!

The few real names in the following stories are the people I could get a hold of who gave their permission to have their moment splashed out for all to see. These individuals are the true humourists, fully ready to laugh at themselves before laughing at others. Some will not be voicing any objections as they are dead; and although I would like to be able to ask them, my meek powers don't extend this far.

In this respect I hope your enjoy what I have written for it is the world many of *us* live in and these are the people we have to deal with.

DEATH & OTHER MEDICAL MATTERS

Happily, Martha our vodka toting friend does not appear in this section of the text - well not yet anyway!

Most would agree the subject of death is not usually linked with humour. Let's face it, people die, it is regrettable but more often than not it is the ones left behind who end up messing up the situation. After all blaming the deceased for anything would be inappropriate so for the following anecdotes it is the living who bear the brunt of our amusement. Well most of them do!

Death is not commonplace in aviation but it rears its head from time to time. It is very seldom it involves an aircraft mishap. Usually, it is simply a matter of transportation, for this is what we do: transport people – mostly alive, but occasionally dead. Then there are the other relatively common medical issues which any normal person might think of and a handful of some less common situations.

How many in your party?

Visiting lodges in Africa can be an expensive proposition as some of them charge a hefty price for providing you with your moment in the sun. This unnamed lodge in Botswana was no exception, being in the US$1,800 per night price range. This story took place in 2007.

Our party, who we will call Mr. and Mrs. Smith had been flown into camp by an intrepid Irish pilot we will call Paddy, who was also due to stay the night in the lodge. Paddy started his flying career a little late in life, much like me. Unlike me he is only five foot two and at least I have managed to maintain a full head of hair in comparison to his well-manicured chrome dome – yes, lots of sunblock.

The Smiths were pushing into their eighties and Paddy, being roughly half their age, was a perfect dinner companion so he accepted their invitation to join them. He had a wonderful evening, drinking fine wine with his meal and finishing off with a glass of port before bidding the couple goodnight.

Paddy departed the following morning on his next flight and yet another overnight in a nearby camp. The following day he was back to collect the Smiths and fly them on to their next lodge. He was looking forward to seeing them again as he had enjoyed their company and thought it *grand* to be flying them again.

When he arrived at the airstrip one of his colleagues was already on the ground by a larger aircraft. They greeted each other and then Paddy asked what he was doing there as he did not appear on the schedule for the day. His colleague explained someone had passed away in their sleep the night before and he was flying the body out. The pilot had been in the business a while and this was not his first experience flying a body. He was waiting at the airstrip for the police and the doctor to finish up. Anytime there is a death the Police become involved to satisfy the legal requirements; from there a natural death moves forward as normal.

With a glance at his watch Paddy realized he was running late. He was halfway across the parking when he spotted Mrs Smith sitting at the edge of the airstrip, waiting for him, or so he thought. He headed towards her calling out, "Morning, it's me Paddy, come to take you to your next camp!"

His colleague, realizing what was afoot, made a mad dash towards his Irish colleague to stop him before he reached Mrs Smith. You guessed it: it was Mr. Smith who had passed in the night and some dolt in the office had forgotten to take the Smiths off the normal schedule when they moved them to the *special schedule*. Mr. Smith was still on his way to the airstrip, although he was travelling horizontally in the camp utility vehicle.

At this point Paddy had made it all the way and was standing before the lady all he could say was, "I am sorry for your loss", which she hardly acknowledged as she was too upset to know what was going on.

It's just the Flu

As it happens life produces some tragic moments, a warning this story is not funny and does not have a happy ending but in my view needs to be told based upon pure medical complacency. An English mining engineer took a contract in Tanzania. These third world contracts can be somewhat lucrative but often the conditions you work in are not what some might term homey. Nevertheless your contract usually includes everything you might need; accommodation, food (in some cases), travel to and from your home country, and of course all of your medical and hospitalisation needs.

The Engineer had been there barely one week when he contracted what seemed to be the flu. He went to check and the doctor said it was the Flu and gave him some medication. After leaving the medical professional's office he started discussing his symptoms with his work colleagues and twenty-four hours later his health had gotten much worse. He reappeared at the Doctors and said he wanted to be tested for Malaria. *No, it's not necessary* was the response, it's just the Flu – more medicine.

By the time Paddy and another pilot were dispatched at night to collect this poor bastard and get him out of the mining camp it was essentially too late. He made it into the aircraft and to his destination where he was taken to hospital; he died roughly twenty-four hours later. The Flu he had been diagnosed with was actually Cerebral Malaria; Malaria is bad

29

enough but in your head it is a fast killer and if not caught early on the results are pretty permanent – death! If the Mine's medical facility had just tested him immediately they had a fair chance of arresting the disease and saving the guy; the cost of the test was roughly $25. Maybe there was an accountant running the company.

Leos Takeaway

If one had to attach a name to the King of the Beasts the first one which pops to mind is Leo. Every kid knows *Leo the Lion* and most of us are convinced Leo wouldn't hurt a soul.

A long, long time ago in a lodge far, far away, Leo's alter ego made his presence known and he was hungry. This lion had been hanging around this particular lodge for several weeks. From time to time animals do this, sometimes it's an elephant or it could be a pack of wild dog. It may be a primal instinct of sorts: the animals might identify the spot as somewhere their ancestors used to hang out, hunting or breeding, and now they see some idiot has built a Lodge in this place which has messed with their *chi*. Another reason animals can hang around a Lodge is they have worked out there is food there.

As an example, there is a camp on Chief's Island, Botswana, called (quite logically) Chief's Camp, run by Sanctuary Lodges. In 2012-2014 there was a big female Hyena which hung around the common area. Imagine my surprise one night as I enjoyed a fine South African Pinotage at the bar and out of the corner of my eye I spied, (less than four metres away), this Hyena, sitting like a dog on the main deck, staring at me. I made inquiries with the bartender, who assured me it was quite normal, she usually turned up at this time in the evening but departed just before the guests rolled in for dinner. I guess she didn't like crowds.

As I see it, *the human being* is the weak point in all animal encounters. For carnivorous beasts the situation is perfectly clear: they want meatas their main meal of the day, or a snack, depending on the size of the object. So when in the bush and as the higher form of life you should chose to be careful, use caution or you may be assessed as *on the menu.* Hence the importance of following the Lodge's rules (more about this later).

However, as all human beings know, if an actual danger exists for a long enough people tend to get used to it and lower their guard, become complacent so to speak. This is what *may* have happened on the day a member of staff met his demise. He was walking alone, which is something to avoid wherever possible. Leo was hungry, noticed the moving buffet and this was the end of the staff member. Well, not quite: there was enough fill a very small cooler box (an *Esky* to you Aussies). This is what one of the pilots was handed when he went to pick up the remains with the police officers who had come to establish the cause of death (no medical degree necessary in this case). Although it was good this person was able to give back to nature it should be noted there is a strict *do not feed the animals* policy!

A few weeks later, Steve Hollingworth (a very real pilot who flew all over Africa - more about him later) is flying past the airstrip this camp uses. He needs to make a position report (essential for letting others know where your aircraft is) so he calls out "Alpha Echo Romeo…" (AER – the aircraft's registration) "…east abeam Leo's Takeaway".

Needless to say this joke did not go down well with a few of the pilots: they felt it was in the *too soon* department. After a short and heated discussion Leo's Takeaway was closed for an additional six months of mourning before the radio call was used again. I know, I know, please don't shoot the messenger.

Blanket approval

In Tanzania in late 2013 a pilot was overseeing the loading of his aircraft at a remote airstrip when he was presented with a rolled up blanket as part of this family's hold luggage. The pilot who we will call Herb is a slender young lad from South Africa, who when I knew him chain smoked cigarettes at a rate which ensured Philip Morris Directors would receive their annual bonuses. Herb is an excellent pilot and a polite young man with a solid set of ethics – someone who you can trust to date your daughter and she would be returned to you intact – if I can phrase it this way.

Today Herb is questioning the family regarding the unusual method for transporting their blanket. He understood a carpet being rolled up but a blanket seemed odd. In a short conversation devoid of many English words, the message got through which was it was 'custom' to transport '*it*' this way. Herb wasn't entirely sure what the '*it*' referred to. Further inquiries revealed the rigidity of the blanket was due to the fact it held a seven-year-old deceased boy being relocated for burial. Isn't it nice to know there are all kinds of customs you learn about in this line of work?

Before you start using the words like 'disgusting' or 'wrong' let's look at some Western Customs which occasionally raise eyebrows:

Cheese Rolling: Ah yes, the quaint English custom undertaken each year at Copper Hill of rolling a round of cheese down a steep hill and watching 100 idiots chase it, often seriously damaging themselves in the process. Ah, no thanks!

The Finnish Sauna: A national custom of the Finn's which involves a bunch of grown men sitting in a small thatched room with a fire, completely naked, sweating for hours on end. Then finally emerging to jump into a frozen lake and then roll around in the snow. Maybe not!

Lobbyists: The unbelievable aspect of American Culture where one's elected officials get
financial incentives (legal bribes) to vote a certain way for an given industry while conducting official business on your behalf. The same legislators who then point at African and Asian countries and speak at length about corruption. Hypocrisy springs to mind.

Democratic Elections: And, finally, in pretty much every Western country the aspect of your political candidates promising one thing to get the job and then once elected not delivering on it, and in no way being held to account for the fraud they have just committed. What can one say?

Please think about all of this when passing judgement on anyone's Culture and/or Customs. Please also remember, being an Idiot does not fall into either category!

Can I give you a Tip?

To most of us death will come as a surprise. In some cases we will depart this world in our sleep, like Mr. Smith, in others it may come about in a more sudden and perhaps painful way (hit by a bus, car crash, trampled by an errant donkey – this last one is more of an African thing).

On the other hand, as was previously mentioned, some visitors are aware of their health situation and are taking what they believe to be their final trip. They have been sat down and informed of their fate by a medical professional and have decided if they have only so many months, or in some cases so many weeks to live, now is the time to start ticking things off their bucket list. I often wonder how many times this involves a misdiagnosis which has left a person broke and still waiting for their time to come, albeit with some great holiday memories.

We had one lady who was doing a round of the lodges and at each one she would announce upon her arrival this was her last trip to Africa as she had it on the best authority she was for the next world very, very soon.

Her behaviour was magnanimous to say the least: she would ask for a can of Coke to be delivered to her room and the staff member would receive US$50 for her trouble. Game drives were lucrative as she was handing out US$100 tips each to the guide and tracker. The bartender would also receive US$50 or 100 for his deft hand with the cocktails. During her first two-day camp stay it was estimated she went through almost US$1800 in tips. She moved on to the next camp and the money train continued as she told everyone she was moving outsoon (a real upper for the other guests).

In the third camp the tips dried up on the very first day. No, she didn't run out of money, she died. Her doctor had been right, or nearly right, as it seems her time on earth was somewhat shorter than the doctor had estimated. Alas, no refund from the medical professional. By the way, why do they call it *practising medicine*? What would people say if I told them I was a *practising pilot*?

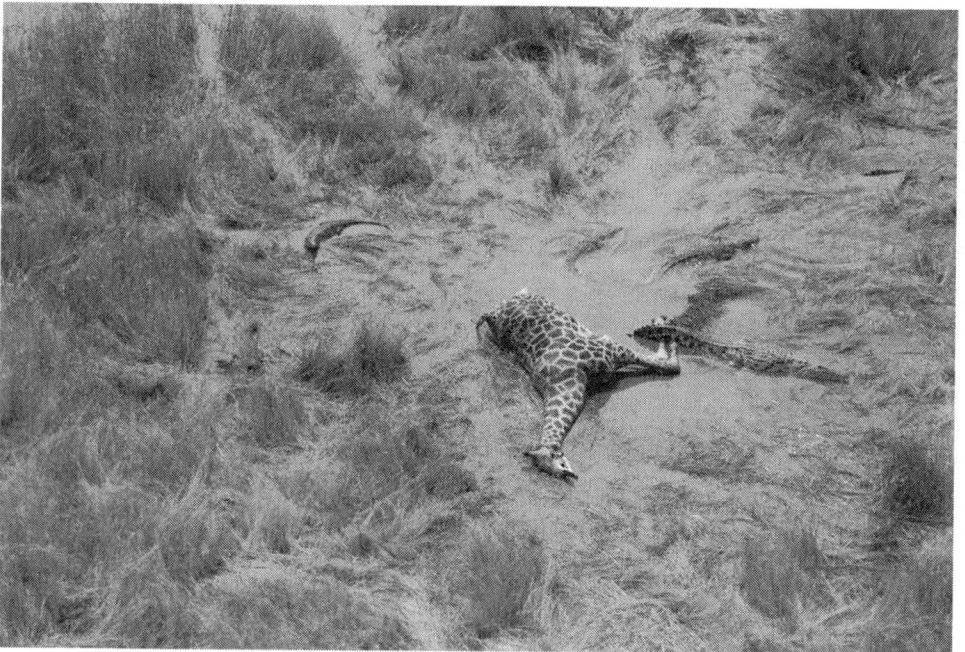

Death is regrettable – but as some people say 'it is God's work'

Over my dead body

A pilot in Maun, Botswana who we shall call Nick - who also appears later in our Special Cases section - has been invited to a Wedding six months before the event. Nick is hesitant to go to the ceremony simply because he is nervous about meeting one person who is also attending – his girlfriend's father – who is also a Pastor of the Church.

In this spirit Nick says he will try to attend but has been reluctant to fully commit. The week before he starts hedging, saying he can't get the time off work, this sort of thing. The girlfriend is less than impressed with Nick's attitude. It is now the day before the big event and she has gone ahead to help organise things – Nick has remained behind. Nick knows he has screwed up and starts to rethink his decision, the problem now is he needs to figure out how to get to the other side of the country to be there for her. He meets a couple of pilots who have just flown in to carry out a Med-Evac or medical evacuation.

One of Botswana's Medi-Evac Aircraft

Botswana has an excellent *free health care system* for its people and if you cannot get the medical help you need where you are the government sends an aircraft to transport you to where you need to be – this is also FREE OF CHARGE! Hopefully some American legislators are reading this and maybe you'll study this system for affordable medical care for your own people; or you can just continue to let the Insurance Industry Lobbyists milk your citizens to death. No I am not a *socialist* this is a convenient label people attach to any programme which helps people and they decide they don't want to support!

Anyway, these two pilots have come to collect a lady with a life threatening illness. After Nick explains his transportation problem one of them makes a passing comment:

"We could take you back with us as crew but with the patient and the Medic there won't be room, sorry."

Nick understands. A couple of minutes later the pilot's cell phone rings and there is a short conversation after which he hangs up.

"Well if you want a ride we can give you one now. But we're leaving almost immediately."

Nick enquires about them not having any space in the aircraft – not a problem, as regrettably the lady just died and she won't be coming along after-all and neither will the Medic for obvious reasons. Nick enjoyed meeting his future Father-in-Law – the Pastor - and it was apparently a lovely ceremony. The Lord really does move in mysterious ways!

JOKES

Pilots play practical jokes. The places we work can get a bit boring and this is the way we mix it up a little. Sadly not everyone sees the funny side or thinks through the entire joke before they start.

These guys in an unnamed East African country used to have Arab Fridays. They would dress up and go drinking and clubbing. Needless to say there were some raised eyebrows and from time to time a few terse words!

German humour

Meet Ted Poppek (yes, he's very real), a guy who has an incredible sense of humour; still this can let you down from time to time; and was just a little misplaced on the day in question. Ted is one of the pilots who worked here a few years back who undertook his flight training in New Zealand. He is a solidly built lad who did his national service in his birth country of Germany, but he is also 50% Kiwi. Now for Ted to make the money to get his commercial license he worked as a bouncer and club manager in South Auckland,

New Zealand.

For those of you who have visited New Zealand it is a truly peaceful and stunningly picturesque place. But like all such destinations it has its areas which are not what most would call tourist friendly. South Auckland would fit this description perfectly and is what would be considered in most countries as a true working class area. Debates in this part of the country on a given subject might be settled with a fist fight followed by a trip to the hospital – or possibly the morgue if it were a particularly heated debate. Ted being a ginger (red head for you Americans) probably didn't endear him greatly to the predominantly Maori and Islander clientele of these drinking establishments by not only being an outsider but also….., let's say being European - to be politically correct. Nevertheless he managed to make it through relatively unscathed, arms and legs attached, and his faculties intact – therefore no brain damage – well maybe a little as you will see in some of our stories.

Ted's two American clients who had just arrived off their international flight were complaining they 'needed to get to camp'. Ted apologized profusely for the delay at airport security and assured them they would be there in a timely manner. But it seems the clients were a little hard of hearing as the moaning continued all the way to the aircraft, through the safety briefing, and even when they were finally buckled in and ready to go. Now in the front and about to start the engine, Ted turned and announced, in the heaviest German accent he could put on:
"Attention! We are now leaving for *thecamp*; you will be in *thecamp* in fifteen minutes!" While he was speaking he had placed his hands together in almost a prayer moment but was strumming his fingers in what might classically be referred to as an evil gesture. The complaining stopped, the wife went very quiet and the husband announced:
"Do you realize we are Jewish?"
Ted said he immediately felt flush, stammered out an apology, explaining he was just trying to lighten their holiday mood. Of course Ted being German was not helping the whole situation either. After the fifteen minute flight all three had a little chuckle at the airstrip regarding the awkward moment. Ted apologized again, was given a US$20 tip,

with an unspoken rebuke regarding certain jokes in the form of a slow nod while he and the husband not only shook hands but locked eyes, and all parted on friendly terms.

Ted even managed to convince the owner of the Charter Company he worked for to name their new aircraft after him.

Just be Gay

Okay this is my disclaimer. I do not have anything against homosexuality; I feel it is a personal choice. This said it is not something which has ever interested me – sorry guys, as I am a bit of a catch. Not everyone has the same broad-mindedness. As is human nature some people make fun of people who have made this choice. Furthermore I am just telling you a story and my sum participation in this incident was me saying the whole thing was a really bad idea.

So we had an English pilot who we will call Tim, working in Maun who enjoyed playing pranks. Although he has a good sense of humour, we were a bit surprised to find out he was behind some of the jokes which were going on. If you were stupid enough to leave your Facebook account open, and then step away from the computer you could often return to find your profile picture changed to include a romantic moment (photo-shopped) with you and a horse or you were now in a relationship with Mark or Steve with an accompanying photo of said individual lying on their bed in a Thong; things like this.

Today Tim has found a new website named gaydar.co.za (now gaydar.net). Obviously this is what it sounds like and is a Gay Dating website based out of South Africa. Wikipedia gave the following description:

Gaydar is a worldwide, profile-based dating website for gay and bisexual men, women and couples over the age of 18. Although many of the individual profiles are publicly accessible on the Internet, to gain more functionality and interact with other users, a registration is required and a guest profile must be created.

It was founded in 1999 in Cape Town, South Africa by London-based South Africans Gary Frisch[2][3] and his partner Henry Badenhorst, after a friend complained that he was too busy to look for a new boyfriend.

Tim is not Gay, although we are not sure how he found the site. In addition he is from England, some of whose people can be enigmas concerning their public vs. private sexuality – sorry I digress.

Tim is on the website when I enter the pilots' room and is discussing with another pilot the new account he has created; I ask what is going on and he explains. Halfway through the explanation I am already shaking my head in disbelief. Enter another pilot we will call Ben. Ben has no idea Tim has just created an account on the site using his name – yes, his real name, profession, geographical location, etc. The site has selection boxes for sexual preferences which I will not go into; Tim has decided on behalf of Ben to tick most of the boxes. At this point I am saying this is not only a bad idea, but may have ramifications for Ben beyond the obvious ones. Unfortunately Tim is hard of hearing during this conversation.

Twenty-four hours later Tim's hearing has improved shortly after he opens the account and finds Ben has four people from the Capital (Gaborone) who have decided he is their soul-mate/flavour of the month. Tim has had a re-think and decided to delete the somewhat dishonestly established account. Before he does, he screenshots the account page and slips it in to Ben's documents tray. Ben is away, but when he returns there is a bit of an explosion which needed to be settled by purchasing a few cases of beer; fined for going too far.

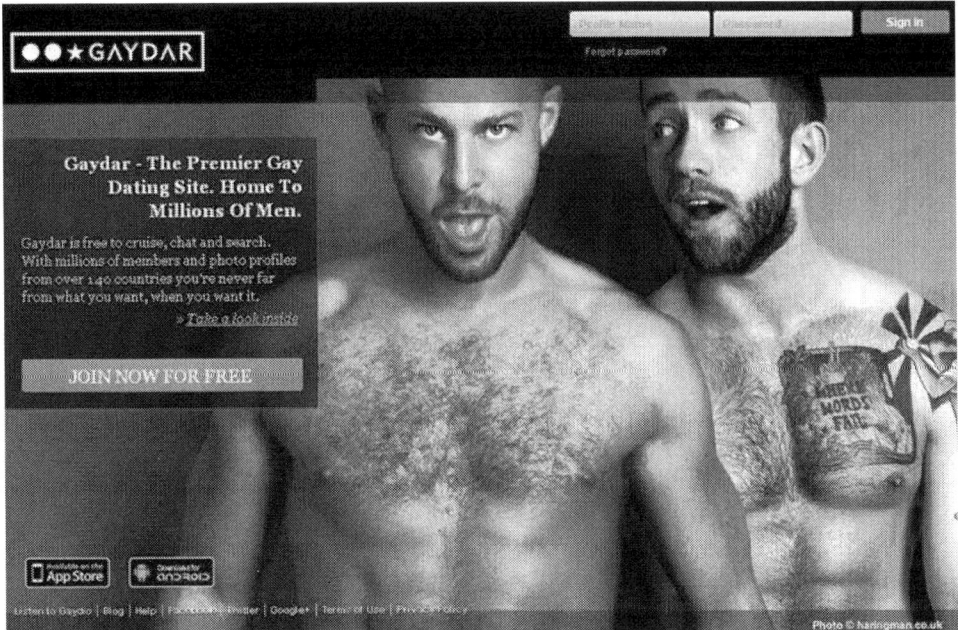

A family email

As Tim's pranks continued they escalated. You are probably wondering how much further Tim could go from a Gay dating website for his co-worker. Tim FRAPED (Facebook Raped) three further pilots accounts where these pilots entered varying relationships with everything from a Pig to one of them being in a relationship with an ashtray. To be fair it was a really nice ashtray!

Tim is one day away going on leave. He will jet off to the U.K. to visit family and friends and this is about the time I find his Hotmail account which he has left open on the office computer – pretty stupid huh. I normally do not involve myself in such matters but as Tim was working his way through all the pilots in the company I felt my time would come. With this in mind I wrote an email.

Hi Guys,

I love all you guys and it is with a heavy heart I tell you I have not been fully honest with each of you.

I AM GAY.

I know this will come as a shock to many of you, well most anyway, but I feel the need to be free and want you to support my decision.

That's it, I hope we can all still get along as if nothing at all has changed because I am the same person you knew and loved last week. The only thing which has changed is your knowledge that I look at men in a different way. I look forward to seeing you soon.

Love Tim

I then selected every person in his address book who had his family name and also a couple who did not. Tim returned from flying later in the day and I just told him to check his Sent Items. Apparently Tim did not like this email and family aside one of the names I had selected was his ex-girlfriend. Oh well, the damage jokes cause.

The following day Tim was rushing for his international flight. You guessed it, he left his Hotmail account open again.

Hi Guys,

In follow up to yesterday's email not only am I gay, I am also stupid. I am getting on my flight now, see you all soon.

Love Tim

Tim sat in the aircraft while it taxied looking at my text regarding email number 2. I felt it was only fair to give him a heads up. Apparently he was asked several times by relatives regarding his sexual preferences and had to explain in detail how the email came in to being. One Uncle said 'I'm not convinced but I'll leave it at that'.

When Tim returned from leave he was a little more low-key about his jokes. But he is still a great guy or is it gay guy.

Take a raincoat

Condoms have a variety of uses other than what they were intended for. As an example the military use them over the end of the barrel of a weapon to keep out water and other contaminants. They have their uses as survival equipment – look it up if you don't believe me.

Originally they were designed by Catholics (I'M JUST KIDDING), they were designed by someone to prevent pregnancy. These days their usefulness has been extended to cover more permanent and/or life threatening diseases. In 2012 the South African Health Department decided to go on a nationwide Condom drive to promote AIDS awareness. They handed out a one page fact sheet with a free condom stapled to it – straight through the middle of the device. Stupidity beyond believe!

Meet Darren who has just loaded his passengers and managed, as he put it, to strategically get a *really hot chick* in the front seat next to him. He is just starting his take-off roll when something drops into his lap, looking down he sees a condom. As he accelerates more condoms start raining down on him. He is airborne now and one last condom bounces out and off Darren's right arm and straight into the lap of his front seat passenger. Darren stares at where it has come to rest – pretty much over her vagina. He then realises where he is staring and looks her in the eye instead. There was an awkward silence before he starts apologising.

It wasn't him, it was one of the other pilots who thought it would be funny. To be honest it was funny, but on a Freight or Staff flight – not a flight with guests. As I said we need to have fun, but be professional at the same time.

Meet my doctor

As has been said we get some annoying and rather retarded questions. Many people question why it is they cannot sit in the co-pilot's seat and my view is - you can sit there. The only exception to this moment is IF SOMEONE IS ALREADY SITTING IN THE SEAT!

Please do not ask me to sit in an aircraft seat which is already occupied as this question shows a fundamental lack of intelligence which should take you back to those puzzles and games we did as kids – you know a Round Peg goes in Round Hole. Recently I was asked a question similar to this and the word "Why" was included; I decided to use something new.

"*Why* does he get to sit up front"?
"Oh him, he has to sit there, he's my Doctor and he travels with me everywhere".

Just remember all of the vacant seats are available and if you cannot grasp this concept it shows a certain Vacantness on your part.

The meat is hard

Nick has an assignment. His girlfriend, the Pastor's daughter, is hungry, so Nick has driven to Sports Bar for the Tuesday Burger special – buy one get one free. Now if you visit Maun this is a great meal as these burgers are huge and come with a multitude of toppings as well as salad or chips.

As is habit here going out to a bar to get food and doing exactly what you are meant to do does not happen as it should. Tuesdays are a busy time and Nick runs into Ted the German. They have a few beers while Nick awaits his food; as it is busy he needs to wait awhile. More beers and Nick is off to the toilet which is about the time the two take-away burgers arrive. Nick returns and Ted suggests another beer; okay, one more but Nick indicates he needs to go *soon* as the girlfriend is calling and he needs to get back. They have a few more drinks, and then Nick gets hungry so he eats one of the burgers, still one more drink before he finally disappears home.

It's late, the girlfriend is in bed and Nick does what many guys do in this situation, apologizes about how busy the place was and how he couldn't get away as they had a work matter to discuss, etc. The girlfriend isn't buying any of it, but it doesn't matter as she is really hungry. She sits up in bed and her burger is handed to her; she opens the container to find a semi-wet rock. She yells to Nick in the other room "okay jokes over where is my food". Nick appears somewhat bewildered and stares at the rock.

It's only the next day he sees Ted who admits it was him. Initially Ted didn't remember the incident, and then the light bulb went on and he started apologizing. When Nick had gone to the toilet Ted was hungry, so he *borrowed* one of the burgers (his words), and he and another pilot ate it as a joke. Of course they couldn't leave it this way so Ted found an appropriately sized rock (from the outside pond) and placed it in the takeaway container, something with a similar weight so as to mimic the now missing burger. Yeah I know, sort of a dick thing to do but hey you have to have a thick skin and an abstract sense humour to survive working here. They were going to order another one but as time marched on they completely forgot about their little prank. When it came time for Nick to actually go, Ted and the other pilot just bid him goodnight. Because Nick had already eaten his burger there was nothing for her.

Now, Nick's girlfriend is African, so do you think this qualifies as another African going to bed hungry?

Straight or curly

Vibrator; I agree this is not normally a word you would see at the beginning of a sentence but I felt there was no way to ease you into this one. Now for the uninitiated a Vibrator is a female sexual toy shaped like a penis and as it sounds, the item vibrates. If it doesn't you need new batteries or you are the proud owner of a Dildo. Anyway it's a concept which was developed for women who might be at home (probably waiting for their burger to appear) and who have decided to have a solo masturbation moment, you know *get themselves off* whilst dispensing with all the fumbling, bullshit conversation, and beer breath.

As has been alluded to we have female pilots here. One of them had her sister visiting who apparently had a sense of humour, although our female pilot wouldn't necessarily agree. Our female pilot, who I won't even offer a phoney name, had just spent a week with her sister and was now back to work. She was going through airport security and the female security officer asked her to open her flight bag. She complied, and they searched the bag. Out came a Vibrator with the accompanying and very serious question "what is this?"

I must say Female pilot was quick although a bit embarrassed; "it's a hair curler". The now, three, female officers at the checkpoint just starred at her. So she dove in to the moment, jamming it in to her rather short, straight hair and mimicked the action of curling. There was a short conversation in Setswana (the local language) and then nods of approval for the device. 'It's so small', 'what a great idea', those kind of comments. Finally one of them asks *'where can I get one'*. Female pilot just said she wasn't sure as hers was old, she would look for the receipt when she could. She then hastily packed up her flight bag and ran off to work.

Yes there was a rather loud and somewhat emotional conversation with her sister later in the day.

Professional Help

When I first started working as a pilot, I worked for a company which had only a few aircraft and only serviced a couple of photographic camps. Their main work, however, was for the numerous hunting operations which took place in Botswana before it became a taboo subject. We dealt not so much with the prim and proper but rather with the gun-toting grim reaper with shit loads of money and a passion for moving things off the planet. Therefore I was trained by people who were used to being a little more direct with clients, a little more brusque, so to speak. I was the new old guy, mentored by even older guys, so in the absence of any other example I followed their lead.

At the time there were six different charter operations of varying sizes in Botswana, which made a total of 60-odd aircraft on the field. From time to time your own company might not have a plane available to get the clients to a lodge on time and this is when the *Sub-charter* comes into play.

The company which had run out of aircraft would ask a competitor to help out. Kind of a daily ballet of 'I'll scratch your back, you scratch mine'. In a couple of days the roles were often reversed so it made sense to help and it keeps things moving smoothly and to schedule for all the passengers. I was flying four passengers for another company to a beautiful lodge up on the Botswana border with Namibia, a place called Kingspool, in the Linyanti (highly recommended). According to plan, I had collected the two couples off their international flight. One of the ladies didn't seem to be well; she kept mumbling to her husband.

This job has taught me much about human nature, body language, and people's fears. On this day I knew something was up. I asked if everything was ok and she said something about feeling sick; but to be honest I wasn't convinced this was the sole problem. By the time we got to the aircraft she had taken a turn for the worse; she was happy neither with the size of the aircraft nor the flight-time (45 minutes). In fact she started to get quite wound up and I used my company's version of customer service. The conversation went something like this:

Woman: I don't think I can do this!

Me: I start each morning thinking the same thing but I find as I go through the day it gets better. Usually, anyway.

Woman: You asked if *I* was all right. Are *you*?

Me: I'm great, except for the chronic back pain, all the medication I'm on, and the fact people say I am a bit paranoid. I'm fine......, *why what have you heard*?

Woman: Oh my god I can't be here! I can't get on the plane! *You need help.*

Me: What a co-incidence, my ex-wife used to scream that at me all the time, but since I started the therapy I think I'm doing much better.

At this point her jaw drops and she's speechless, staring intently at me. I gave a rueful little smile hoping she would understand it was all for a laugh. It was her husband who spoke. "He's just joking with you". I looked over the top of my sunglasses and said,

"Madam, you are on the vacation of a lifetime, maybe it's time to lighten up a bit. What do you think?"

She was a bit more relaxed but, alas, it didn't make her passage with me any better. Apart from the panic attack she was, in fact, physically ill (bad food maybe) and vomited all the way to our destination.

It's my first time

A lot of ribbing goes on among pilots and one of the well-known jokes is to wish a pilot luck with his *first flight* and of course you need to do this in the presence of his passengers for the desired result. This has received mixed reactions from the guests – but it's all for a bit of fun.

Meet Rick who has just returned from leave and has been bush flying for a year or so. Another pilot swings by:

"Hey Rick, first flight, congratulations!"

"Yep," responds Rick. "First flight since the crash, I hope it all goes well cause I'm a little nervous."

Seemingly this did not go over well and the three guests hurried away. They eventually returned being reassured it was just a joke. Yes, we have weird idea of what constitutes a senseof humour.

'Ensuring' a safe flight

As I have said some of our humour can be rather abstract and as I see it Religion should be left out of aviation (I'll explain later). However, on this day in 2007 the pilot was, well, let's call him Richard. Richard is an older South African pilot with a lot of wisdom, a penchant for jokes, and a pronounced limp. He has collected his four passengers (two couples), arrived outside his aircraft and he is shortly to load them all for their flight. He calmly gives them a short briefing and then looks at them all very seriously:

"Now if you could all join hands."

The four look at each other while Richard immediately grabs the hands of the two people on either side of him. There is a small hesitation with the rest of the group which is addressed with little gentle verbal prodding from Richard in the form of comments like 'come on, come on' and 'don't worry it won't hurt.' Everyone finally linked together Richard starts:

"Dear Lord, I ask you bless this aircraft and those who travel in her. In the past – undoubtedly with your help - she has been a sure craft to me so we seek your assistance once again she will carry us safely to our destination. We also ask………"

Well you get the idea. Richard had his head down the entire time and did not once attempt to steal a glance at these four (yes, five of us saw the whole thing). Three of these people just stood there with their mouth's hanging open. Richard then calmly finished with an 'Amen' and announced 'boarding would take place now.'

Just so you understand I could not do this with passengers - simply because I would be incapable of keeping a straight face through the whole prayer. Richard was much more professional and to be honest it was a lovely prayer.

I can't breathe

The Cessna Caravan has a Service Ceiling; this is the maximum height the aircraft can operate at which has been approved by the Authority (in this case the U.S. Federal Government). For the Caravan this is 25,000 feet above the earth. For a small non-pressurized GA aircraft this is a long way up. In order to do this Cessna installed an oxygen system otherwise the pilot and passengers would drift off to sleep due to a lack of O2.

Many of the older Caravans still have these systems but they are not in use principally because there is no need for them. Our aircraft operate at much lower and more user friendly altitudes so our passengers can breathe without the system. Still many of these aircraft still have the oxygen masks in a small compartment in the cockpit. A game some of the pilots play is to pull one of these masks out and slowly mount it over their face, this makes you look like a World War II fighter pilot. This is best done when people are dozing. Eventually, someone wakes up (it is usually the person in the front seat area) and out of the corner of your eye you can see him staring at you. It always becomes too much and there is a tap on the shoulder with a conversation which goes something like this:

"Excuse me".
Remember to take a deep breath from the mask before removing it.
"Yes"
"What's that"?
"It's an Oxygen Mask"

Put the mask back on and take another breath. Now the person is staring at you and you can actually see them rationalizing through the information. I have had people sit back at this point and just say "Oh, okay" which I don't really understand. But more often than not they usually continue:

"Shouldn't I have one of those?"

Yes 'I', not 'we' - as in the rest of his family or fellow passengers. Ah, selfishness, it's everywhere. This is when you respond with a simple question.

"Are you flying the plane"?

This is about the time the pilot produces the other end of the mask, which is a tube and needs to be attached to something to make the whole thing work. Usually passengers see the funny side of it but there have had a few adverse re-actions. Please relax guys, if we want to suffocate you we'll use the traditional method - a pillow, promise!

ANIMAL INTERACTION

This pilot overnighted to find there had been a bit of a battle raging while he slept. Seems some Lions had wounded a small Buffalo who had decided to use the aircraft as a backstop. The pilot came out in the morning to find this and what was left of the animal nearby.

Every profession has its anally retentive bastards, who are so serious that a grin from them would involve surgery and the compulsory paperwork. In aviation we have these people as well, both license-holders and want-to-be pilots who usually work on the ground. Luckily for us there are the *other ones,* who make our work memorable. The humorists and the jokers.

Let me be clear, the latter group does not include pilots who do not take their jobs seriously: those idiots appear from time to time, and when they do, many of us will do our best to either educate them or failing this ensure they do not continue in the industry. The *other ones* I am referring to are the pilots who bring a bit of joy to us on a day to day basis and don't dwell on the tiny setbacks which happen in all professions. Those pilots who patiently educate the less experienced and take advice from those with more of it. We must enjoy our work and even laugh at times, both at or with our colleagues, for untimely comments or mistakes made. Animals have played a part in these moments.

Livestock

Up on the east coast of central Africa a pilot (call him Arthur) is doing the *round the houses* run for his company. Arthur was born and bred in Edinburgh, Scotland some forty odd years ago, dons round rimless spectacles for any hope of seeing, usually sprouts closed cropped hair, is about five foot five and when I knew him had a developed mid-rift. He is well-mannered, patient and polite; in a word, a gentleman. But if you are unnecessarily rude to anyone in his presence he will give you a quick sharp verbal warning; and if the behaviour continues he has been known to knock a person flat; so please don't let his size fool you.

On this day Arthur is given a straight forward schedule which requires him to go from airstrip A to B to C to D then refuel and repeat the journey backwards. At each location he will deposit or collect his charter company's paying passengers for the day. Some of these passengers are international guests visiting nearby wildlife lodges and some are locals travelling for personal reasons, such as family or business.

So far it has been a normal day with normal passengers until on the last stop of the return leg. An elderly gentleman, dressed in a rather well used black suit, black shoes, a dress shirt of sorts and an old Fedora style hat – circa 1960s presents himself. The gentleman arrived ready for his flight: he brought one small carry bag, well within limits, and *one live goat*.

Arthur, as civilly as possible, attempts to explain to the elderly gentleman that *the goat* cannot come but communication is limited. Arthur speaks English with a heavy Scottish accent and the old timer's English was well below standards. The conversation, such as it was, went back and forth with the pilot politely saying no live animals could be carried on a commercial flight and the old man explaining, in his own way, he needed the goat with him for his onward travels – fresh milk, maybe for the coffee service.

Finally Arthur seemed to have got his message through and turned to close up the aircraft; when he turned around again he was just in time to see the elderly gentleman pull a long knife from his bag and quickly run it under the goat's neck. The poor animal went limp, dropped to the ground with an ever-expanding pool of blood now forming around the carcass. Arthur stood there a bit shocked while grandpa cleaned his knife. The old man then pointed at the goat and asked "OK"?

Arthur searched his memory for the words he had used with the old man – *no live animals* could be carried on a commercial flight. The goat was promptly wrapped up and placed in its own hold and the flight continued. Really, what else could one do at this point?

It is hard on me too

Maun, Botswana, is a town which has essentially built itself over many years. Initially through the hunting industry but now this has evolved through the businesses which support the Photographic Lodges in the Okavango Delta. Maun looks a lot like what I picture a Wild West town did in the United States in the 19th Century (minus the guns).

We do have several main tarred roads which have developed over time but most of our roads are sand tracks. It is not classified as a town or city but as a village and is situated in the Ngami-land Tribal area and the village classification allows the owners of livestock to let their animals wander free around town. In other words, if you do visit Maun do not be surprised if you come across groups of horses, goats, donkeys or cattle wandering through the centre of the place. So with all this traffic it is only sensible to lock one's gate lest you wake, as I did, to find three cows in my little 2x3m front yard, munching through my small garden. As if this weren't enough, it seemed all three cows had been at the local Indian restaurant recently for they had deposited a thin layer of brown liquid through the yard. Now, domestic livestock not only roam around quite freely consuming our gardens, blocking traffic, and creating fertilizer but they also, like the wild dogs and lions on the airstrip, have natural urges: we call it sex - for them it's mating.

On my way to work one morning there were two donkeys in the road (as is their wont). Anyway Donkey One (liable, remember?) is chasing Donkey Two through the traffic. Donkey One is in a highly excitable way, which is rather impressively displayed for all of us to see. Eventually Donkey Two makes a manoeuvring error and attempts to escape the chase over the bonnet of the vehicle in front of my taxi. Donkey One sees his opportunity and dives in. For those who have ever witnessed it (and I hope never have to again), the sights and sounds of donkeys mating is unique - but it pales into insignificance compared to the wailing of the poor car owner who now had significant hoof marks and the enduring image of Donkey Kong taking place over his polished black Mercedes (yes, we have some of those over here too). The taxi driver and I overtook mid-coitus, and he couldn't resist commenting,

"Well, there's something you don't see every day".

I spent the rest of the day chuckling but also spared a thought for the poor bastard who would have a bit of explaining to do to his insurance company. If he had been quick he could have videoed the event – just to ensure the claim was settled! I wonder if the claim falls under the Act of God section of the policy.

Maun in the 1970's and how she looks in 2016, as you can see – a bit of growth

Pin the donkey in the Tail

Rape is a serious subject and there is definitely no funny side to it but on occasion the victim may not be who you might expect. Before I arrived in Botswana there had been a couple of newspaper articles regarding a local rapist picking on certain victims – it seemed he was only interested in donkeys. He was eventually caught after having had his way with three animals and was sent away for his crimes.

Another guy was also charged with a similar crime, but his defence was a little different, 'he and the donkey were in love, so it was consensual sex'. The judge was a little suspicious of this claim, so the accused asked to call the donkey as a witness, to corroborate the facts. The judge felt the accused was attempting to make an ass out of the Court and denied the request, sending Lover boy off to serve his time with the rapist. Do you think prison will bring out the beast in both of them?

'Serial donkey rapist' caught

Maun's legion of donkeys will breathe a sigh of relief at this news!

A "serial rapist" is being treated in Maun General Hospital after allegedly raping three donkeys.

The unnatural act took place in Botshabelo ward on Sunday, police said. Tests are being carried out to see if the man is not mentally disturbed and pending the outcome of the investigation, he may be charged for practising bestiality.

According to Maun Police station commander, Moitally Thokweng, three donkeys were involved. Immediately it was reported to the police, the man was taken to the hospital and admitted.

If the man is charged, he can face a term of seven years in jail for committing an unnatural offence.

The suspect is currently not in police custody, but he is part of the investigations.

Two years ago a similar occurence took place in the town, when a man was arrested for raping a donkey on the banks of the Thamalakane River.

A bird in the hand...

I took off out of Selinda airstrip in 2008 and just as I got airborne a tiny bird flying across my flight path decided to turn right and head toward me and it was all over in a millisecond. Unfortunately he didn't quite clear the propeller tip and was partially shredded - except for one wing and some guts which bounced on to the lift strut.

My former feathered friend – a truly sad and unexpected funeral, Selinda, Botswana 2008

Due to the airflow the guts immediately hardened on to the right side lift strut but the bird's wing did not, so it flapped around a bit. I looked across my passenger for an assessment, no visible damage, good. I exercised the Pitch Lever (controls the propeller) no vibrations, all seemed to be functioning. I decided to continue on and this was about the time I pulled out my camera and snapped a picture. Out of the corner of my eye I could see my passenger glancing at the small wing flapping around and then he would turn to look at me; then he would look back at the bird wing, then me, then back.....
Eventually he tapped me on the arm:

"You hit a bird."

Obviously I did, as you just saw me take a photograph of the whole thing – moron!

"Yes I know, occasionally it happens."

Silence. I could almost hear him thinking. Then:

"What are you going to do about it?"

Are you kidding, so what's your plan Einstein - stick the aircraft in to hover mode, so I can go outside and inspect something which is less than a meter from where I am sitting?

"Well we won't be pulling over," I replied. "But don't worry, I'll deal with it at the next airstrip."

Twenty-five minutes later I was trying to pull this debris off the aircraft. It did take me a while as it had hardened to the strut like concrete. The same passenger felt the need to stop by as I was doing this and remarked:

"You should try to avoid hitting any more birds," before turning and wandering off to the camp vehicle.

Certainly sir, I shall try to be more careful in future! To the general public: maybe think about what you say before you say it, were not aiming for the things!

When it does go very wrong this is the outcome!

Aero Commander vs. Marabou stork – shall we call it a draw - June 1974 Lake Ngami, Botswana

C208B Grand Caravan vs Eagle on Take-off Stanley's airstrip, Botswana 2010

Having George for dinner

In 2015 Paddy, another pilot who we will call Andre, and I are on leave in Malawi. We are visiting our friend (and part time male stripper – see Allegations of Theft). Prince who now lives in Malawi with his beautiful wife and their two children. We have all left the bustle of the Capital Lilongwe for the peace and solitude of Lake Malawi.

If you ever get the chance, go to see the Lake. Snorkel, Scuba Dive, take a week, it is well worth it. Lake Malawi is the third largest Lake in Africa and it's enormous. It's also stunningly beautiful and is packed with almost every conceivable fish you might find in an aquarium; principally because the lake is where most of the world's Aquarium fish come from.

For accommodation there are a few ways to go, but we discovered a First Class method with Backpacker prices. This information probably piqued your interest. The Lake has numerous huge, beautiful houses (six to eight bedrooms) you can rent one for anywhere from US$200 to $350 per day. Our little group rented one for $250 between the six of us; forget your calculator its $41 per person.

The house we rented sits on the Lake, has a swimming pool, a Bar, DSTV (Cable), a full kitchen, a private beach, and all of the water toys required to enjoy the Lake. For a little extra, it also has a couple of house servants to take care of things like cooking, cleaning etc.

As an example we awoke on the third day and decided to spend the morning on the Lake but really wanted Fish & Chips for lunch. After voicing our request to the house staff, thirty minutes later six fishermen appeared on the lawn with live fish and we selected several of them and handed over a bag of potatoes. Two hours later we returned to find our food all cooked and on the table.

Most of the Lake properties are situated in and around small fishing Villages therefore there are no defined supermarkets as such - so eating needs to be planned. After three days of fresh seafood we opted for a change and the women handed out the responsibility to us men to sort all of this out – so technically they bear some of the responsibility for what happened. They stayed at the house and we drove in to the village to do the shopping. We looked at the availability of beef or pork and based upon the general hygiene of the establishments, or lack of it, finally opted for chicken.

Now you'll be happy to hear the only chicken you can get is fresh, it's so fresh it's still moving! So this is what we brought back, a live chicken. There were several on offer and the largest was a black one – but after a short discussion we felt buying, killing and cooking a black chicken in Africa could be construed as politically incorrect – Prince concurred with our assessment so as a compromise we got the slightly smaller brown one! Sorry it must be the air, but we seem to have a propensity to name things which really just shouldn't be named. On the way back to the house we decided to call our short lived friend – **George**.

Meet George

During dinner George was the topic of conversation with all of the accompanying snickering. After all he had behaved like a champion throughout his death row journey back to the house and never made a fuss in the kitchen. As we spoke of him so highly the ladies were quite inquisitive about who George was and they indicated they wanted to meet him. When we broke the news that George was basically dinner it didn't go over too well. One of them actually stopped eating and left the table – oh well, this meant there was more for the rest of us – this is the glass half full mentality. Take the time, go to Malawi the people are wonderful and the chickens are friendly too!

I'll have the fish

Lodges here are great, obviously, or they would be hard pressed to stay in business. Having said this everyone has been to a Bar, Restaurant, or Hotel which they would never go back to; it just wasn't to their liking.

Occasionally there are Lodges which guests just don't mesh with. They're nice but the kids aren't happy as there is no internet (No research done by the parents before booking), there are no Air cons (no research), it's too hot, there is too many insects, too many rules, we have to fly in an aircraft, no cell phone signal – yes no fucking research. I could understand if it were the 80's or 90's but now you have the Internet which can give you some idea of what information or needs will be catered for, so maybe take a little responsibility, rather than booking yourself in and then complaining about your situation.

Having said this, it is very rare when a Lodge does not meet even the most basic requirements. Enter an unnamed Lodge in an unnamed country which works on a budget. I understand, all businesses work on a budget, regrettably this Lodge has *under* budgeted on food. Portion sizes or maybe just supply seems to be a major issue; guests are complaining, some even leaving the Lodge early to move on to the next one.

Today, three guests have also made the decision to leave the Lodge, but they have made it a little late and are unable to fly out of the camp until the morning. They demand to see the Manager, "What's for dinner"? He shows them, and they are clearly not happy regarding the meagre amount they have seen for the three of them. They discuss it amongst themselves and tell their guide they don't want a Game Drive today – they want to go fishing!That's what they did, they fished all afternoon so they would have enough food to eat dinner! Really, have the fish it is the only thing on the menu.

Loading Guests

Many of the Rules we have for flying in the bush or staying in Safari Lodges have been developed over the years around one subject – Safety! We undertake these procedures and systems because it is the safest method for all of the people involved.

When you arrive or leave a Lodge you normally do so by aircraft. A Lodge staff member comes to the airstrip 10-15 minutes before the aircraft lands, drives up and down the airstrip to check it is clear of everything, and then parks halfway down the strip to ensure this doesn't change. The aircraft then arrives, the pilot checks the airstrip them self. The staff member on the ground waits as an additional set of eyes in case something tries to run on to the landing area during this rather critical phase of flight. It is a simple system and the whole thing works rather well.

Unfortunately, no system is perfect and occasionally all the eyes in the world don't see that one wild animal leap out. Regrettably we do have some aircraft vs. animal moments where neither party comes out unscathed.

The following photos are part of a series which can be found on the Internet and were taken by an American Helicopter pilot Shane Patrick who we really miss here. Shane was attempting to get pictures of the dust blowing up through the aircraft wingtip vortices on landing. He recorded a little more than this for the Insurance Company. In the end it was Zebra vs GA8 Airvan. Just as the aircraft was in the flare (landing) was when the animal rammed it from behind and to the right, snapping off the right Main gear. The pilot gently placed the left Main gear down allowed the aircraft to decelerate and eventually it popped on to the ground and ground to a halt. Everyone was fine – even the Zebra, if you can believe it. The animal sat on the airstrip for about an hour, somewhat stunned, and then stood up and wandered off in to the bush. The aircraft was recovered and repaired and is flying again.

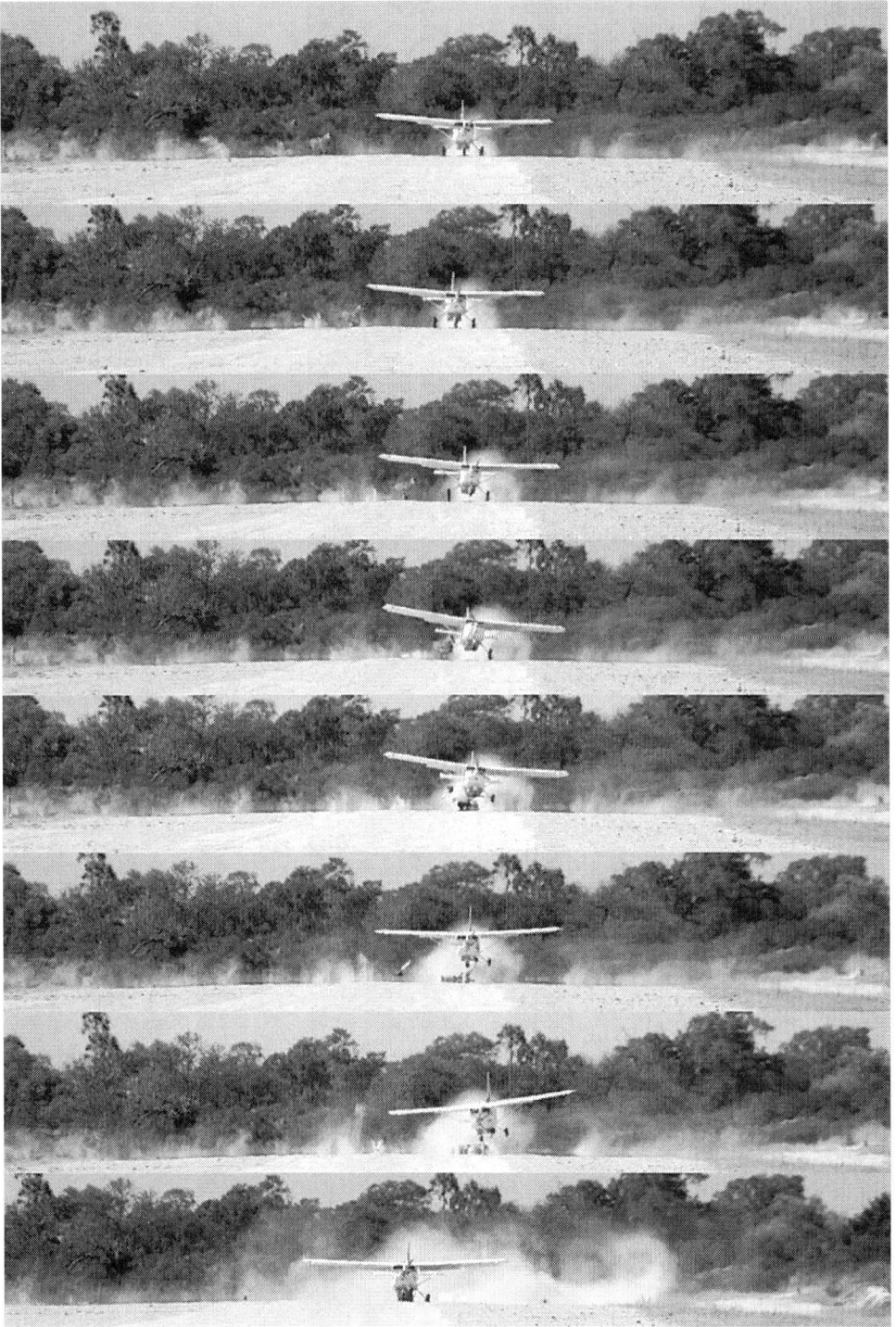

So these are the safety rules in place for you the visitor. In 2011 nothing like this happened and the system worked perfectly, well *almost*. Paddy had arrived at Piajio airstrip (Chief's Island, Okavango Delta), had squeezed his Cessna Caravan in to the small parking area and was preparing the aircraft while the Guide drove down the airstrip from his mid-way parking spot. Most Guides, when they arrive to drop or pickup guests park a reasonable distance from the aircraft – not too close and not too far. If you are here for a while you can tell by the Guide's parking if there is another variable involved.

Paddy has seen the guests and yelled out 'morning'. He is opening up the engine cowls, the doors, and is generally moving around outside the aircraft. The Guide drives up very close to the aircraft, much closer than he would normally park and the passengers just sit there without moving. Just so you know, for most of us, this is odd Guide behaviour.

The Guide is out of his vehicle and is pulling the bags off and throwing them on the ground while Paddy starts wondering what is going on. At this point all the bags are on the ground and the Guide jumps back in to the driver's seat. He bids each guest 'goodbye' before all five, as a group, flee the vehicle and race the 1.5 meters to the aircraft, rocketing up the stairs into the cabin. Not one of them greets Paddy and all of them seem to be in a big hurry to get in the aircraft. Paddy looks at the Guide and asks him what the problem is. The Guide doesn't respond.

He then collects the bags from near the tail and loads them in the aircraft and the Guide sits safely in his vehicle. Paddy moved to the pilot's door and stands on the small ladder, half in and half out of the aircraft looking at each of the five faces in the cabin, bidding them 'morning' again and announcing he needs to give the Safety Briefing. Not one of them is paying attention and all of them are looking out the left side of Paddy's aircraft.

"Guys, are you all right"?
"Lions, right there, in the bush. Look"!

With this Paddy turns to see a reasonably sized female appear from the scrub less than three meters away and wander past the aircraft's tail up to the nose and into some more scrub where she plops herself down. The journey brought her within one meter of Paddy's legs. Seeing her coming Paddy entered the cockpit rather quickly and sat staring as she wandered past. It is only then the Guide yelled out 'lookout, there are lions'. Paddy's immediate thought was this information could have been dispensed much fucking earlier.

He now had a small problem as the entire aircraft is open and in order to close it he will need to step outside. Lions can be somewhat lethargic when they want to. They have been known to sit under trees or bushes for hours at a time and everyone could clearly see her sitting four or so meters away; it's not like you can wait her out. So Paddy took a deep breath and left the cockpit, raced around the aircraft and at some point he grabbed the Caravan's tail-stand.

This is a long metal pole which we attach to the back of the aircraft for ground operations (loading and unloading) and it basically prevents the aircraft from tilting back on the tail and damaging it. This could happen if two or three rather FAT people (no other way to put it) were in the back of the aircraft at the same time. In answer to some: *'but don't you tell them one at a time'* – yes we tell them a lot of things regrettably not everyone listens or I would have 75% less material to write about.

Paddy has the Tail-stand and this is about the time the other two Lions make their presence known. They are still lying at the rear of the aircraft, about a meter and a half from Paddy, where the female had appeared from. Paddy now has the tail-stand out in front of him and is rushing to finish closing up the aircraft. Then he hears the game vehicle start and the Guide drives off down the airstrip – FUCK. Paddy is now alone with the Lions!He eventually got it all done and jumped back in but the system might have taken a few hits on this particular day. The guests said they got some great pictures though.

I feel like a run

Obviously much of the world's population are in awe of Africa and her animals. But we should all remember many Africans live in these environments and on a daily basis interact with the Wildlife. For some Africans wildlife interaction is something they do when on leave (vacation for you Americans).

Camping is popular in most cultures – camping in a Game Reserve with Lion, Leopards, Elephants, Giraffe, Hyena and Wild Dog, to name a few can present its own challenges and concerns. When you decide to camp under these conditions there are certain safety aspects one might include for the group. I know people like to exercise but when in the Bush you need to curb your yearn to run. If you run animals will assess you as food. The following was posted on Facebook in June 2016. I have obscured the names involved – but the stupidity is obvious.

THIS IS A POSTING FROM 4X4 COMMUNITY.
Next thing we know our lions will be shot for being lions!

On the 2nd of May I went for an afternoon game drive from the Moremi North Gate. At about 5pm I came across something I had never seen in a game reserve. There were 5 sub adult homo-sapiens out for a fun run. They were jogging along looking very happy and unconcerned with the potential danger. At my point of interaction they were more than 1km from the Khwai Gate heading further into the park. I assume that they all returned safely to camp. The parents of these children obviously care little for the park rules as generators were run from sunrise to late into the evening. Some South Africans should know better and respect park rules.

NOTE: You see what I mean about people breeding. Now there will be more of these morons and less lions!

Don't play with my food

I sat outside my room early one morning at ChobeChilweroBotswana (another Sanctuary Lodge) and was watching a troop of Baboons picking their way across the grass. Obviously there was some nut or fruit which was dropping from the trees and it seemed the troop liked it. Also on the lawn were about four dozen Banded Mongoose eating the same condiment. They were of course a little wary of getting too close to the Baboons. Well, all of them were but one, it seemed this big male Baboon and one of the Mongoose selected the same morsel to eat and went for it at the same time. I watched in a split second as the Mongoose was there and then he was airborne. The Baboon, without breaking his stride, grabbed the poor little thing in his right hand and flicked it away from his food. The movement was so quick it would have made and Baseball or Cricketer envious. The Baboon never even looked up as the poor Mongoose sailed through the air about two meters above the ground before crashing down the lawn some twenty meters from where he had departed. There was a squeal from the Mongoose and it disappeared; the Baboon continued its breakfast. As you might imagine, I was rolling around in tears!

I don't like your face

Many of the Lodges here have both indoor and outdoor showers. It is quite pleasant to freshen up before dinner looking into the African bush, sometimes at an Elephant, while cleaning off from a day of wildlife spotting. One Lodge here was having a small problem, all of their outdoor showers had mirrors and some of the guests would return to find the mirrors smashed. When this had happened upwards of seven times to three different rooms the Manager decided to set up a Go-Pro and establish what was going on.

It was the second day when he discovered the issue, a Baboon. Apparently Baboons would drop in to the open bathing areas most likely out of curiosity. Now, as the Baboon had arrived alone he was a little surprised to turn and see another Baboon staring at him; he would then shriek and punch at this other Baboon which of course shattered the mirror instantly. I agree, Baboons are really ugly!

My room makes me dizzy

The first time I overnighted in Zambia I stayed at a beautiful place run by Sanctuary Lodges named Sussi&Chuma.

Sussi&Chuma – Sanctuary Lodges, Livingston, Zambia sits on the beautiful Zambezi River

Many of us know the name David Livingstone who was a 19th Century Scottish medical missionary and African explorer. There is a lot more to the man than this which also includes a moment in history when Henry Morton Stanley and he met with Stanley uttering the phrase: 'Dr. Livingstone I presume'.

Chuma was a young African boy Livingstone rescued from slavery. As the boy had no family he knew about he choose to remain in the employ of David Livingstone.Sussi, another African, came into Livingstone's permanent employment some years later. When David Livingstone died, both Sussi and Chuma decided to move the body. They took it from Chitambo Village (in today's Zambia) and carried it all the way to Bagamoyo on the coast of what is considered as Tanzania. There they handed it to the British Authorities for it to be returned to England. Sussi&Chuma Lodge is named after these two remarkable Africans.

The Lodge is stunning. All of the rooms are on stilts sitting about two meters above the ground and about the same distance from the Zambezi River. On the first evening I stayed there we all had a lovely gourmet dinner with many fine wines of which I had enjoyed a couple of glasses. It was time for bed and I bid all a good night, entered my room, conducted the obligatory pre-slumber customs and then jumped in under the sheets just short of 2130 hours.

I hadn't fully dropped off but was certainly in the dozing portion before one entered REM sleep when I was awoken and found myself staring at the ceiling through the mosquito net. Something wasn't right - the ceiling appeared to be moving. Now anyone who has ever been really drunk knows this feeling as nothing will stay still; the problem being I wasn't drunk. I swung my legs over the bed and stood on the wooden floor – yes the room was definitely moving. I adjourned to the balcony and looked over the side and found the source of the oscillation, a Cape buffalo. There were in fact about ten of them under my room. One of them appeared to have an itch and had decided to use one of the supports for the room to rectify his problem. It must have been a hell of an itch because the room continued moving for another thirty minutes which I could remember. In the end, having established the issue, it was sort of soothing and I eventually dropped off to sleep. Africa, something new every day!

Careful on the pre-flight, I found this in my wheel well Maun, Botswana 2007

BAGS & AIRCRAFT vs. COMMON SENSE & MANNERS

Let's discuss some of our more rude and/or idiotic passengers. This section encompasses things which touch on a passenger's initial flight with their Charter Company. Many of our passengers come here on Safari so they are not here to ride in a Charter aircraft, they are here to go somewhere; for us pilots this means getting them to a Safari Lodge. Just like a normal airline there are certain rules; for Charter operations these usually centre on the size of our aircraft vs. the size of their bag.

The accommodation in Namibia, Botswana, Zambia, and Tanzania is spectacular. They are not hotels; they are traditionally referred to as **Lodges.** Operators' today cringe when they are referred to as *'camps'* as it tends to send the wrong message or image, so in general use of this term is often avoided. People, however, do still call them 'camps', which stems from the turn of the century when going on safari meant organizing porters, other manservants, cooks, food, rifles (normally you would be going hunting), and livestock to carry all of the required equipment to go to a chosen destination and set up camp. Think *Out of Africa – Meryl Streep and Robert Redford.*

Back then going on safari was for the rich, or eccentric, depending on the way you looked at it, and in those days they took trunk loads of stuff with them as they had unlimited manpower to carry it.
These days we take you to much more comfortable places and have small General Aviation aircraft to get you there so you can't bring a *trunk;* in fact Charter operators make it very clear what you *can* bring. Soft-sided bags of a specified dimension, no wheels: information your Agent will have given you when you booked. And of course, you'll remember to collect your bags when you arrive off your flight and pass through Customs....,or will you?

Sandibe Lodge Botswana - & Beyond

Travelling norms

Most of us who have travelled are fundamentally aware of some important responsibilities; one of these is we are required to carry our passports with us at all times. Picture someone from Mexico or Egypt standing in Los Angeles or London saying, 'But I left my passport at the hotel': these days it would always be good for a quick trip to the Police station just for the authority's piece of mind. Yet seemingly many Western visitors who would agree with this scenario are the same ones who wander around Africa without their passport. 'I wanted it to be safe so I left it at the hotel'.

The funny thing about Rules – they're everywhere and they apply to everyone. So with this in mind and for the slower readers let's have a state the obvious competition:

1) Always carry your Passport it is your proof of identity, no a Driver's License is not acceptable.

2) The rules of the country you are in are the rules stipulated *by the government* - normally referred to as The Law. They should be complied with regardless of whether you agree with them or not. Comments like "but this isn't the way we do it back home" should be muted on the indisputable fact –you are not in your country!

3) Upon arrival and immediately after passport control you usually pass through the Green (I don't have anything) or Red (Yes I'm honest but this probably won't work out for me) Customs formalities. Of course for these moments you need to have your luggage with you. But you know this, unfortunately it seems not everyone does!

The traditional gateway to the Okavango Delta is Maun, and the number of passengers arriving here who go through passport control, straight *past Customs* and out into the terminal to meet their Lodge representative *without their luggage* is roughly 15%. Only then do they inquire when their checked luggage will appear. To those people I say - wake up! The responsibility of claiming and presenting your bag to a Customs representative is yours and yours alone. I say this because on more than one occasion we have had people ask us *why* they had to collect the bag themselves – I don't know, maybe because it's *your bag*.

Everybody has 'personal baggage'

In 2007 I witnessed one gentleman screaming at the poor lady meeting him after he discovered his bag was still sitting in Customs because he had breezed past these officials and made it to the Arrivals area. The screaming was to punctuate the point and consisted of the sentence -"the system in my country is much more organized and the people there would have sorted out my bags more professionally". I wasn't sure if he thought African's were hard of hearing or just this lady hence the need for the amplification. I decided it was neither and he was just being a prick.

I have my limits to people's rudeness so on the day in question I stepped in to point out at one time I had lived in his country and at no time at San Francisco, LAX, Honolulu, Denver, Houston, Chicago or JFK do the airlines or any other agent retrieve and present your bags to Customs, then leave them on the kerb. I then went on to suggest he lower his voice and return the way he had come to undertake his responsibility to claim his luggage and present it to customs. Some may say my behaviour was rude, but I am going with direct.

On this occasion (yes there have been many others) the client was unhappy with my 'insolence' and initially rejected my suggestion, so I provided him some additional motivation. I pointed out if a traveller enters any country without presenting *everything*they brought with them, by law, this constitutes an *illegal* entry. Such an entry could raise serious suspicions and lead to an even greater delay for him, especially if someone higher up the official ladder were informed of it. I proffered this was the direction I was fully ready to pursue, having witnessed his "very rude behaviour", and included "you would really make my day by keeping your voice down and stop treating the lady like a servant". There was a short silence before the conversation abruptly ended, he disappeared and when he returned with his bag he was, happily for all, a new person.

That's not mine

Some of you may have noticed a worldwide propensity these days to use the phrase 'but it's not my fault' to literally any situation where a potential problem pops up. It's as if we as people could not possibly make any mistake. So you know, I make them, as do other people working with me. Yet a good deal of our guests do not, seemingly they are perfect; this must be really nice.

From time to time we have people rush through Baggage claim grabbing the wrong bag. This occasionally extends to the point where the bag makes it all of the way to the aircraft or even the Lodge before the mistake is discovered. In the end it's fine, it happens; all I can say is, if you do make this error make sure you handle it some measure of maturity.

In 2015 one gentleman claimed his bag, presented it to the Charter Company's Porters (Ground staff) and the pilot (me), it was labelled with the Charter company's baggage tag, he proceeded thorough the Departure lounge to a vehicle to transport him to the aircraft. At the vehicle he again identified the same bag (to me); only when he got to the aircraft did he say – "that's not my bag, what have you done with my bag?" He then turned and proceeded to start screaming at the Porter who was assisting him. – "I knew it, typical. I knew this would happen and something would get stolen."

My immediate thought was - You knew what - crime happens everywhere or just here in Africa, you know with Africans? When he had completed his rendition of a four year old, I then asked him to escort me back to the terminal to look for the bag. He rudely refused:

"Your staff lost it, why should I get involved. You can work it out yourselves. I'm staying here".

With this he folded his arms across his chest and took a step back; yes, extremely mature. Keep in mind there are eight other people (nine if you include his wife) waiting to board the aircraft and go to camp, its 35C (about 100F) – so this idiot is delaying all of them purely through a lack of cooperation.

This grabbing the wrong bag happens a lot and the usual solution is Customs. It's uncommon for both parties to grab the wrong bag at the same time. So Customs usually has the missing bag as the other party would not claim it as their own. On this day my immediate thought was this, so I grabbed the errant bag to take it back to the terminal and the guy said, if you can believe it.

"Where are you going with the bag?"

"Sir I am going to look for yours".

"Well I'd rather you left this onehere, okay?"

So it's not his but I can't take it - Yeah, real Twilight Zone territory. As you will see in the coming pages I can have a bit of a short fuse when it comes to illogical thinking, today was no exception.

"Just confirm this is your bag?"

"I have already told you it's not mine."

"And will you be accompanying me to the Terminal to locate your bag?"

"No! Were you not listening to me?"

I could see him building to another round of screaming but this crap doesn't work with me. Most people scream at someone to set them off balance or make a scene thereby ensuring they get what they want – if you doubt this think of a child, it's the same concept. If you want to try immature stuff like screaming with me go right ahead.

"So if it's not your bag, then you have absolutely no say over where it goes or who handles it, are we in agreement? Now if you'll excuse me I will locate the problem."

I had a pretty good idea where the problem lay. It was this guy's thought process which he had developed somewhere between birth and two minutes ago. When I arrived at the terminal I walked straight in to Customs and there was an identical bag. I had a short conversation with the Customs ladies who were very accommodating, but they still needed to see the owner. I radioed the Porter at the aircraft and told him to please grab the gentleman and drive him to Customs; the guystill refused to leave the aircraft. I got in the vehicle I had come in and attempted to calm myself during the 2km drive back to the aircraft.When I arrived I could see the other passengers were now very irritated as this whole fiasco had occupied upwards of 15 minutes of their time. In theory we should have been close to landing at their airstrip but we were still standing on the apron in Maun.

"Sir, your bag is in Customs. You need to return with me and claim it in front of the Customs Officer before they will release it. Please get in the vehicle."

"Why is it in Customs? I gave it to your Ground staff – why did they take it back to Customs?"

Once again, we return to the Twilight Zone. Yes, as soon as we were presented with your bag we rushed it through the screening process and ran and hid it in the Customs area – just to piss you off. Then we found an identical bag and drove it to the aircraft, hoping you wouldn't notice. But, hey, you caught us! Yeah this all sounds quite rational to me – what do you think?

Eventually he got in the vehicle and drove back to see Customs. Both bags were side by side and he visibly hesitated when deciding which one was his. Yet when he returned to the aircraft he was vocal the Porters had lost his luggage. You know what they say when people oversell stuff.

Ill-informed

All travel 'Agents' who book a Camp for the guests, my apologies, *lodge* (*bad* habits), are required to come here regularly to see exactly what it is they are selling – a sort of a visit to the factory to check product quality. It's a great perk for the Agent as everything in the lodges is included in the price (accommodation, food, activities, even alcohol). Because of the size of our aircraft the Agent isrequired to tell you certain thingsand one of them concerns your travel bag.

Please note I did not use the word *suitcase* because they are not generally allowed. You have to make special arrangements (well in advance) for Mr. Samsonite to be your travel companion. This is not done to inconvenience you but to assist us in getting you to the Lodge safely, comfortably, and with no additional charges. While we understand huge bags come in very handy if you are disposing of your spouse's body, they will usually not fit in our aircraft. If you opt for the body option then please go ahead and bring the suitcase but you will need to fork out in advance for a luggage seat; which seems fair, after all as it is your spouse's last trip.

When a guest shows up with a suitcase the Charter Company will ask them to repack –
most companies supply a repack bag. Each and every day we encounter guests who have
either refused to listen or regrettably their agent has omitted this critical holiday
information. The latter is not the guest's fault and although we empathize it does not
change our situation – the bag just won't fit in the aircraft.

In 2008 a German couple arrived: the husband was six foot two, slender, and well dressed
as so many Germans are. He wasn't fat but with his height he would have been in the
hundred kilo area of the scales. He presented his suitcase to me which easily reached his
waist and at a push could have been used as a tall coffee table.

I went through the obligatory baggage weights and dimensions conversation which I was
sure he had had with his agent, something along the lines of *'stick to the limits unless you
are prepared to pay for additional charges such as a bigger aircraft – if we have one
available.'* This guest was adamant he knew nothing of this; the agent had not mentioned
it. Furthermore it was not his problem, (seemingly he needed his mobile closet); that was
that *take them to camp*! For some reason, (it may have been his lovely wife's face which
jogged my mind), through my fog and haze I managed to muster up the memory of these
two from the previous year, but before I could say anything his beautiful wife said it for
me.

"I remember you, you flew us last year to Khwai River. Remember, dear?"

His face changed colour a bit, sort of a soft red. Rage or embarrassment – I wasn't sure.

"Ah," I said. "So you have been here before and understand all the luggage
requirements?"

At this point the husband seemed a little less staunch on his suitcase ignorance and the

83

repack bag was presented and grudgingly used.Madam, if you are out there, I thank you from the bottom of my heart! I don't know if it was a *fauxpas* on your part, but you made my day: to get you there safely, without any further argument and, most importantly, the look on your husband's face was, to borrow MasterCard's catchphrase, priceless!

As an example this is luggage for 5 people staying four days in a Lodge, please try to remember you are here to spend time in the Bush to commune with Nature - it's not a costume ball.

The luck of the Irish

Late in 2007, roughly six months into my flying career, I met an Irish family, from Dublin. The wife, a pretty petite lady with soft red hair who I could easily picture baking a Shepard's pie in a small farm house in the country, two kids; who were remarkably well behaved, and a lady I took for the grandmother; just a picture of a family. Unfortunately Dad was what one might term *a rude bastard.*

Back then we pilots didn't normally meet and greet the clients: the company had a member of staff for this, so I would wait to hear from them before arriving at the Terminal to collect my passengers and fly them. This particular day I decided to accompany the young lady on duty and see how all this was all done – sort of self-training. Frankly, the whole thing was a bit of a zoo: it's not the operators fault, it is just we have a really old airport and it was designed for another era. So as I had not really done this before I decided to watch the other pilots (different companies) and this lady. I stood there taking it in: Yes, this makes sense, all straightforward. Then my guests showed up. I was standing roughly a metre away watching our young lady and when she was finished I stepped over to introduce myself. Dad was last with the introductions.

"Well, nice of you to make it". (This was said with heavy sarcasm.)

I was a little taken back "I'm sorry?"

"You've took your time. We've been waiting here for you."

Regrettably I have used this type of approach in a few conversations in my life (I think it was when I was a teenager) and since not one of those conversations went very well I soon stopped doing it – more self-training. Any of us who have gone down this socially inept path learn quickly it's rude, unnecessary and moreover, generally makes you appear foolish. For these little moments in life when people speak to me this way I choose *not to ignore them.*

"Yes I do apologize for the *nine seconds* you had to wait; I was standing over there while this lady was greeting you."

There was a few moments of silence while he had a look where I was pointing. Then he turned back and I continued.

"I am also sorry but you are going to be a little further delayed as this lady is now going to discuss your luggage."

The young lady took over and went on to have a very frank, but polite, conversation with the family regarding the seven hard suitcases and three soft bags they had brought for the five of them for the *two days* they would be spending in the Lodge. I stood by, observing the father as I could see which way the wind was going to blow. He kept interrupting, the lady would then politely continue and he would interrupt her again. This went on for a while before the conversation finally came to an end with:

"….and I am sorry but all those details would have been in the booking information we sent you".

The wife was apologetic and embarrassed. She was sure she had read everything but hubby immediately chimed our Meet and Greet lady was '**wrong**' and **'no it wasn't in the booking paperwork'**. The lady then asked if Father Irish might just retrieve the paperwork so we could all have a look.

"Why? I've told you it's not there."

She looked at this gentleman and said:

"Yes, of course, but we are still going to have to ask you to repack your bags into smaller bags for the aircraft".

"We don't have any smaller bags", Dad shot back.

"Don't worry sir, we can supply these bags for you", she countered.

"How much?" Now, when he said this he folded his arms across his chest and started slowly nodding, as if to say *'so this is your game, is it – more money?'*

"Sir, there's no charge. And we will store your bags here until you return from the bush".

There was a short silence as Irish had run out of excuses. It was then he decided to reuse one of them.

"Nope I don't think its fair you asking us to repack when we haven't been told about any of this."

So far I hadn't said much of anything, I knew this Meet and Greet lady, she had been in the business a lot longer than I had; she had had good training and successfully dealt with difficult clients before. However, most companies do not give *asshole training* and I could see this was the territory the guy was quickly moving into. So I stepped in.

"I am sorry, but the reason for the repack situation is I am pretty sure all of this cannot fit in the aircraft I am flying today. Even if it does, we still need to fly you safely out of the small airstrip we are taking off from when you finish your stay".

"You didn't tell us".

This moron just kept repeating himself. I really felt sorry for the rest of the family, so I proffered a solution.

"Right, let's see the booking paperwork. If it is truly not in there I will make a plan and somehow get all of this to your destination".

From the look on his face he knew I had him cornered but he wasn't done yet.

"No, there's no need to look. I know it's not there so there is no reason to get the paperwork out. I want to go to camp and I am not repacking. None of us are".

His wife attempted to speak to him and he just held up his hand and said 'No' quite loudly, much like I have seen some parents speak to their children. When she made a second attempt he shut her down even more rudely (basically shut up as he was dealing with it). The Grandmother's eyes tightened and locked on to him. I was guessing this was his motheras amother-in-law would likely have stepped in if their daughter was under this kind of attack. Keep in mind the kids are standing right there listening to it all. All I could think was what a c**t. Based upon his language and principally on the way he was speaking to his wife I got a little angry and my patience wore out.

"Okay, I'll take them. No problem - we'll take everything".

His expression indicated this was not the response he was expecting.

"Really?"

"Absolutely. But there's one condition, Sir: once we leave the terminal it's a done deal. We take everything, there's no changing your mind or asking for repack bags when you see the size of the aircraft. The aircraft is loaded the way *I* want it to be, there will be absolutely no criticism of how I handle the luggage to get it in the aircraft and no further discussion regarding any luggage aspect of your flight to camp. Agreed?"

Meet and Greet lady was staring at me in shock as if to say 'what the hell are you doing?' I didn't wait for an answer from this rude bastard and got our porter to take all the bags to the X-ray machine. Once everyone was safely through, the group and I trekked across the apron to the little Cessna 206.

The Porter started to load the aircraft; the soft bags went into the Cargo Pod first. They made it easily. Now the small Samsonite hard cases were squeezed through the door. These I actually did not think would even make it through the little door. Unfortunately they don't just need to make it through they need to be pushed to the opposite side of the Pod.

The little cargo pack under the aircraft was where I needed to fit all this rude bastards' luggage

When Cessna designed the 206 it did not have a Cargo Pack or Pod on the bottom. The feature is what is known as a Mod (Modification to the original Type Certification). So the underside of the fuselage is not flat but curved and the bags needed to get past this curve to the far side of the Pod's storage area.

The porter who was trying to squeeze these bags in finally looked at me and shook his head so I stepped in and took over. I positioned the handle of the bag outward toward me (so I could yank it out on arrival), then put my foot against the bag, held onto the lift strut and used my body weight to push the bag further in. I did this three more times. On the last two bags I heard a plastic cracking noise. Oops, oh well, he wanted them in camp! One big bag was then placed pretty much in the door but it wasn't quite in, so I put my knees on it and helped it along: more cracking.

"I think you are breaking it", the guy said in a very small voice.

I ignored his breach of the established rules and continued loading. Then I got everyone in, but made sure Dad sat in front with me. While we taxied he was looking worriedly around.

"Is all this okay?" Yes, there was no trace of the brash confidence he had demonstrated in the terminal.

"All what?" Remember there are times when ignorance has its uses.

"The small plane, all the bags and us?"

"I'm sorry, I thought you and I had an understanding about the luggage subject."

"No, I mean is this safe?"

"It's a little late for this conversation isn't it?" It *was* safe, of course, just a little packed. My feeling was he didn't deserve the information.

"So it's not safe?"

"Didn't say that."

"So what are you saying?"

"I'm not saying anything at all. It's you who's been doing all of the talking since we met; and now you want my opinion? Funny, I seem to remember trying to give it to you in the terminal. Excuse me I have to speak to the tower."

I didn't, but I was tired of this guy. We took off and flew the twenty minutes to the family's destination. Everyone got out and I started unloading all the bags: three of the cases were cracked but I ignored this and handed them over to the guide.

"Thanks very much for flying with us and enjoy your time in camp".

This I directed to his lovely family. Then I looked back down the700-metre strip we had flown into staring at the trees at one end and commented to the guide.

"Wow, those trees are getting taller and taller! One day it will be a big ask to clear them on take-off". It never would but he didn't know this; I looked back at Irish who was staring at me.

"Have fun in camp", I said again.

I wanted him concentrating on the trees for the next few days. I made sure it was me who went back and picked them up. Of course we left the trees intact, but it might have been a new underwear moment for him.

This is luggage for two people staying two days in camp. How much stuff can you wear?

36 is less than 20

In 2009 at Kasane Airport I met two Italians who needed to be flown to Gunns Camp. They were a lovely couple, polite, very pleasant, who had only just got married three days before. I congratulated them, handed over their tickets then asked about the bags. They pointed to *a single bag* which looked like it housed a dead body. I discussed the luggage requirements, a total of 20kg per person (including hand luggage) and the husband assured me the bag was under the limit at 36kg. I indicated I was a little confused regarding his rational which was 36 was less than 20kg.

"But there are two of us, so 18kg each and we are still four kilograms under."
He smiled away, and I didn't have the heart to tell him this line of thinking was approaching clinical stupidity, so I opted for a different angle.

"So if you were a family of four you would have brought an 80kg bag?"

He looked at me a little confused.

"But that would be just…silly."

Yet here we stood having this conversation! The mind does boggle doesn't it?

PS - Please follow the luggage guidelines: it not only assists us but also guarantees your own peace of mind during your stay.

BELT UP

Obviously when you fly you need to wear a seat belt, you would think this is not a difficult concept to understand as we all do it each day in our cars. This area of the flight frustrates me no end, but these are personal issues for which the regular counselling I receive is helping.

Now, it is true certain areas of aviation tend to produce some complicated systems for preventing deceleration trauma, but on the whole General Aviation seatbelts are fairly straightforward. There is the actual belt bit which goes around your waist - which is why it is called a seat BELT, and then the shoulder bit crosses your torso from one shoulder to opposite hip, aka a shoulder harness. Aircraft do not have the kind of belts where you open a car door and the thing slides around the frame of the door, no, ours require some minimal effort which may involve a spark of electricity between a few brain cells: you pick up both ends and join the male and female parts together until you hear a click. The whole thing is designed to stop you moving: it's not rocket science.

So, on the Seat Belt issue I am a lot less tolerant, that's right, *less* not more, when being barraged by questions which revolve around whether an individual has their safety belt attached correctly or indeed whether *they have to use it at all.* For those passengers who are unsure about their belt, its fine: I much prefer the *'can you help me?'* approach. I'll happily assist, using it as a chance to find out something about the person, such as where they're from, if they are enjoying their stay, if it's their first time here and so on. Flying can be stressful for some and I think keeping the whole event light is important. But having no idea what you are doing and then refusing to ask for help will not endear you to me. So here are a couple of individuals who did not use my preferred method.

Is this right?

One lady had successfully done the waist portion of her belt and then wrapped the shoulder harness, which is a single strap, around her throat – twice, only then enquiring if it was correct.

My response in these situations is to try to educate, I am very helpful this way, which I normally do by asking the passenger what a seat belt is there for or what it is designed to do. I have received varying answers to this question and one of my favourites is: "because it's the law". This is not *itspurpose* it's the legislation behind the device. The correct answer is: to restrain you if there were a sudden change in velocity. In other words if we were going very fast and then we suddenly stopped - sometimes referred to as 'a crash'.

So my next question to female Darwin nominee number 8 is this: 'what's going to happen to your neck if we stop really fast?' A few seconds went by before the light bulb went on and then she sheepishly removed the strap so I could show her where the unit actually went.

I can't figure this out....

People often get frustrated around aircraft because they feel they should know what to do next but they cannot figure it out and are often reluctant to ask for help. Kind of like the guy who drives around with a map, obviously lost but who won't ask a soul for assistance, principally because the wife or girlfriend next to them has suggested it. I think this is called stubbornness, or pride, ego; something like this. *Please* just ask for the help – really. It is however, nice to know, this more than often *male* related disorder extends to females as well.

I had one lady who was a very young sixty with a beautiful soft purple tint in her hair and a set of diamond earrings with a matching ring which would have easily cleared Malawi's World Bank payment for the month - if she so chose to donate them. The lady clearly could not figure the belt/harness arrangement. I was hunched in behind her offering help, but she couldn't hear me because her emotions were spilling over and she was focused on the belt ends in either hand. When she finally realized I was there she shouted,

"I can't figure this out! It's impossible! I guess I'm just stupid - what do you think?"

Only one thing entered my mind so I responded with it:

"I was instructed not to argue with the clients."

It was immediately apparent she did not find my response amusing; but her husband who was on the other side of the narrow aisle was hysterical. It didn't improve her mood or feelings toward me when I pointed out him wetting himself. This may sound rather mean to you but it ended up with everyone in the cabin, including this lovely lady, laughing so hard there were tears. I of course could not join in – it would have been inappropriate, plus I had to fly the aircraft.

I can do it!

Returning to the men and maps analogy, I would need a Cray supercomputer to count how many guys have entered my aircraft, clearly couldn't figure out the seat belt arrangement, will not ask for help, and refuse it even when it is offered. They more often than not turn belligerent if you attempt to interfere with their holiday version of solving a Rubik's Cube.

In the beginning I was not as assertive as I am now, - for those who know me, please stop laughing, there was a time. Early on I had one gentleman delay my aircraft while he insisted he wanted to work the seatbelt out for himself. I treated him as tenderly as possible rather than wound his ego. As a result I was severely reprimanded for running unacceptably late and it was then I chose to adopt a different approach.

As in anything in life, we evolve in order to survive and nowadays I just do the belts myself drowning out objections with as much chatter as possible, thereby ignoring the protester by speaking politely, but more loudly than they do. It is a much more efficient and less stressful use of my time and helps me stay on schedule, but you still get the argument from people who indicate they don't want me touching them. In some cases the objection is valid as there are real phobias. Nevertheless these comments more likely stem from the frustration and resentment at the fact they had to have it done for them like children. In cases like this you can always proffer the *trust concept.*

"Sir, it's just a seat belt, I am sure you can *trust me* with it.After all I will have your entire life in my hands in a few moments so the belt is the least of your issues."

This needs to be followed by a small smile and a wink. I have found this tends to break the ice for the moment – most times at least.

Do I have to wear a seat belt?

I have been asked this more times than I care to remember by passengers, usually followed by, "Why do I have to wear it?" This type of thinking kind of makes you wonder how the individual is still alive, had children, you know, made it through their work lives? I certainly wouldn't want to car-pool with this jackass if they always sat behind me.

The first, polite, answer to this is: "I am sorry, you *do* need to wear it as it is not only a legal requirement but also for your safety". This stems the flow of enquiries on this issue with about 95% of all people; but then there are the 5%ers. Persistent haggling by this group regarding this survival requirement generally leads to the development of a more succinct discussion with the pilot, followed by polite insistence and finally culminates in something like this from one pilot named Steve Hollingsworth:

"Oh, you're right, I completely forgot; we're the only airline in the world which is approved to fly passengers without seat belts."
This guy looked dumbfounded at Steve, "Really?"
"No. Now put the belt on or you can step out of the aircraft and maybe take the next one, which by the way, has a remarkably similar restraint system and pilot."

Being Big-Boned

I understand people come in different sizes: this is why we have adjustable seat belts. But everyone must realize eventually the belt comes to an end, right? I mean the aircraft manufacturer can't construct a never-ending seat belt on the off-chance Fat Bastard will show up for a flight.

So, it's 2007, I am doing my usual, belting in an Australian lady who hadn't taken a break from complaining since I met her in the terminal:

"It's too hot"; "why is the terminal so old?"; "Immigration were rude"; "why are you taking my bag, am I going to get it back?" - No it's a bag napping and this is the last time you will ever see it; "what do you mean I have to get my passport out again?"; "we need to go through security but I just did it like two hours ago" - yes darling, that was South Africa and this is Botswana. Anyway, you get the idea.

We have now reached the aircraft: "it's so small"; "how is everybody going to fit in?"; "is it safe"; "*I can't fit in there*". YES, finally she had said something which made sense. You know, she was absolutely right, she was unlikely to fit in the aircraft.

In order to get a sense of the physical depth of the woman I was looking at you need to picture a South African or New Zealand Rugby player, a Prop or a Forward, too you Americans pick your biggest NFL Line-backer. All of these guys usually stand over six feet (about 1.9 meters) and often weigh in the 130 kilogram area. Now, whoever you have pictured retain the weight, and make her about 5' 5" (1.6 meters). Yeah, wow, sort of round with bulges which look remarkably like arms and legs.

With some effort, I did manage to finally squeeze this lady into her seat and as I said was belting her in but was having trouble getting the male part of the belt to reach the female part, principally because no one makes seat belts you can measure curtains with –it's impractical. There's no polite way to say it – her FAT was in the way of me doing my job. I kept telling her to breathe in and then I pulled really hard and on the forth go I finally heard the click.

To be fair she did look a little uncomfortable and she said to me "I can't breathe". I looked - her chest was going up and down. "See, you're breathing". I was about to close the door when she added:

"Your seat belts are too small."

"Well, that's one explanation."

She looked at me oddly. "What would another one be?"

"Sorry I won't tell you madam, but its twenty minutes to where you are going so if you figure it out let me know on arrival".

She never did tell me - maybe she still hasn't worked it out.

Some of the very large things you will see in the Okavango Delta...or possibly trying to get in to the aircraft!

You can't make me

Steve Hollingworth was a pilot in Botswana in the early part of this century. I could accurately say he was an educated and a very worldly man with a great sense of humour. You will note in all cases I have presented him in the past tense and this is not a writing error. Tragically Steve was killed in an aircraft accident on the border of Cameroon, West Africa, in June 2010 and is sorely missed. But more about him later as he does appear in several areas of this book.

In 2008 Steve'spassengers were a father, mother and a seven-year old boy from New Zealand. Unfortunately the kid refused to put the seat belt on and the parents seemed uninterested in the dispute. Finally, Steve said the aircraft wasn't going anywhere until the belt was on. The parents finally got involved, they apparently started speaking gently to the boy, coercing him, offering him hints of future rewards (bribes); Steve's actual thought was: who the hell is running the house they came from? The boy relented, put his belt on and shortly after this they were airborne. Ten minutes into the flight Steve receives a tap on the shoulder and it's the boy, belt off, arms out like he's at a revival church yelling;

"What are you going to do now Mr. Pilot"? Steve motioned to the father who promptly shrugged at the boy's disobedience. Obviously he'd seen it all before, hell, seen it, the two parents had *created* it?

Let's stop here for a discussion on gravity. We all have a rudimentary understanding of the concept. We jump and a force above us pushes us back to earth. In space there is no gravity so you just float around. Did you know you can alter the forces of gravity given the right dynamic? You may have seen it with astronauts in a NASA aircraft floating around for several seconds. Now, back to the story.

Steve then called out to the parents, "Are your belts on tight?" He received confused nods. He then started to push the control column forward creating what is known as Negative G's or a negative gravitational force. The parents were unaffected due to the fact they were wearing seat belts. The boy, however, was now floating up from his seat and screaming. Steve then pulled back on the control column and this smart ass kid was promptly planted back in his seat, suitably terrified. Steve looked over and yelled; "PUT YOUR BELT ON NOW OR THE NEXT ONE WILL HURT." There was frantic movement and the belt clicked home. Problem solved. You see - Parenting, it's not difficult!

Note:

As an aside for you 5%'ers, what a lot of you fail to remember is since 9/11 the worldwide aviation community has promulgated legislation which is pretty harsh regarding <u>non-compliance on a commercial flight</u>. Yes, this includes <u>every commercial flight,</u> even the 'little ones', as a lot of the aircraft we fly are referred to. Just throwing a thought out there. But, hey, feel free to test the boundaries. The Industry is starting to lose its patience. I don't suppose you'd like to be a test case: it comes with a fine and a free trip to prison. I am sure you'll make some new friends and possibly get a rectal exam!

AIRSTRIPS

Some of our airstrips have their little challenges

Ninety nine percent of all people *fly* into and out of the Lodges in Zambia, Tanzania and Botswana: this is why we all have jobs and for this we are very grateful. To fly in and out, these people need to be driven to and from the airstrip. The ones leaving need to await the arrival of their winged chariot and the same vehicle which transports those people there will fleet away the new arrivals getting off the aircraft. For some who are passionate about flying or filming an aircraft this is the momentfor them to seemingly participate. Sadly, in some cases, this participation can lead to the aforementioned thought-process which can set you up as a Darwin award nominee.Just so we are clear, if any of you Darwinians are reading this please note none of us have any interest whatsoever in being associated with your coming award. The fact I could be harmed or even killed in the crossfire, so to speak, also makes me furious with myself for having been stupidly unable to avoid this year's moron.Yet these potential award-winners can be difficult to spot. Here are some examples;

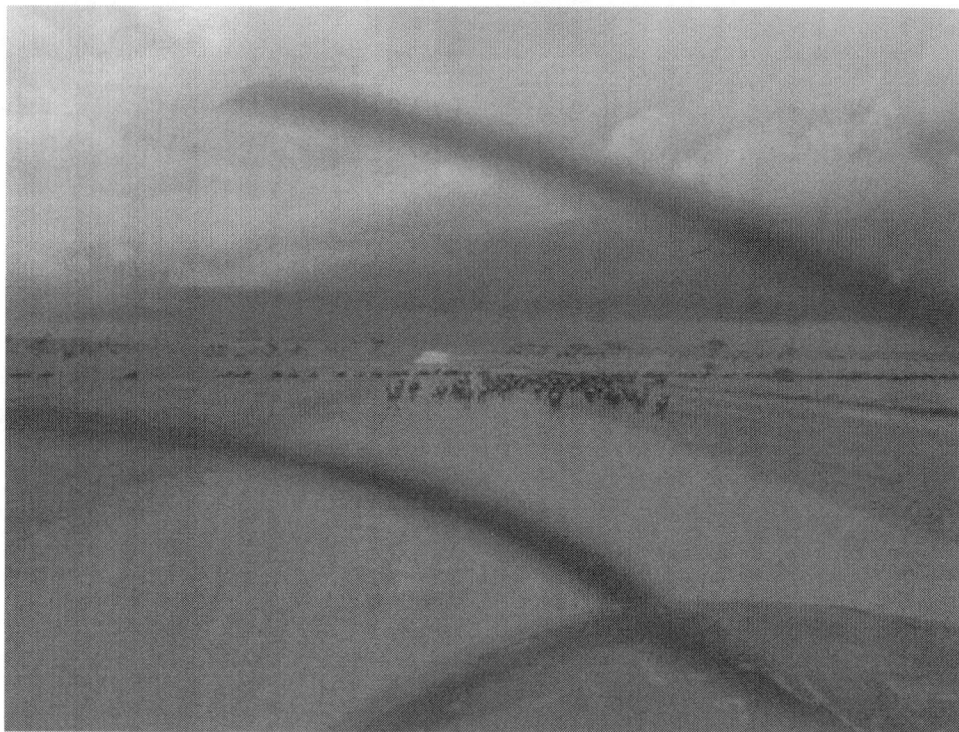

Seronera airstrip, Tanzania where a C208 pilot awaits a Wildebeest heard to finish crossing – just a small delay. This airstrip also services larger aircraft.

Tens of Thousands of Wildebeests migrating across Tanzania's Serengeti

Welcome to our village

A Cessna C208B Grand Caravan (pilot plus 13 for perspective on size) on a U.N. contract is landing in the Sudan; as it touchesdown the entire village runs onto the airstrip waving and shouting to greet the aircraft. In order to avoid killing anyone, the pilot swung left off the runway, through a ditch, thereby snapping off the nose gear which caused the propeller to impact the ground, which, in turn, shock-loaded portions of the turbine engine and other accessory drives. Luckily for all, there were no injuries.

Roughly two months and US$650,000 later the aircraft was operational again. Keep in mind the insurance pays the repair cost of the aircraft but not the down-time when it wasn't able to make a profit. So it is not just about someone paying to get the aircraft back!

Now, I suspect what some of you are thinking: 'But they are poor African villagers, living in the middle of nowhere, uneducated, probably don't understand what an aircraft is, big bird', and so on and so forth. Okay, fair comment, a bit bigoted maybe, but I'll let it pass. So let's move on.

Rifle Range

It's 2009 and a Cessna 206 with three people on board is landing at a bush strip in Botswana to collect four guests and fly them to their next camp. The pilot is about to put the aircraft wheels on the airstrip's surface maybe 10 feet above it, at an approximate speed of 75 knots (130km/60mph), when 400 metres down the airstrip Fred today's moron from the good old US of A leaps from his game vehicle in his Darwinian moment.

Before the guide can stop him he runs onto the runway so he can get a front-on shot of this aircraft closing in on him at high speed. The guide yells he must come back NOW! But alas, the people of Botswana are lovely, friendly Africans and things like giving orders or yelling are for most of them not really part of their cultural chemistry. Fred ignores his guide's warnings and continues taking pictures as the aircraft bears down on him. Fred is clearly a member of the 5% as well as being an idiot. Fred obviously endangered himself and all the people in the aircraft but luckily for him there were no dire consequences, much of it due to the pilot's quick reactions as he added power and did a go-around to position for another landing.

Now, you might ponder how a man who has, supposedly, received sufficient education to earn enough money to come on safari cannot see the possible problems of running out in front of a fast moving object. My thinking was perhaps Fred should consider spending time at a local rifle range: there are plenty of fast moving objects there and he would certainly get a great view if he stood in front of them (not apologising for this one).

Anyway, just so you know, the guide almost lost his job over the incident as the safari companies expect these professionals to control their guests just like we pilots have to: sort of like parents with children. But when we cannot control them and something goes wrong we are sanctioned – we can lose our jobs, our licenses and, in some cases, our freedom or even our life.I thought the idea was to employ people in need of jobs, you know, Africa and all that, not get them fired.

A Facebook moment

At times there are several aircraft at a given airstrip and as any pilot will know, a lot of aircraft in close proximity means the possibility of someone getting injured, so your danger senses are heightened. Mine are finely tuned out of selfishness: injuring or killing someone creates a lot of paperwork, and I hate paperwork.

A pilot friend of mine in his youth used to be a coach-builder (manufacturing buses and such) and when he was an apprentice one of his responsibilities was to put the 'Please keep your head inside window' stickers below each window. He hated doing it, considering if you were this stupid then you deserved a quick trip off the planet.

On this particular occasion I am outside my aircraft at a bush strip just as one of the other pilots starts their engine on the opposite side of the parking area: this seems to act like a pistol shot for the London Marathon for two guests who leap from completely separate vehicles - they don't know each other yet respond identically – maybe stupidity is a communicable disease. They run to a position roughly five feet in front of this poor pilot's spinning propeller, wielding cameras to catch *the shot*, get *one photo* they can post on their Facebook page – if they live long enough to do it.

I was caught flat-footed, but two pilots who were closer ran after the two guests in an attempt to stop them. The pilot involved immediately shut down the engine. The obvious question is *"what the fuck are you two morons doing?"* but decorum needs to come before hostility so everything is done politely, inquiries made and so on.

As was said, they were trying to get the perfect shot and both of them were livid with the three pilots who had ruined their photographic moment, yelling complaints and some quite strongly worded abuse. They were also stomping around like a six-year-old does before retreating to their camp vehicles, threatening to complain to our respective companies.

I'm not sure how the complaint would be worded and I am still waiting. Something to the effect of 'we were denied the ability to endanger ourselves and others.....', would be a great start. Am also not really sure what to say: more Darwin nominees?

PS

I am sorry; one of these stories was purposely altered. In Sudan there were no villagersas they seem to have the basic and *uneducated* common sense to stay away from an aircraft during landing; it was actually several goats which ran in front of the aircraft causing the pilot to avoid them; yes the accident happened, January 2010, Walgak, the Sudan.

Note the imprint of the nose wheel in the ditch – ouch!Remember flying in Central Africa presents a lot of challenges – the U.N. aren't there on vacation

Think of it this way, if I had not altered the first story to establish a mind-set, or prejudice, you might not have believed the other two. Everything else is true; Fred does exist, hopefully exploring a rifle range somewhere; see you on the next trip Fred, if you make it. Still waiting for the complaint letters from Darwinians 15 & 21; but I am patient.

As for the above aircraft, a brilliant team of engineers over a period of six days in the blazing heat of a Sudanese desert painstakingly replaced the Pratt & Whitney Engine, the Propeller, Nose Gear and any number of other accessory drives. They then obtained a Ferry Permit to fly it back to its approved Maintenance Facility. She then spent a further sixweeks under maintenance scrutiny before being successfully returned to service. I can assure you accidents here are beyond rare despite all the crap you read in the newspapers. For those of you non-aviation types who are a bit shocked at all of this, remember our aircraft get *thoroughlyinspected*each 100 hours of flying (200 for Turbines) which for many Charter Operations here is every 6-8 weeks – this is means on average a major inspection on each aircraft takes place seven times each year. For some perspective compare this to when you last had your car serviced?

When the floods come some of the airstrips can get smaller!

A VISIT TO THE CAMPS

We are very fortunate in our work as we occasionally get to stay in the five star lodges we fly the guests into. This means apart from the flying interaction with guests we sometimes have the opportunity to have dinner, breakfast, or even go on activities with the same people we have transported.

I won't mince words; roughly 20% of these people are really interesting and thoroughly enjoyable individuals who have stories and life experiences which I can only dream about. When I am fortunate enough to spend any time with them I usually hang on their every word. Even if I found out later what they had told me had been embellished, it would still be considered good entertainment in the same way a movie is.

So this covers 20% and then there are the 75% who are really just a blur: they don't say much, do their own thing or are just devoid of the ability to socially interact with others. No harm done, they're not here for me and after all it's their holiday. This leaves 5%. It is unfortunate for the planet this five percent even exist. For myself, I don't really care, as I have already had to deal with them and unfortunately have to grin and bear their presence; the alternative is I quit my job.

Believe it or not there *can be* many more precarious situations in the Lodges than there ever would be in an aircraft if you don't listen to instructions. A pilot can easily monitor a guest in the aircraft but in the lodge or out in the bush on a game drive, there is what might be called *broadersupervision*, with people having a little more mobility. Before we speak about clients who don't listen, you need an understanding of some of the basics.

Understanding the Lodge & its Rules

Eagle Island – Belmond Safari's Botswana

Rules are everywhere. I know it's a pain, but think of it this way – they also *saveyou* from having to witness someone showing up for dinner at the Savoy in London wearing a red Speedo or watching somebody else having a Brazilian poolside at the Peninsula Hotel in Hong Kong. So when it is your turn for *the rules* just deal with them. I don't care how much you 5%ers are paying to fly to a swanky African lodge and stay there - don't be a dick - follow the rules.

When you arrive at these beautiful luxury lodges you are immediately sat down for a briefing to apprise you of the lodge *safety* regulations. This is the very information which will save your life *should* a moment come. Try not to think of it like an airline emergency briefing: the one we all just read or listen to our music (myself included) because we've heard it all before. This time you definitely need to listen.

Basically these are all open lodges, which means no fences, which means wild animals wander through the camp twenty four hours a day. This is nature at its rawest and more importantly it is what the clients have come to experience. True, predators tend to hunt at night so daytime is a little safer but still, while they may not always be plunked down next to your room, or wandering down the path near it, they can be. Plus, it is not only predators which can upset your stay: elephant, hippo, zebra, and giraffe can ruin things in a painful way.

A few years back a giraffe in a prominent Victoria Falls hotel charged two guests, flung one across the open space with its neck while kicking the other in the chest. The guests were 30 metres from the animal and both were elderly, basically minding their own business; obviously the giraffe took umbrage with something and closed the gap to address the issue. As far as I know they both recuperated well. And this happened in a *hotel:* the Lodges are far more open than this. So there is no walking around at night without a trained member of the camp staff to escort you. Dealing with these animals is possibly like dealing with a rabid child, with sharp teeth, so leave it to the staff to escort you and make the appropriate decisions.

Emergencies, your room and the Air Horn

After the rules session you are shown to a stunningly beautiful room which has all known bug sprays as well as an air horn for any critical emergencies which could arise late at night after everyone has gone to sleep. Remember you cannot go outside: just blow the horn and someone will come and assist you.

So there are any number of reasons to blow the air horn; heart attack, panic attack, stroke, dizziness, shock, a burn, the inability to breathe...you get the idea. These are real emergencies where the use of the horn, night or day, is encouraged.

Use of the horn for an inability to find the bottle opener, one of the many light switches, to get something ironed - you should have planned ahead, or because there is a small or even large wall spider - completely harmless - does not constitute an emergency. Remember the bug spray and I am sure you can work it out.

Can you hear me?

The most idiotic use of the air horn to date was in 2013, with a man, funny huh - let's call him Heinrich, to avoid a lawsuit, who hails from a European country which is neither Austria nor Switzerland.

As Heinrich tells it on the day in question he looked out and found a small male elephant next to the deck of his room. He told *the doctors* he moved quietly outside to get a better look – then the Elephant attacked him; so he used the Air Horn to try to scare the animal away. Unfortunately, in his description of the incident Heinrich omitted a few small details. These details were filled in by the housekeeper who was on the deck of the next room watching this idiot's behaviour.

Heinrich did indeed look out his door, he then disappeared back inside reappearing a few seconds later pointing the Air Horn at the Elephant. He slowly moved across the deck and closer to the animal, basically sneaking up behind its shoulder, which can be a blind spot for the animal. According to the Housekeeper at this point the animal did not appear to know he was there. She then said he deliberated pressed the top of the device whilst pointing it at the poor animal's ear. If you have ever used one of these horns you know how loud they are and they shake you through to the bones.

Needless to say when the horn went off Jumbo was not amused with the whole event; in fact he was more than a little upset. To show his immediate feelings the now hearing-impaired elephant spun round, grabbed a very surprised Heinrich with his trunk and threw him against a nearby Leadwood tree. To finish off the bush massage, the Elephant stomped on Heinrich, breaking his pelvis, his femur and his tibia before tossing him around a few more times and then strolling away. The only lucky part of this encounter is Heinrich is alive – lucky for Heinrich anyway, I'm not sure about the rest of us. Now when I heard all this and had recovered from laughing so hard I thought I had hurt myself, I had just one question: 'what kind of a retard thinks scaring an animal with an air horn is in any way acceptable?'

This is a true Darwin candidate and clearly a member of the 5%, alas for us - not dead – remember at some future date he may breed, then we will have more of these idiots running around! Of course Heinrich needed to be flown straight out of camp to the nearest suitable hospital which, by the by, is far away so it took him some time to get there. Apparently the flight from camp was not as smooth as Euro-zone Nominee 7 would have liked – just remember a pilot flies through the air, he does not control it. But as they say a little pain is good for the soul,right? I hope the hospital was equipped with a suitable psychiatric ward, because the physical damage aside, it's really not the originating problem.

Activities abound

Other than sitting in the luxury of the camp, people on safari have all come to see animals and in order to do this game drives in Namibia, Botswana, Zimbabwe and Zambia are carried out in open-framed vehicles - no windows. Relax - research has shown the animals see only the vehicle. Nevertheless, there are a few safety measures to go with this research.

So as passengers on a game drive it is simple: no sudden movements to break up the animal's image of the vehicle; no standing up or poking any part of your body outside the vehicle's structure; no loud talking, just orderly and polite behaviour. In short: don't get yourself noticed. All of this is thoroughly briefed; yet you still get the following conduct and questions.

Questions

Some of the questions our long-suffering guides have to answer is:

"Can I pet the - Lion/Cheetah/Hyena/Leopard" (take your pick).

Who the hell wants to pet these?

The answer to this is hardly surprising: 'No, you cannot', simply because each of these *wild animals* sees your hand, and the rest of you, as a meal, not a peace offering or form of affection, so keep your hands to yourself.

However, you will still get people who will try to get out of the game vehicle, this pretty much gets them noticed by the animal, so they can get a closer look or, as if this serves as justification, get a better picture. This is with the animal standing less than two metres from the vehicle and the offender sporting an enormous zoom lens on their camera. As far as I'm concerned these Darwin nominees can go ahead and pet away – all of the

Lodges have an indemnity form and if you 5% don't want to listen to instructions – over to you.

"When are we going to see a polar bear"? No bullshit this was what was asked at Kanana camp in 2007. I'm no expert, but don't polar bears live in the chilly northern latitudes? I certainly have yet to see one wild in the Africa bush. Maybe it's worth making a little effort, you know do some research as to what might be seen on safari. It does save one from being focus of the *raised eyes* moment.

The husband of the lady asking the question immediately called his wife a *stupid cunt;* yes a bit of an awkward moment for the rest of us, and hardly necessary. It all transpired at the fire before dinner and Carl, the Camp Manager, and I chose this moment to run off and refresh our drinks. Obviously this type of language and behaviour is not common amongst our guests; but when it happens what can you do, because as I have said being rude or stupid is not a criminal offence.

One young lady yelled during a flight to camp, "I saw a tiger, I saw a tiger". I said she didn't, which upset her to no end - I guess being told she was wrong did not form part of her upbringing. She insisted on me circling back round so she could prove her point so I suggested she tell the rest of the passengers about her sighting. An informed soul in the back yelled, "There are no tigers in Africa", which brought a rush of blood to her face and a prolonged silence for the rest of the flight.

"Why are there so many bugs in Africa"? Now, this is a bit rich, coming from a Thai lady, as I have actually lived in Thailand and bugs are one thing they are not short of. Maybe it's the size of our African ones which is a cause for concern.

A completely harmless Dung Beatle. It does however spend a lot of its life in the shit, so to speak.

"Ooh, these animals stink! Who washes them?" So sorry, this is Ronald's month off, he's on his annual leave. He is the one solely responsible for ensuring the animals bathe regularly, won't let anyone take over while he's away. Are you kidding?

"Do giraffes hunt in packs?" Umm, No-oooo. Giraffes are herbivores, a vegan, by human standards, so they eat bushes and leaves and things. They are not prone to ripping their fellow animals apart. Another good case for a bit of pre-safari homework.

At the landing strip we have a windsock, which shows us the direction the wind is blowing as well as how strong the wind vector is. It is at the top of a 3-4 metre pole stuck in the ground. It looks quite similar to a giraffe's snout, but not enough to warrant the question: "Is that where the camp feeds the giraffes?" The camp is there to observe wildlife and no feeding takes place save a Darwin participant climbing out of a vehicle to try to pet a hyena. In these cases it is useful to have your video ready if you are interested posting a YouTube hit.

"Are zebras nice?"*Are zebras nice?* The guide was not sure if he had misheard and asked for the question to be repeated. After repeating the question, the guide confessed to still not understanding what was being asked. The three words were repeated in a more aggressive and louder tone, because speaking louder always accomplishes a fuller understanding of the question; but still the guide was at a loss regarding what the woman meant.

Think hard about what you ask before opening your mouth as you may be in time to stop your foot slipping in. All of the animals here are wild - hence 'wildlife', and all of them have defence mechanisms and survival instincts - so no matter how soft and cuddly they look they will assault you in the most grievous way possible and with everything they have if they feel in any way uncomfortable, threatened, or trapped. How do I know when they are feeling any of this? I do not and I cannot as I have no knowledge of what is going on inside an animal's head – neither do you. For this reason observe them from the distance your *professional* guide decides is safe, and with this be content.

Note: Prior research really is the best way to make the most of your African experience. It is certainly worth doing a little. Also, if you are the kind of person who feels the need to fill any silence with chit-chat, you would do well to temper this part of your persona and enjoy the moment, the solitude, and the wonder of the great outdoors. I know the rest of the guests will applaud your decision.

They look nice to me

Wild Dogs avoiding the heat, Piajio Airstrip Okavango Delta, Botswana 2012

What's in a name?

Many of the guides have traditional African names and since they are African this makes perfect sense. Some of these names are quite difficult for foreigners to pronounce so staff, especially guides, have taken to changing their names to make things easier for guests – sort of a working name. How they choose the name is a mystery to many of us, but it seems a lot of thought, or incredibly little, depending on how you look at it, has been taken to come up with their new title. Here are the names of some of the guides and in some cases Taxi drivers in one African country:

Gin & Tonic - this is one person

Mighty

Adolf *

Hitler * (maybe not ideal for the Jewish market) *

Lost (yes he's a Guide)

Virgin

Lover

Dick (he could have gone with Richard)

Never

Now

Fridge

Lovemore (a popular boy's name in certain countries, if I had a daughter there is no way this kid would be anywhere near her)

Pro (No, it stands for Problem, if you can believe it – yes this guy quite casually told us his mother named him this)

In many cases it might have been a good idea to run the name past a few close friends before the final choice was made. But they are not the only ones who have interesting names: the guests, too, come with a colourful list. I know, I know, a guest was born with their family name and had no input regarding their given name. But in most countries you can apply officially to have the name changed or at the very least altered. You think I am exaggerating?

Kuntz:

There were a number of different aircraft at the airstrip when Steve went to collect these people, so upon arrival he just politely inquired, at the top of his voice, "I am here to pick up Kuntz, are any of you Kuntz, I am looking for 5 Kuntz?" Heads turned, hands covered mouths; you get the idea. Guys, no judgements, the pilot was just looking for his passengers: not his fault if people have either an interesting name or others have a dirty mind.

Stiffly: His first name if you can believe it - Roger.

Wank: I know, it doesn't mean the same thing to everybody.

Virgin: "I am looking for the Virgin party" or "I am looking for Virgin, a group of 4"!

Bastard: Imagine yelling this out at the airstrip.

There are many more, but hey, let's give them a break. After all, they live with this every day.

PILOTS IN THE CAMPS

None of us are perfect and with every interaction we have the potential for an epic fail moment. It is just a question of whether we survive with our dignity intact or in some cases if we survive at all.

Everyone's a contender

It would be unfair to pick on the multitude of morons in this book without including myself and my own failings. So in this spirit let's start this section with something I did early on, and to this day I don't know why. One silly mistake and my Darwinian moment both transpired within two hours of each other.

I was on my second overnight at a place called Kanana, a truly beautiful place in the Okavango Delta, Botswana. Before you turn in for the night, the serving staff will ask you what you would like to have to drink at the wake-up call. This is the moment when your guide comes early in the morning to politely rouse you from your slumber. This usually happens in complete darkness, so you can be ready in time for the morning activity, usually a game drive. To take some of the sting out of this early start, they bring you a tray of coffee or tea and some rusks (biscuits). On this particular morning before my nominee moment, I had tea. As a helpful thought I decided to assist the staff by putting the tray outside the tent when I was finished with it. I then discovered putting anything which is not nailed down outside is not a good idea. The baboons at this camp found the tray, smashed the teapot and cup, consumed the sugar, twisted the silverware into puzzles, and made wood chips of the delivery tray. This, of course, endeared me in so many ways to the camp manager, Carl.

Now to describe Carl, I would say he is a big burly South African (Afrikaans descent) , a man who is not afraid of food and who is an incredibly nice guy, warm heart, with a real Santa Claus look about him. He is the type of guy who, given the right reason, could smash an individual into the ground to defend a child, then scoop the youngster up and have their complete confidence they are safe in his arms. I can also say he was remarkably tolerant of my somewhat naive and more accurately stupid decision regarding

118

his crockery.

My stupid moment over and the Darwinian yet to come; my flight was scheduled for later in the morning so after breakfast I decided to explore the camp. I was delighted to spot an elephant wandering along the one of pathways the camp uses to get to a series of tented accommodation. It was fascinating to watch such an enormous creature negotiate such a narrow avenue. I decided to follow and get a picture. You may not know this but elephants walk pretty silently as well as quickly. So I was pretty much trotting behind him to keep up to get *my photo* - I know, what was I thinking? The path curved to the left and I saw him step off it to go into the bush; I also saw my opportunity as there was a large tree there. I snuck up behind the tree and then stuck my head out looking through my camera viewfinder - CLICK. However, unbeknownst to me Mr. Elephant had become aware of my presence, had already turned, and started to charge toward me when I snapped the photo.

This is my photo, he doesn't look happy does he? Anyway I am lucky I lived through my stupidity.

It was about then my *flight responses* kicked in and I was off back the way I came as fast as my legs could carry me. On my sprint back down the path I met a guide who wondered why I was running and all I could scream was "ELEPHANT, ELEPHANT!" At this very moment the guide started running as well. I had yet to learn running is a big no-no and you are supposed to stand your ground. I was new and had not gained this knowledge yet (yes, more ignorance). What excuse did the guide have? Well, once I had started the ball rolling the big male wasn't interested in slowing down. I had pissed him off, and he wanted me, anyone else was just in the way, so the guide wasn't going to hang around either.

After this I had yet another meeting with Carl: it seemed two incidents in one morning were a bit much for anyone staying in the camp, let alone a visiting pilot. The meeting was much like being called to the headmaster's office - discomforting. From that moment on I sat down and dutifully memorized the do's and don'ts of bush behaviour.

Guys, keep it Clean

Behaving properly in public, as our mothers used to impress upon us, is important if we want to create a positive image. Some people don't care, others take it too far, and then there are the rest - to each there own!

A pilot's behaviour in front of guests will often reflect on the company. As I have said we are very fortunate in our work, flying to so many of these beautiful and expensive lodges and from time to time being allowed to stay in the camp for the night often called a 'night stop' or 'overnight'. In all but a few Lodges, we are essentially treated as if we are a guest: assigned a guest room, access to the front of house areas and there is even the possibility of a game drive or boat trip; it is really quite a treat.

So, Ted the German and a guy we'll call Carlos, from Europe somewhere, I can't be too specific; a slender well-kept man in his mid-thirties. Both are on an overnight at Deception Valley Lodge (DVL) – despite the nuances of the name it is a really lovely place with some thoroughly amazing staff. The two pilots have been cautioned by someone akin to their mother - this usually means the owner of the company, they are to be on their very best behaviour as they are flying eight VIPs, all Agents. Agents are the people who are responsible for directing business to the lodges; they also decide their preferred Air Charter operator – so they are kind of significant. This owner waxed on about the importance of making a good impression and sums up the conversation with a very clear message: "Don't fuck this up"!

Everything was under control with Ted and Carlos upon arrival at DVL. They are sent off to their shared guest room, which turns out to be the honeymoon suite. Both pilots are exploring their new habitat and Ted, already naked and displaying his accompanying ginger chest hair, discovers a bathrobe which comes down to very sexy mid-thigh length. He continues looking for more treasure. Meanwhile Carlos, who is roughly six foot two inches tall, has stripped down to his tight white underwear, also sexy – from Stevie Wonder's perspective, and he has donned an attractive pair of white slippers to off-set the underwear. It is at this point Carlos discovers the Louver in the shower and with it he bounces into the main portion of the room where Ted is still rummaging around and brandishing the Louver like a sword, hollers:

"What the Fuck can we do with this?"

Ted spins around and stares at Carlos. They both suddenly have the feeling they are not alone and sure enough, a glance toward the sliding glass doors reveals the lodge manager and all of the Agents staring into the room. Remember the Agents are here for work and are inspecting everything, which includes the Honeymoon suite. After several seconds of awkward silence the lodge manager chokes out: "Okay, well, uh......, we will leave you two to your own devices".By dinnertime everyone was laughing about the moment, though a couple of the agents were convinced the two were a couple.

PS - For the record neither pilot is gay and the writer accepts no responsibility for convincing the sceptical; Carlos is in a committed relationship and Ted believes you need to be committed - if you are in a relationship. At the time of writing Ted is available on weekends in Papua New Guinea for Bachelorette and 'female' birthday parties – Speedo provided.

Sounds of Silence

Whether you go to Namibia, Botswana, Tanzania, or Kenya, going on Safari is something you must try at least once. It is popular with couples and often comes at the beginning of married life: enter the honeymoon.

Each room in a Bush Lodge is secluded, cut off from the view of others so guests can do their own thing, with or without clothes. Any accompanying sounds to these activities will usually be drowned out by the sound of nature - but not always. Air density is acute in winter, which causes sound to travel great distances in the crisp night air, as one pilot discovered.

Paddy, had turned in early, jumped straight into bed, and snuggled up to the hot water bottle which is placed there to keep you warm on these chilly winter nights. If a person hasn't been warned about the hottie they generally rocket out of bed on first contact with it, taking it for a furry bed companion. But not Paddy as he was a pro in this aspect.
One generally drifts off to the, for the most part, quite soothing sounds of the bush, crickets or the harmonic sounds of the painted reed frogs. But on this particular night something a little different was making noise. It started off as a grunting noise: a hippo, maybe? No, more like a cape buffalo, then he realized there was a consistent tempo to the grunting and it was getting louder. Certainly sounded like some animal was getting worked up about something; then the grunting turned to:
"Yes, yes, yes, right there, don't stop, oh baby I love you so much, so much – Aahhhhh".
And silence.
It's perfectly natural, we all do it, ok, some less than we would like, yes more therapy for me. The following morning Paddy was at breakfast table next to the newlyweds and happened to be drinking his orange juice when camp manager stopped to ask them if everything had been to their satisfaction last night. On hearing this, Paddy choked, spraying the juice all down his front. Everyone looked at him somewhat concerned. "Sorry, just went down the wrong way", he spluttered. I hope for the couple's sake it didn't.

Cane and unable

But it's not all young newlyweds who come our way. Some regard their safari as a last 'hurrah' before they meet their maker. In many of these cases the older traveller seems rather melancholic as they attempt to relive their past African adventures. Take a man we'll call Parker, who claims he is on his last trip and as such is hammering the whiskey and sodas from roughly 10 AM onwards to ensure he gets where he is going fully pickled.

On this day in mid-winter 2015 I meet Parker at Selinda Camp in the Lynyanti area of Botswana on the border with Namibia which is run by Great Plains. It is a beautiful Lodge set in the flood plain, and a favourite stop for many. The whole area is renowned for good, consistent animal sightings. Parker has arrived the previous day and I meet him at pre-dinner drinks on his second evening.

Parker is about six feet four, a solid man, well-built and a former professional guide. In my view he has aged well for his seventy odd years but clearly might not be in his best frame of mind. Parker joins some other guests for dinner: a family with a couple of kids between 12 and 14. Dinner goes reasonably well except the manager has to keep reminding Parker to go easy on the language as there are children at the table. Parker's repertoire consisted of a few *fucks*, a couple of *shits* and one really loud *cunt:* well to be fair there was only one there.

After dinner Parker suggests a fireside nightcap but strangely everyone else seems keen to go to bed. The manager, Parker's guide, myself and a fellow pilot on an overnight move toward the fire. Hey, I am always up for a laugh.

Parker walks with a cane, but these are notoriously hard to handle when drunk. This is immediately demonstrated at the fire when Parker swings the cane to point at something and cleans out his full glass of whiskey and soda; a replacement is requested and shortly delivered.

Parker sits and stares at the dirt in front of him, eyes open, but no movement. Now there is silence, literally no one is speaking. Two minutes goes by and my fellow pilot starts to ask a question of the manager but Parker is back, slurring out some vital piece of information.

"You know many yearsssss' ago in this area......I once........there used to be......ah Fuck it!"

Frankly I was disappointed with the information as I have heard all this before, somewhere, and was expecting something new. We all look at one another, stifling a laugh. Parker is away with the fairies again and his cane is in action - don't worry his whiskey is safe. Parker is drawing in the dirt in front of him and he is sketching quickly. A minute of frantic movement goes by before he exclaims:

"Giraffe...........it's a Giraffe - What a fine looking giraffe!"

Now he looks at it more closely and his face contorts a little. It seems he is not happy and rubs it out. Something else occurs to him and he starts furiously drawing again. As he does this he keeps up a deep conversation – with himself.

"Last trip to Botswana... final jolly... time to die, yes, time to die. Not needed anymore...time to go..., Africa no more."

This sounds rather sad to us, but Parker is still drawing frenetically in the sand and when he is satisfied with his artwork he yells and points with the cane:

"Scrotum.......that is a scrotum, see? It's my ball sack!"

With this he stretches, cane and all, and there goes his replacement whiskey and soda. I actually don't know how he managed to get so drunk as most of his tipples ended up on the ground. At this point my colleague and I are having a lot of trouble keeping straight faces. But we are saved from appearing rude as Parker has decided to call it a night. He springs up halfway but plops right back down again. Second attempt brings success, except for one problem:

"My cane...my cane...where the FUCK is my cane?"

Not to worry, Parker, it's hanging off your forearm. He locates it and his guide helps him walk the few steps to his tent, #3, right there next to the fire, just 5 metres away. We watch as it takes a full five minutes for him and the guide to complete the distance, then another three minutes and he is up the two steps and through the door. Good night Parker, sleep well, old chap.

Since the floorshow is over my colleague and I bid everyone good night. We retire to our room which is #4. Yes, Parker and I are neighbours, oh joy! I wash my face and brush my teeth, as does my fellow pilot, Mum taught us well, and we are both now in bed, lights off. Not Parker, who we can clearly hear, hell the whole camp can.

"Light switch, switch, switch…where the FUCK is the light switch! Ah, here it is (click).You turned it off, you idiot…FUCK, quick turn it back on (click) that's better, not again…don't do it again."

Parker is once again in deep conversation with himself and this carries far through the cold night air. The two of us lie there staring at the ceiling, seems the floor show is now Lux Radio Theatre. Parker continues.

"Shirt off…off…off…shirt *offffff*"

Now we are not sure if this is some Jedi manoeuvre: you know, maybe he was using The Force, or was he was wearing voice operated clothing? Either way it seemed to work as roughly four minutes later the conversation with the shirt over, he had moved on to his pants. This took a little longer and there was some language which I hope, for the sake of the children, was not used at the dinner table. Finally he targets his shoes, which explains why he had such trouble getting the pants off. Twenty minutes has gone by when he starts wandering around his room - endlessly. Just so you understand the rooms are lovely and spacious but it's not a warehouse. We were just beginning to wonder where this night-time stroll was leading when his toe came into contact with a piece of furniture.

"Ahhh FUCK, fucking toe, god it hurts…fuck, fuck, fuck".

The two of us couldn't take it any longer and we both burst out laughing. Parker immediately stopped talking to himself and called out:

"Hello…hello, is there someone there"

I whispered to my fellow pilot we could have some fun. I suggested calling out in a kind of 'spirit' voice: Paaarkerrrrr…Paaarkerrrrrr, do you remember me Parker? Now my roommate was really muffling laughter but warned me against it in case the poor old bastard had a heart attack. I decided this was good advice and then just lay there listening.

He eventually quietened down but it took him another fifteen minutes.Parker, wherever you are, thanks for the evening. We will never forget it!

Midnight snack

Two young Kiwi pilots were on an overnight, 2 nights this time, together at a Lodge in Savute, which is in the Chobe National Park, Botswana. They had arrived early on the 24th, disappeared to their room with a bottle of Jack Daniels and some Coke, one drink led to another, they lost track of time and missed the evening meal.

By midnight they were starving and made their way through the darkened camp to the kitchen, where in the fridge they found a whole cooked ham: Score! So they tucked in and polished off all three and a half kilos of it. What a great way to start Christmas Day, they mused. Yes, our two lads had just consumed the Lodge's Christmas Lunch.

The discovery was made a couple of hours later by the chef when he arrived to prepare breakfast, and needless to say, he wasn't happy. The upshot was the charter company involved adopted a policy of never allowing more than one pilot to stay in a given lodge at a time - a policy which has since been relaxed.

Smoking can be revealing

Some of the lodges are in a small town called Kasane, near the border with Namibia, Zambia, and Zimbabwe. It is an area of the country called the four corners because essentially this is where the four countries meet. Here the lodges are a more like hotels, nice but not quite the bush.

Chobe Safari Lodge is one of many major Lodges which sit on the Chobe River. Today Ted is staying in one of the rooms at the Lodge. He has just showered and decides to have a quick cigarette so he drapes one of the smallest towels in the bathroom round his waist and steps through the front door - *why not onto your private balcony, Ted?* He lights the cigarette and hears the soft click of the door closing. As he takes his first drag the penny, but luckily not the towel, drops: he is locked out, semi-naked.

He edges down the outside corridor to the end, where he can see the barman and beckons him over. The barman was somewhat reluctant to move, but Ted can be convincing. As he approached Ted his reluctance increased. Ted begged the barman to go to the front desk and get a replacement key so he could re-enter his room.

"Ah, unfortunately this is against lodge policy," says the barman. "Security measures require you go to the front desk yourself." Ted pleads with the guy, pointing out his scanty attire. The barman is adamant: it is Ted who goes, or no one. So Ted puts his best face forward and casually strolls through the entire bar and dining area in nothing but his hand towel wardrobe circa 2014. There were a few cat calls and some whistling during the journey, but no proposals. When he presents himself at the front desk the young lady there greets him:

"Welcome to Chobe Safari.... But you're naked!"

Ted confirms the sighting and explains the problem. She understands completely: guests lock themselves out of their room all the time, though they are usually fully dressed. She will make a new key in 15 minutes. Ted enquires about the delay?

"I'm afraid the system is down and will only be back on line in about 15 minutes. Please go back to your room and wait for me outside."

When Ted goes back to the lodge now everyone greets him with a broad smile and has no problem recognising him even with his clothes on.

ALLEGATIONS OF THEFT

I think everyone at one point or another has stolen something: a bar of soap from the hotel or maybe the temptingly fluffy bathrobe; a piece of pie from the staff fridge; or pens from the office. Then there are those people for whom these types of 'thefts' are mere Child's play.

But lets just say you are strictly the *courtesy soap* kind of thief just going about your daily routine, minding your own business when you are suddenly accused of taking something significant. Having watched *Law & Order* or *Criminal Intent* you might defend yourself with a simple: "I didn't do it"; but for these examples you will need slightly better justification than this. For these stories I will explain the three categories of tourist we have here.

The first keep a good eye out on their stuff (bags etc.), why? Because it is their stuff and therefore their responsibility. They don't guard it like someone's virginity but they behave cautiously and carefully: the correct travelling mentality. These are the people I like to deal with because they practise common sense!

The second group are the tourists who leave their stuff lying around, and I mean everywhere. They park their bag outside a shop and go inside to browse for three minutes and are surprised when it is not there when they return. Some of them expect other people to be responsible for their luggage even without informing these others of their new duties. "Oh but I thought you were watching my bag" – yes of course, I came on vacation to watch your shit – how thoughtless of me shirking my duties so soon after arriving!

I fully agree people should not steal but travellers should also try to remember the contents of your small personal bag/purse may represent **two-month'sexistence** for someone in the Third World, and an empty stomach can be a powerful motivator.

The third group are tourists who are looking for a *free*, or *discounted holiday*. Now how would they get this? They allegesomething has been stolen so they can either claim on their travel insurance or more often than not browbeat the service provider - Lodge, Air Charter Company, ground Transfer Company, and so on - into giving them a discount. They feel this is what they deserve since "the whole sordid matter has ruined their

Holiday experience".

These accusations necessarily cause collateral damage (i.e. someone often needs to take the fall, and maybe lose their job through the allegation). The finger is usually pointed toward a housekeeper, a camp hand, or a driver but from time to time we pilots join this group.

Stealing across borders

Meet Prince, yes my friend who is now living in Malawi. Prince is a black African - *sir, I object to the reference to skin colour – overruled; as it goes to the mind-set of his racist passengers* - is seven months into his flying job in Botswana and today he is flying two clients from an airstrip in the Okavango Delta to Kasane for Customs and Immigration and then on to Livingstone Airport in Zambia.

He greets the clients at the airstrip and picks up their two bags. The clients hold on to their personal hand-luggage and watch Prince as he loads the bigger bags in the small cargo pod underneath the aircraft. The two South Americans then climb in and the aircraft departs for the roughly one-hour flight up to Kasane.

On arrival Prince retrieves the bags from the cargo pod while the clients stand there watching, with their hand-luggage glued to their bodies. Prince looks around for the porters who should be coming to help him but as there aren't any in sight, he escorts the two passengers to the terminal, where it is immediately, and I mean immediately, discovered 3000 Euros is missing. The money was apparently in the larger bags the pilot handled and not in the bags the clients grasped throughout the flight as though they contained a cure for cancer. The pilot is accused very directly: "what have you done with our money?"

Let me give you a little background on my friend Prince, who I have known for almost eight years. He is a well-educated Zimbabwean, whose command of the English language and most aspects of life would rival any schooled person in the first world; he has in my view had a good upbringing is a thoroughly honourable person and I would trust him with my wife or girlfriend. He is extremely diplomatic and patient, qualities his father and mother seem to have instilled in him over many years; along with a great deal of integrity and manners.

His first reaction to their accusation is a bit puzzled and he actually asked the two how he could have possibly taken any money since he was with the guests and being watched the entire time. But Mr and Mrs South America are convinced Mr Africa is a thief. So logic is thrown aside they get the Airport Police involved and all adjourn to an interview room.

After thirty minutes and a search of the suspect pilot the police say they have no evidence with which to proceed. If the couple wish to fill out a formal statement only then can they move further and look into arresting the thieving pilot. The couple decide they will proceed with the statement. They are then informed they will need to stay in Botswana and not continue on to the Zambian leg of their holiday until all the official signing, stamping and what-have-you is over with. This could take better part of the day at the very least.

There immediately follows a short rapid conversation in Spanish, the upshot of which is they have changed their minds and decided not to file a formal accusation. This also leaves Prince in the awkward position of having to fly them a further 20 minutes into Zambia and escort them through immigration there. It's not quite what I would have done but he's a bigger man than me.

So a short while later, in another country, having safely arrived with their *thief of a pilot* they are standing at immigration when the husband announces he wants to see the police because their pilot has stolen money from them – and so it all starts again, maybe its Groundhog Day? The police arrive, listen to the allegation and they all go off to yet another interview room for a chat.

Mr. South America is speaking, actually yelling: always a bad move, about his missing Euros and keeps referring to Prince as 'this black pilot', which was probably not the smartest move in front of the Zambian official. The police point out the alleged crime was committed in Botswana, outside their jurisdiction, so there is nothing they can do. Mr. South America 2010 is having none of it: he wants Prince strip-searched. The airport police commander says emphatically:"No, absolutely not, the matter is closed, will everyone go now please." But by now Prince is at the end of his tether and forsakes his usual diplomacy, so he starts yelling;

"YOU WANT A STRIP SEARCH, LET'S GO!"

And with this he starts pulling all his clothes off: shirt first, shoes and socks next, then the pants, and finally the underwear. Needless to say the airport police commander is less than impressed with his interview room being turned into a strip club. He shouts at Prince to stop; but Prince is beyond hearing any of this. He lifts his arms and has a good look in the arm pits – 'IS THE MONEY THERE? NO!' He reaches down a lifts his up his scrotum. 'NOT UNDER HERE EITHER.' He then spins round, bends over and spreads his cheeks so they can have a good look up his ass. 'DO YOU SEE IT IN THERE? NO!'

About then the shouting stops and the room is very quiet; Prince makes the most of the Zen moment to grab his underwear and start collecting himself. His usual calm is restored, although his 26 year record of diplomacy now has a slight dent in it. The airport police commander repeats 'the matter is closed' and wishes the South Americans a good stay in Zambia. He beckoned Prince to accompany him outside for a quick chat regarding the strip act - possibly a few suggestions on improvements.

Two days later the wife calmly reported the money had turned up in her bag. No apology, just a FYI email. More than likely their angle was the insurance claim but since their plan had gone a little too public they reported the 'discovery' of the money so they then could try it somewhere else on some other poor bastard.We officially reported the whole incident and the two to their agent with a special mention to alert their insurance company. They are now banned for life from the camp operation who had accepted their holiday booking. Adios idiots!

This is Prince – he allowed me to use his photo but stopped short at the use of his name – sorry ladies he's married

Ten Thousand reasons

Different companies have different ways to interact with passengers. This particular unnamed company likes the personal touch so the pilots meet the clients in the airport terminal and then see them through the mayhem which can be encountered at most international airports.

Today, a Thursday in 2015, a pilot we will call Chris, has what would be called a simple schedule: a 25-minute flight into the Okavango Delta with group of five guests and their guide. This appears as 5+1 on his schedule to denote the breakdown of people. The guide arrives, identifies himself, and then the first three guests arrive from immigration: an American husband and wife and a British lady travelling on her own. While waiting for the arrival of the other two, the American wife realizes she doesn't have her suitcase: I guess *where she comes from someone else would claim the bag on her behalf.* The bag is quickly retrieved and now it's here she is impatient to leave. It is explained we are still waiting for two more passengers but she presses the issue with the guide and the phrase "well, it just doesn't seem fair as we are ready to go" is used. Chris steps in to point out if the situation was reversed and it were she and her husband who were still in the immigration queue, wouldn't she want us to await their arrival? The logic of the argument sinks in and she calms down – Yes, it is exactly like dealing with a child.

An interminable twelve minutes go by before the other two eventually show up. The impatient American lady makes it very clear the small grey box with shoulder strap she is holding is of great importance and must stay with her at all times. She explains it is a breathing machine as she has a lung issue which must be attended to three times a day. This sounds serious and the guide quickly checks his paperwork but can find nothing relating to this piece of medical equipment on the booking form. Because of the remoteness of some of these places, lodge operators are required to ask about dietary needs, allergies, and any medical conditions.

Upon hearing this Chris, in his usual irritating attention to detail, asks about the voltage, as Americans use 110Vs and most of the rest of the world uses 220V. She assures us there is no need to worry as she only purchased the unit when she got to South Africa where the problem appeared to begin, on the first morning of the trip. The group proceeds through the metal detector and x-ray before heading to the departure lounge. It is now time to board the bus. But wait! The lady is missing her breathing machine. The guide shoots off and seconds later reappears with this incredibly important machine which *she left at the security checkpoint.*

The passengers board the bus, get to the aircraft, take off, and fly to camp. Upon arrival Chris carefully briefs the clients to take all their personal items from the cabin of the aircraft. He himself will unload the hold baggage and make sure it gets to the vehicles. The passengers exit the plane and Chris inspects the cabin. Ah, there it is - the fucking breathing machine – as she keeps leaving it everywhere Chris surmises it was possibly a suicide safari? The machine is dutifully taken over to the vehicle and Chris hopes he has seen the last of those two.

Back in Maun Chris has refuelled, done his paperwork, secured his aircraft, and undertaken a post flight inspection for oil leaks, any potential bird strike damage, to have it all ready for tomorrow. What he hasn't done is look in all the seat pockets. Then the radio call comes in two of the guests - no prizes as to which two - have left a small purse in one of the seat pockets. The purse is immediately located by a porter and, following procedure, an inventory is taken in the office so the company has a record of what was there: in this case it was some receipts and two passports.

On Friday the purse is flown to camp by another pilot and delivered to the guide for our two friends. On Saturday Chris draws the short straw and is flying Mrs. Dozy and her husband (and their group) to the next stop. Before he takes off there is already a problem: the two guests want to know "*where is our purse with the passports*". It is pointed out their purse was delivered to the camp the previous day. "It's not possible" they say. "We never got it". Frantic calls are made to the Canadian pilot who had dropped it off. It was her day off but the company needed to clear up matter at once. Yes, she had given it to the guide and this information was communicated to the camp. As Chris gets airborne out of Maun the message comes in 'the Dozy party' has located their travel documents elsewhere in their possessions: problem solved. The flight continues, Chris drops them all at their next camp, carefully inspects the aircraft – nothing in the seat pockets and no breathing machine in the back. The suicide watch can be called off; and he can fly on.

On Monday the owner of the company says he needs to have a word with Chris and they adjourn to his office. Seems a complaint has come in concerning two guests are missing a purse - no, the purse was found and returned, passports and all. No, this complaint centres on a missing purse with US$10,000 in it. Chris and his chief pilot, who was sitting in on the conversation, start asking questions: this wouldn't be the two Americans who arrived on Thursday, stayed at camp A and then moved on this day to camp B. Yes, the very same.

It was carefully explained that not only had Chris not touched the purse he had never even set eyes on it. Further questions revealed the complaint came in on Sunday with the alleged offence being committed on Thursday, the day of arrival. The complaint states in writing 'I saw the pilot open the purse and take the money.' Chris points out if this had been the case, any normal, rational person would have hollered, "Hey stop" or "stop thief" or words to this effect. What did not seem normal or rational was an email after four days of silence.

The company owner is now more than a little suspicious about the complaint but as is custom Chris must write a report. The lodge operator's senior management is now involved and at the end of the American couple's trip they are carefully interviewed by one of the managers. The woman is adamant: Chris took the money. The husband refuses to makes eye contact throughout the interview and does not say a word. The questions are asked and then re-asked, producing different answers each time. By the time he is finished said manager has three stories – not one – of what happened: but they all result in the same outcome: Chris took the money.

Chris's take on the incident was either she never had the money and was too dozy to remember or she had a hold on the family's purse-strings and the husband saw his opportunity, took the $10,000 and let the wife believe it was the pilot. According to what the Manager could determine she was on the anti-malaria drug Larrium; which has been known to cause hallucinations, and some strong sedatives, so she was clearly out of it. It was unfortunate this caused the pilot to be accused and put in a very unpleasant situation but I don't think people really think of these things.

Just remember false or unfounded accusations can have personal ramifications in the form of slander – these have the potential to lead to amounts which exceed US$10,000 – if you know what I mean.

PRIVATE FLIGHTS

We get a lot of visiting pilots, usually private pilots from South Africa: this is the aviator's version of a road trip. It involves them dragging their aircraft out of a hangar, dusting it off, filling it with their family. They then depart for a remote lodge more than likely in an adjoining country. Botswana, Namibia, Zambia, Zimbabwe and Mozambique are popular destinations.

You can rent an aircraft like this to fly around Southern Africa, please just follow the rules.

A private pilot is legally allowed to fly for fun, which means he cannot receive any money for the operation of the aircraft. They are often referred to as *weekend warriors*, basically because most of them fly only on weekends and have a day job elsewhere which funds their hobby.

As with anything you do, regular practice is required to keep your hand in or as pilots say – *keep current*. Flying every other weekend would be enough but some of these private pilots pursue their hobby a little less frequently, which makes for some interesting moments and demonstrations of abysmal airmanship.

Airmanship often defines your aviation commitment and how other pilots see you. It is best summed up with the following ideals: etiquette, common sense and safety. Airmanship is being aware you are not the only aviator in the vicinity and so should take other pilots into account when you are flying. The opposite, in fact, of most car drivers' behaviour; except maybe in Germany or Switzerland.

A private pilot also needs to remember he or she is operating in a variety of airspace: put another way, sometimes they are on the motorway and sometimes they are on a side street. When you are operating in densely occupied airspace you need to be on top of it and concentrate. Sadly, not everyone does this, usually because they aren't proficient enough – not current.

Some even attempt to drive against the traffic flow with sort of a *do as I please* mentality. This causes commercial pilots no end of worry and the occasional incident ensues.

I can say what I want

As mentioned before, rules are everywhere and they are no more prevalent than in aviation: I believe we have a rule for everything. One of them is this: when you use the radio do so with essential information only and think about what you say before you start saying it. This keeps the calls short and professional.

Imagine you are at Target or Costco and, as you wander through the cavernous structure someone gets on the PA system to tell you about something which might be important to your shopping experience, such as a new product the household can't do without; you know an automatic cheese slicer or coffee growing kit. These calls are similar to the professional calls made by aviators with good airmanship, be they private or commercial pilots.

Then, still enjoying your shopping experience, you hear another garbled announcement without much product information. The message is poorly formatted and delivered, as if some trainee has gained access to the store's public address system and is trying it out. Welcome the private pilot with poor radio skills and/or airmanship.

These types of radio calls go on forever, thereby blocking the frequency for other users. Requests to keep the calls concise are ignored: they go on spouting useless information other pilots do not need to hear. When these pilots fly as part of a group of aircraft it is usually worse as the chatter is often non-aviation and done on an open frequency about the lodge they are going to or how *'lekker'* (good) their dinner was the previous evening. Needless to say, although we might applaud Henie's decision to have the pork ribs and steak combo, currently we are at work. To do this we need the radio frequency which Fatty is blocking and therefore don't give a shit what he had for dessert after his quarter cow and half pig starter.

When we do manage to make contact with the offender we usually get some form of resistance to our polite request to Henie which is 'please follow the rules'. Most of these idiots are definitely 5%ers and have obviously missed the Airmanship portion of their training.

I stop where I please

Just because you are staying at a lodge does not mean you automatically have the right to use their airstrip – yes let this sink in – an airstrip is not the carpark outside a hotel! It is a private airstrip and permission must be sought, which is something most of these private flyers don't understand, or even bother to check. What is more, many Private Pilots often feel the airstrip has been built just for them and so they show up and just park their aircraft wherever they like. Kind of like if I showed up at your house and parked in your driveway, garage, or better yet on your front lawn? One idiot parked on the runway as he said he didn't like the look of the parking area. "I'll only be staying two days", he reassured us. Not to worry, these moments are not an Airmanship issue, they centre on a complete lack of intelligence.

This selfish behaviour gets mixed reactions from pilots. Some complain to the camp operation which own the airstrip (*the high road*), while others feel a more personal, direct, and anonymous hand-written note might be the way to go (*the low road*). Still others just fix the problem themselves (*the in your face road*).

In 2008 at an airstrip which will remain unnamed, a private pilot had just finished securing his aircraft and was about to head off to the lodge when two charter pilots from the same company landed, with two more due in two minutes: they were flying in a big group of tourists.

The private pilot had parked his Cessna 172 in an extremely inconvenient place - the middle of the airstrip's parking area. It was pointed out to Private Guy this was an operational airstrip and he needed to move to a corner of the parking area. The whole thing was done politely but firmly in accordance with good airmanship and manners.

He said "No way am I going start up my engine and move the aircraft". One of the pilots said they would happily assist by helping to push the aircraft with him; it seemed this offer was also out of the question. "You'll just have to work around the aircraft", he said, mounting the camp vehicle in readiness to go. Steve approached the vehicle:

"There are two options here; you can go to camp now, enjoy a beer, and pretend this conversation never happened or you can lend us a hand to move your aircraft – it is your choice, but it is a choice you need to make now."

Private guy just stared at Steve and then said he was *off to the lodge*. Steve smiled. "Enjoy your time at the lodge and don't you worry about your aircraft. Bye now."

The camp vehicle started to move but Private Guy suddenly seemed less sure of his decision: he kept looking back at Steve who just smiled and waved at this guy until it was out of sight. Ten minutes later, four pilots using their brute strength relocated the aircraft to a spot he probably would not have considered: between two bushes under a lovely tree, completely out of the parking area. The airstrip could be seen from the new location: now Private Guy was a *real bush pilot*!

Parking at the pumps

Lets just say I pull into your favourite filling station to get gas, climb out of my car and lock it while the attendant pumps away and then I just disappear. This wouldn't annoy you, would it? Then I show up one hour later to pay for the petrol, I've done some paperwork and had a coffee. You'd be ok with this, wouldn't you? Especially if your filling station was at the crossroads of three major motorways (*freeways* to you

Americans): this wouldn't be a busy filling station, now would it?

This is another irritating and illegal practice which some private guys cannot grasp; basically that there are other pilots around attempting to work – for this we need fuel. This has happened so often I have lost count and in the old days we just took the law into our own hands pretty much as Steve did. We pushed the aircraft off the pumps and into the grass nearby. Needless to say some of these private pilots were a little unhappy when they showed up again. On one occasion this aviation idiot took a swing at one of the pilots he *thought* was involved in his aircraft's relocation. The pilot successfully blocked the punch but did not return fire. He simply pointed out to private guy he was in breach of any number of civil aviation laws and, also, if he chose to take further physical action he would be sufficiently injured to allow for a free tour of the local hospital. This information seemed to solve the matter and private guy disappeared never to be seen again.

Whose country?

Imagine I took off from an airfield in the United States, radioed the appropriate official and told them I was going from A to B (within the U.S) but that at some point I was just going to cross the border into Mexico because I wanted to look at what the Mexicans were going to see from the other side after Trump finished getting them to build a wall. Don't worry, I am not going to land, just invade their airspace for thirty minutes before I come back, this couldn't possibly cause any problems, could it?

One brainless South African pilot was flying from Vumbura in the Okavango Delta to Kasane in Botswana. The town of Kasane borders Namibia, Zambia and Zimbabwe and is close - about 20 minutes flight time - to Victoria Falls, a beautiful natural wonder of the world.

Captain Dense announces to the air traffic controller that he is shortly going to be travelling through Kasane airspace to land there but he will be detouring through Zambia to look at Victoria Falls. I am listening to his radio call and shaking my head in disbelief; my loadmaster (crewmember) actually called him an 'idiot'; something unusual for Batswana to ever say.

140

The controller thinks she has misunderstood so asks the pilot to "say again", or repeat, his last request, which wasn't a request at all. He does and she tells him it is not possible as it is illegal: he may land in Kasane and file a flight plan to the Falls if he wishes. The pilot insists: "Look, you don't understand, I am not *landing* in Zambia, just going for look. Do you *get it* darling"? Wow, not condescending at all.

She repeats it is not possible: he may *not* enter Zambian airspace to look at the Falls. After several seconds of silence he comes out with, "Fine! I will just go through Zimbabwe and look at the Falls from another side".

Clearly Captain Dense is the one not *getting it:* you can't just fly into another country without their permission so he needs to wake up and learn the rules, it's not a difficult concept. This guy relents only when an operational pilot tells him why it won't work. Yet he should know simply because part of getting his license is to pass an Aviation Law Exam.

My feeling was he wasn't going to be told by some local person; *yes I mean Black*, what to do. But he should also understand if he breaks the law and ends up in prison there would be a few local people telling him what to do in a much less polite manner, if you get my drift.

Small talk is better than no talk!

One pilot who we will call Mark, was on his way to Khwai River Airstrip in Botswana, when he was cut off by another aircraft. Now, getting cut off by an aircraft is not the same as getting cut off by a car. Cars operate in close proximity to each other while aircraft do the exact opposite, so if this occurs in the air it means either one or both of the pilots did not see or hear the other.

Of course, we should all hear each other because we are constantly making radio calls to let other pilots know where we are, this is done for safety reasons. In this case Mark had been cut off by an aircraft which had not made *a single radio call* and turned out to be part of a group of five: luckily for him he had caught the tail end of the chaos. Mark landed behind the offender and wandered over to find out what the issue was. It turned out to be a group of German self-flyers. These are private pilots who come from overseas, rent an aircraft in South Africa and go on their own flying safari. If it sounds like fun, it's because it is, but this doesn't mean the rules don't have to be followed.

Seems these guys did not know the radio frequencies for the area they were flying in because they hadn't bothered to do any research. There is absolutely no excuse for this because in aviation pretty much everything is published somewhere and if you are not sure you can always ask. These dimwits had decided to skip all of this and proceed directly to - *we'll fly around and dispense with the small talk*; you know the legally required stuff.

It goes without saying Mark was a little upset at almost being killed but he kept his calm and gave the five a full briefing as to what they needed to do from now on. They took it all on board and were much better throughout their onward travels, but it staggers the mind it could go this far.

Fly faster, as we need to check in

This happened in early 2016 and many of us are still shaking our heads over it. A privately owned, South African registered, Cessna 172 had been on a flying Safari through the Okavango Delta. Basically they had been flying their own aircraft in to a given airstrip, staying at the Lodge for a couple of days, before flying on to the next Lodge.

Now, anyone who flies knows you don't just jump in the aircraft and go; preparation is key, which is part of the previously mentioned Airmanship. You need to take fuel enough for your trip, plus your reserve fuel, you do not land an aircraft with empty tanks for obvious reasons, and if you are unfamiliar with the area maybe a little extra fuel for those just in case moments. You have a Map, you ask for help regarding almost anything and you ask from people who know the area. Unfortunately it seems these morons might have skipped a few steps in the above equation.

We could all hear them flying around, seemingly a straight line was foreign to these Private Pilots. But as was said, they were on vacation so probably wanted to have a look around. That's great 'the looking around' and the time taken to do this is limited in this respect – it's called FUEL. They got lost travelling to at least two of the lodges they were flying too. How would we know this; well when you make a radio call you are going from A to B, then start asking for directions for your destination, which should be in your GPS anyway, and a 20 minute flight ends up taking one hour twenty – it all sounds pretty lost to me.

A week goes by, seemingly they have finished flying themselves to camps and are returning to Maun. They have checked in with ATS (Air Traffic Services) and are on a 4 mile left base, in preparation to Land. This is when the pilot calls a MAYDAY (emergency) and indicates his engine has stopped. He also indicates that he sees a small field and will land the aircraft in it.

One helicopter has just landed in Maun and is unloading his passengers. The company is called and asked if they can proceed immediately for the short trip to the crash site. They have a schedule but this is an emergency and their schedule is immediately put to one side to assist a fellow aviator – this is called Airmanship.

There is a Cessna Caravan on a two mile left base and the Tower asks if they can break right to locate the aircraft and await the helicopter's arrival. The pilot hesitates at this request, seems they didn't want to go because they had passengers on board – yes, this is not really Airmanship – an emergency is a FUCKING EMERGENCY. By law you are required to assist unless doing so would endanger yourself, your passengers, or your aircraft – try to remember worrying a passenger does not fall in to this description. The Tower motivates the Caravan pilot in a somewhat embarrassing manner; sort of with a frustrated tone of disbelief. They depart for the *thirty second* trip to where the aircraft reported last.

Five minutes later the helicopter arrives and the Caravan departs to land. Seems both people in the aircraft are fine. The aircraft successfully landed in the field, momentarily - due to its speed - got airborne again and re-landed roughly six feet up, in a tree. The two South Africans were in a jovial mood with only one concern. They asked if the pilot

143

could fly the helicopter directly to Maun Airport as they were in a hurry. The helicopter pilot asked what the rush was. Their reply:

"We are running a little late for our Charter Flight. We are supposed to check-in in the next 30 minutes to fly up to Kingspool Lodge for three days".

The pilot thought they were joking and made it clear he was at their crash site to collect them as certain staff at CAAB (Civil Aviation Authority Botswana) had just a couple of questions and a few forms to fill out regarding their aviation road trip. Seems these guys were adamant they were going to Kingspool. So, you have an accident and then just go on vacation, wow, I'll give you one guess who won this argument.

Now, at this point, no one can accurately say they ran out of fuel. Funny thing was everyone who went to the crash site said there was one thing absent – fuel, even the smell of it.

KNOWING YOUR EQUIPMENT

It is important that a pilot should know their aircraft thoroughly but in some cases memory fails. We occasionally make silly, human blunders and this is unavoidable for as a profession, we pilots are fallible. Though, having said this, I still meet pilots who think they are perfect – to those people all I can say is 'you'll get a big shock one day, I just hope you live through it'.

Now, for this section I will need to explain some rudimentary aspects of aircraft operation, the little dials and gauges we use and the paperwork required: I have tried not to make it too dull and I feel confident that you will plough through it.

Tailwind operations, off wet airstrips, is common with much of the Charter flying inAfrica

It's not a Golden goose but a 'Golden cock'

Luckily pilots everywhere make mistakes or this book would be half the size! Many years ago in Botswana some Maun pilots decided as long as pilots made mistakes they should be punished for them, but in a manner which encourages the offending pilot to do better and promotes social interaction - enter the Case System.

Now, to be clear, if a pilot does something dangerous or illegal, which usually amounts to the same thing, he does not fall under the 'case system', but under the law, which normally sends him packing. 'Casing' a pilot is about embarrassing them for not giving the job its due attention. Letting everyone know he or she has slipped up certainly accomplishes this, as embarrassment can be a powerful tool. It is a system meant to humble a person before their peers and build the correct aviation mentality through very mild humiliation – ie. 'Remember you are not perfect and double check your work - all in the interests of safe flying and living longer.'

Add to this, the whole system is integrity based and is meant to develop your personal attributes. Because of the remote nature of our work there are times when what you did went unnoticed but under the 'Case System' you are required to report yourself when you screw up. Once penalized you buy a case of beer and the whole group of pilots from your company sits down and drinks the beer with you, laughing *at you;* all of themknowing full well it could be them next week! But beware for those non-witnessed events it is more affordable to fess up, since hiding any transgression will get you a <u>double case</u> offence for not following the spirit of the system.

Some simple screw-ups which will get you 'Cased' are: forgetting to file your flight plan; trying to taxi over your chocks; leaving a seat belt hanging out the door whilst flying; attempting take-off with your pitot cover on; going to the wrong airstrip; picking up the wrong passengers, and so on and so forth.

But as I said, should a mistake happen of a more serious nature we guarantee no one will be laughing. We take our work seriously and being unsafe in an aircraft is a quick way to get yourself ostracized by the group – but not to worry as your social banishment will be short lived as a termination letter usually follows quickly behind any stupid aviation behaviour and then we won't be seeing you again.

One company decided to take it a little further. They have the 'Casing' System year round and also, recentlythey have an award called the *Golden Cock*. This is an annual award given to the pilot who screwed up the worst during the year regarding *case-able offenses*. It is awarded at the company's Christmas party and this year's winner received his award for going to the wrong airstrip, waiting, then taking off and buzzing the camp to wake them up. They did wake up and drove out to see what the problem was. When the pilot asked where the guests were it was pointed out that he should actually have landed at the other airstrip – the one about 1.1 km to the East. Each year we can say the winner is a true Cock, although to be fair we haven't had a female winner yet!

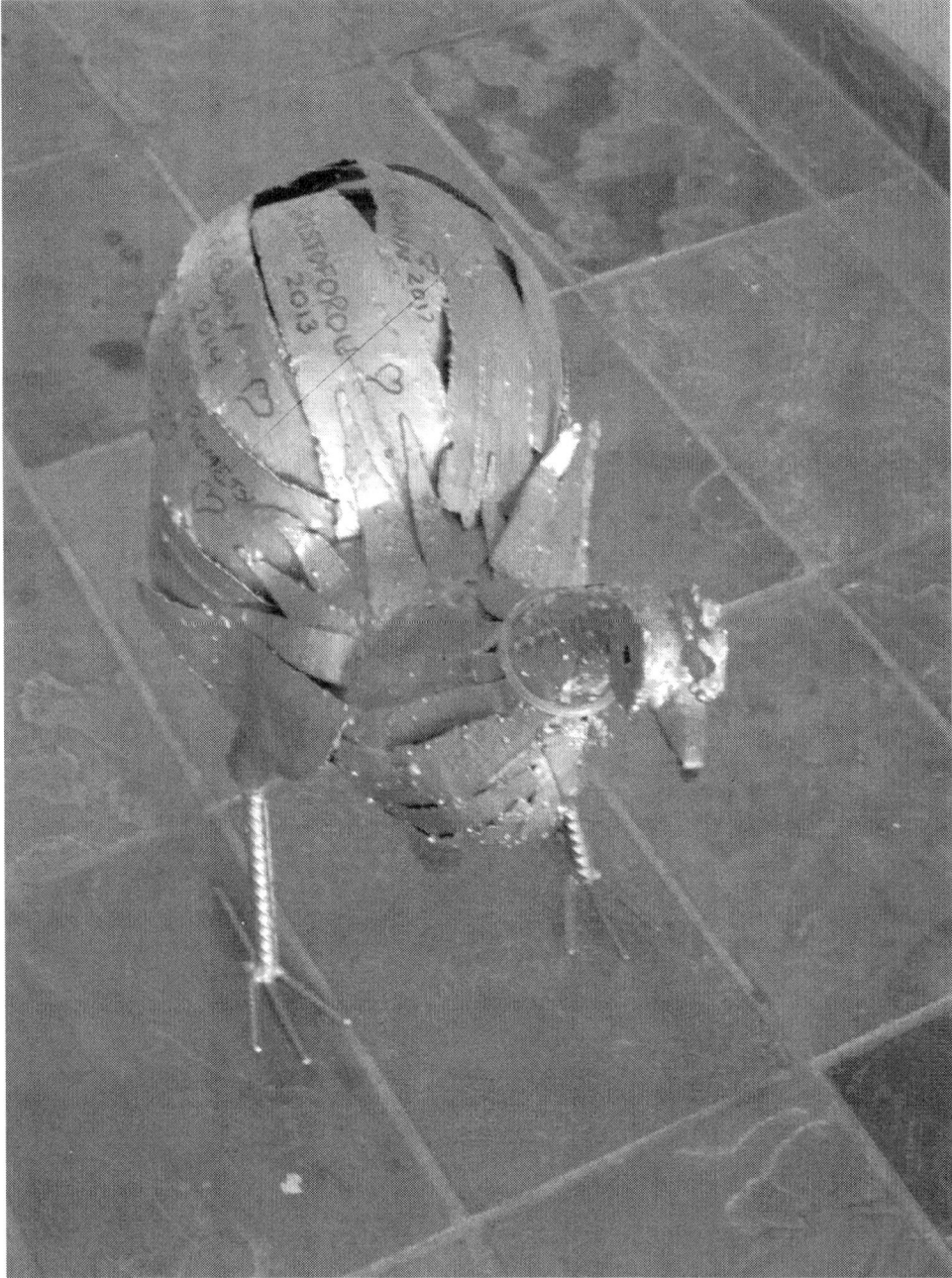

The Golden Cock

It just doesn't add up

When I was younger I used to tell any pilot I ever spoke to that *I* was going to do what *they* did when I grew up. The normal response to this was, "Make sure you're good at mathematics!" I certainly wasn't, but I'm better now, and if you fall into this category too, don't despair as there is still hope.

Because of the remoteness of the areas a lot of these aircraft operate in, areas devoid of any form of mobile phone signal, there is no way to let the office know when someone doesn't show up to get on the aircraft, or if additional people show up hoping to get on, normally these are staff. This pilot's company changed their system so all pilots, on calling inbound to Base, would state the passenger numbers so as to confirm this against the schedule, just make sure the system ran correctly. On this particular day the pilot, Mark, was furious his schedule was wrong and called the office to challenge them on it. He didn't yell, but was clearly frustrated and said he was tired of being handed something by people whose job it was to add things up correctly.

"You have put 9 on my schedule. I picked up 5 at Vumbura, then 2 at Mombo, and 2 at Piajo. It's wrong: 5+2+2=8".
"Mark, 5+2=7+2=9"
Silence
"Mark, did you get that?"
Still no answer.
"Mark"
"Sorry, busy now, speak later, and, er, disregard my last."

Fined one case of beer for not knowing his maths tables. When it came to math's Mark was special; in fact he demonstrated the same mathematical prowess on two further occasions before finally deciding to just keep his mouth shut. I am a little older than some of the others and these days I am truly staggered when I meet people who cannot add simple things in their head – still it can be funny, given the right moment.

Just remember - you can still be a pilot while being crap at adding – you'll just buy a lot of beer.

Identify yourself

In order to communicate in the air with the office, Air Traffic Control and other pilots, we use the VHF (Very High Frequency) radio installed in the aircraft. So the other person knows who they are speaking to, we identify ourselves using the aircraft's registration. In most countries in Africa this starts with the country registration followed by the individual aircraft's assigned letters or numbers. ZS for South Africa, A2 for Botswana, 9J for Zambia, V5 for Namibia, Z for Zimbabwe, and so on.

In this story our pilot was flying A2-AIC, a Cessna 206. We'll call him Kenny, no not real but I can tell you he is now flying for a South African company. Kenny is a young guy in his early twenties with a lot of energy and a penchant for parties. He is excitable to say the least and always has his eye out for a pretty lady, but essentially an all-around good guy.

On this particular day, Kenny, engine running, is about to ask for permission to taxi when he realizes he has forgotten the aircrafts registration. It's fine, it happens, no big deal he just needs to look on the dashboard right in front of the pilot's seat; but Kenny had forgotten this simple detail. He had also forgotten the registration is on the cover of the aircraft's Flight Manual *and* its Tech Log. Even the printed schedule in his shirt pocket would have given him what he was after. But Kenny only remembered the large painted digits down the side of the fuselage. So he opened the aircraft window and tried to put his head out: Epic Fail, as his head didn't fit. Then he opened the door of the aircraft, engine still running, but he was still wearing his headset, so this had to come off. As he twisted his body round far enough to get a glimpse of the number it was only his seatbelt which saved him from falling out the door.

It all went from bad to worse as he had completely embarrassed himself in full view of his passengers and then tried to pretend it never happened. This is not the way to go: if you screw up, take the heat, pay *the case*, and get it over with. In Kenny's situation there were witnesses and any number of questions on the radio before he finally came clean. Penalty imposed - fined one case of beer for being an idiot.

This is as far as it opens so rather silly to try

Ban the Pod

Kenny is not the only pilot to believe his head would fit through a Cessna 206 window. Most of our aircraft have approved cargo packs, which we call 'pods'. They are attached to the bottom of the fuselage to transport additional luggage, and they have a small access, or 'pod door', just below the pilot door through which to push the luggage. This means there is more room in the cabin. It is a perfect arrangement as long as a pilot remembers to close the pod door. If he *doesn't*, then luggage rains down on the flight to the camp and results in upset clients who now have no underwear or, in some cases, private bedroom toys – yes you can bring those if you want.

Meet Mick (it's as good a name as any), yet another South African pilot. Mick is about twenty three, weighs in at the staggering heavy mass of about 50 kilograms and is built like small schoolboy. Most people who fly with him are initially taken back by his appearance but Mick is an excellent and very knowledgeable pilot. Nevertheless we all have our off days.

Mick was already airborne before a nagging feeling started that he may not have closed the pod door. He chose the *head through window* option to check. Mission nowhere near accomplished, his Ray Ban sunglasses were ripped from his nose. Apparently, sticking your head into a light, roughly 200kph, breeze will do this. Mick's last view of his US$120 investment was as they bounced off the tail plane and disappeared into the Delta. So Mick's day ended up tainted rather than tinted (forgive me).

Let's go fishing!

There is a large city called Brazzaville in the Republic of the Congo, in Central Africa. It is home to roughly 1.5 million people and finds itself on a list of cities, along with Detroit, Lusaka and Manila (to name but a few) where it is recommended you should *not go* for a wedding or a funeral - which is basically the same thing. Across the Congo River there is a sort of sister city called Kinshasa in the Democratic Republic of Congo (DRC) which also appears on the same list.

Although located in separate countries, the two appear to share the same level of grime, poverty and a distinct lack of tourism. They also share two other things: they have a shit-load of Non-Governmental Organizations, aka NGOs, the people who help the poor with your tax dollars; and they have remarkably similar weather patterns.

What's the connection? Well, in a country where roads are either non-existent or in a shocking state of disrepair anything which needs to move does so by air. These two raggedy cities are within sight of each other and each has a rather large international airport. Because of their proximity, the weather in one place is likely to be mirrored in the other. One evening in early 2003 our English pilot Steve and his co-pilot are flying a Metro which has just made it into Brazzaville ahead of what could be loosely described as a *perfect storm:* two systems coming together.

Steve had joined for a visual approach just in time and upon landing was glad to be on the ground. But he also knew just how much air traffic was still up there and at least a dozen or so of them were bound for his airport; and the weather had now properly closed in. Since it was a Friday and like anywhere, the rush hour traffic would be heavy for a while, Steve saw no point in trying to make it the hotel just yet. Instead, he decided to get a six pack or so, then stick around in order to listen to and see who would make it in and who would have to divert.

Aviation is all about redundancy, a backup plan or system for most things. For Instrument flying, which is what bigger aircraft do, they carry additional fuel just in case there is a problem at their destination. This fuel is comprised of various groups: *approach fuel*, which is enough for two or three approaches, depending on the company; *hold fuel*, so they can circle high above the airport; and *diversion fuel*, which will allow them to fly on to another destination, should it be impossible to land at the scheduled one.

On this night every aircraft was diverting due to the weather. Then an Ilyushin IL76 joined the fold, at the back of the queue as with many things in aviation – wait your turn. The IL76 is an old high wing, four-engine, Russian military transport aircraft and it is huge. It is similar in size to a 747 but sits lower to the ground. It was designed to move large numbers of Soviet combat paratroops during the cold war. The back of the aircraft opens so these shock troops can disgorge themselves in flight before floating to the ground to murder us all in our sleep and remove our civil liberties – well this was the Cold War thinking of the time.

Now, however, these IL76s and their Russian crews carry relief equipment and food aid to companies who have won contracts, or make money, to assist the NGOs in their mission to save the third world from itself. Just so we are clear, I don't have anything against making money off poverty as long as it is all done out in the open for everyone to see – in this respect I don't think it is. There are a lot of people getting very rich off this type of work all while singing their own praises about being humanitarians.

As an example this is an Angolan Air Force IL-76

Said Russian crew fly their approach to Maya-Maya International Airport, but as they do, each aircraft ahead of them is unable to land and they either conduct a missed approach, thus joining the queue at the back to try again, or divert to another airport. Not the IL76 crew, who, on the first approach, land and then taxi into the freight area only about a kilometre from Steve's aircraft. Highly impressed by this, Steve grabs one of the ramp vehicles and drives down for a chat.

Meanwhile, every other aircraft behind them is still diverting since the forward visibility is less than 100 metres and the cloud base is now sitting halfway down a lot of the bigger aircrafts' tails: in short, in weather terms, it is appalling. No one is in sight as Steve approaches the open access door below and behind the cockpit. He calls out and a head appears slowly, followed by part of the man's body. Steve recognizes a heavy Ukrainian accent when the man suspiciously asks:

"Customs?"

"No just a pilot."

The man relaxes and his other hand appears from behind the bulkhead, holding an open bottle of Russian vodka which is pushed forward. "Drink?" Steve takes the proffered bottle and hands over one of his beers. The Russian seems happy: détente exists again. Steve then wants to know if there was any chance he can come in and look around. Russian number one, who we'll call Sergei, yells loudly upstairs and after a short back and forth with what seems to be the captain, access is granted and Steve climbs the ladder into the hold. Once in, he needs to climb a ladder up to the flight deck which he finds in semi-darkness accompanied by a red hue, with all of the equipment and gyros still humming as the crew carry out their aircraft's post flight. Steve shares out the remaining beers among his new friends, everyone seems happy.

Just so you know, Steve was one of those characters who could talk his way into a Dictator's palace just to say "Hi" and maybe have a spot of lunch. He was rarely offensive and he always displayed a persona of not having an ounce of bigotry whether it involved race, gender, or nationality. Because of this all sorts of doors opened for him and he ended up in the oddest places. He easily made new friends and could quickly calm explosive situations by reasoning with the angriest of people – often in more than one language. He believed things should always be fair – but also was a realist because as we all know fairness does not always exist!

The conversation on the flight deck drifted on and although Steve could speak a little Russian, the crew spoke limited English. Sergei, who had the best grasp of the language, had disappeared. Steve's primary interest was to know how they had managed to pull off a landing on their first approach. It took him a while to explain; he pointed out the window at the cloud base, which was now touching the top of the IL76's cockpit window. He made an aircraft noise and mimicked their approach, much like a child does, and then held up one finger and swept in with his palm to show the landing. The captain finally got it and he and the others had a rapid conversation in Russian and Sergei was summoned; his head popped into the flight deck. They exchanged a few more sentences and then Sergei disappeared. When he reappeared he handed Steve a small electronic device. It was a GPS, the unit was not exactly ancient but a few years old from the description.

Steve thought they were joking. Just so you understand most aircraft have aviation GPS units mounted in their avionics stack, but they are usually clearly marked 'day reference only'. On the other hand it is true many most third world airports have power issues, as well as maintenance problems concerning instrument approach systems. They are much better now, but from time to time systems still die, which is always a problem if you are in the middle of a storm and on an approach. So having your aviation GPS ready is always a smart move. This crew had a different system. It seems Sergei laid himself in the viewing area in the big glass nose of the aircraft with what he called his *fishing GPS*, not even an aviation unit, which updates its position much more quickly. The captain would fly the approach with Sergei calling out left, right, on track, after which the captain would make the necessary corrections then check their profile based upon their altitude. In return the captain would call out these altitudes so Sergei got a mental picture of the aircraft's descent profile. Meanwhile the aircraft would continue its descent as close to the *minimas* as possible before the captain let Sergei know they were essentially there, you know - over the runway.

This will give you an idea of Sergei's office there in the lower nose section – not the company in question.

Minimas are the lowest you are legally allowed to fly on a given approach and if you reach them it is also decision-making time - remember your aircraft is still moving forward, very quickly and the runway is only so long. At this point it seems Sergei would urgently look for the runway, call out when he saw it and judge how many metres left or right of runway centreline the big transport aircraft was before calling out the information. The captain would immediately make any necessary corrections based on Sergei's reported distance and then land the aircraft. The whole system was hare-brained and involved a mountain of trust; yet it seemed to work.They chatted a bit more then Steve decided to bid them all goodnight before Russian out of there. Sorry, couldn't resist.

How I like it

Let me give you a quick explanation as to how most General Aviation (GA) aircraft operate engine-wise. Most *piston-engine* GA aircraft have a *mixture*, red knob which controls fuel input to the engine, forget that for this story, a *pitch lever*, usually light blue or another colour, to control the propeller revolutions per minute or *rpm* and to help the prop control engine efficiency during flight, and you can forget this as well; *bear with me*, I'll get there. Finally a *throttle*, usually black and much like the accelerator in your car, which basically increases or decreases engine power to go faster or slower depending on how you use it, and this is important for our story. I know it is a very basic explanation for you pilots out there but think of the non-pilots. The throttle display is in *manifold pressure* (aka MAP) which is measured in *inches* of mercury or Hg.

A lovely Cessna 210 gets airborne out of PomPom airstrip in Botswana and makes a smooth left hand turn for its next destination. The pilot, a beautiful German lady who we will call Beth, a tall, slender blonde and striking in many respects. She could be known for her temper and although she had *kind of a sense of humour* she definitely didn't understand the nuances of sarcasm or dry humour - not in the English language sense. As Beth takes off she presses the PTT (press to talk) to use the radio and announce her arrival in the air and her immediate intentions for the aircraft.

"Tango Echo November is airborne out of PomPom left turn, climbing 5500 feet for Lebala….", another airstrip about 40 minutes away – think of our work as a bus service of sorts.

But the conversation was not over:

"....you see that's the way a radio call should be done, smooth, no hesitation, just keep the details succinct when you make the transmission......."

This poor young lady was suffering from what is known as a stuck PTT. The button, once pressed, should spring back to its normal position when released, but this one had not. Unfortunately for the young lass in question, everything she was saying in the cockpit to the pilot accompanying her was being broadcast as far as a VHF radio signal will reach – which is line of sight on the earth's surface. For the new pilot this turned into a continuous discussion of aviation procedures and etiquette which lasted over twenty minutes during which time not one of the twenty-odd aircraft flying around could transmit as she was blocking the frequency. The funny bit was when she started her descent she made a radio call, which included good engine management. The end of the call (oblivious to the PTT situation) had her saying:

"We are now going to descend, so good engine management for these aircraft is to reduce the throttle by one inch of manifold for every mile travelled: do you get it? One inch one mile? That's the way I like it, *One inch at a time*."

Now, between you and me, women are always going on about a hell of a lot more than one inch. I listened to this and felt I found a true partner for my life problems...... (Just kidding). Needless to say we were all wetting ourselves in our respective cockpits – I can say this as it is an approved aviation term.

That evening all of us got together in our local haunt, the 'Buck'n'Hunter' (thank you, Jamie and Joanne Briggs, for the good times) and when the lady in question walked in we all could not resist greeting her with:
"ONE INCH AT A TIME!"

On her departure all the pilots chipped in and had a T-shirt made which said "I like it one inch at a time", which she took in her stride. Beth, wherever you are, thanks for making aviation fun, even if it was unintentional.

Gone Pro

The invention of the Go Pro camera has revolutionized what we see on You-Tube and other Internet sites; even the news. We can now mount these little units and get high definition video from some unique angles. Extreme sports has benefited the most as they give the viewer the feeling of being right there during the BASE jump, ski run or any other insane act without the person having to actually do it themselves.

You also get a new perspective of aviation, especially the type of flying we do which is in some really remote areas. It was immediately noted by some in aviation circles these little units could potentially cause safety issues. Obviously the pilot knows it is there and he or she might be tempted to go a little too far in order to film 'that moment', thereby entering the Darwin Zone. Luckily, the companies have recognized this and have essentially banned these cameras - except for some rare and approved occasions.

For those of you not familiar with this camera, each unit comes with its own suction cup for ease of mount and dismount. The cup can withstand high speeds and prior to the ban we have Mick, who has mounted his Go Pro Hero with the accompanying suction cup to the left wing strut. Unfortunately for Mick, he has not utilized the cardinal rule of aviation – the redundant system. Everything in aviation is about having a back-up; but in this case Mick had attached his camera to the wing with only the suction cup.

As he flew along he could clearly see the suction cup, therefore the camera, slowly dislodging itself from the wing. Mick slowed the aircraft, which slowed the process but did not stop it; he further slowed the aircraft; this kept going but of course at some point it had to stop. Aircraft work on forward motion and if you slow them too much you move into an area which could effectively cause an aerodynamic stall (the aircraft stops flying). An aerodynamic stall is also not good for the Go Pro's continued survival. Roughly four minutes before landing Mick's Go Pro detached itself; filming its final flight as it disappeared into the Delta to join his Ray Bans. Maybe next time Mick can use some duct tape as well?

Fire away

When you do something like camping or rock climbing in a remote area it is important to build up some survival skills for the day when you might be lost or forgotten – right? When we drop passengers off at the lodges we sometimes stay the night too, and the camp vehicle is there to pick us all up. From time to time a pilot will fly in alone and a vehicle has to be sent just for him, which is a bit of a pain for the camp but if any of you lodge guys are reading this, we do appreciate it. Very occasionally, the person assigned to this duty forgets or there are insufficient vehicles to undertake the collection.

Enter Mark, a South African pilot whose family heritage is, let's say Mediterranean. So he has a big family, quite a few sisters and most of all Mark is up for almost anything. Today, however, it is not Mark's fault; the whole thing lies squarely with the camp. Mark is scheduled to land at an airstrip at 1630 hours with no passengers. He is on time but there is no vehicle waiting for him. He is not unduly concerned and gets a book out to pass the time. One hour goes by and still no vehicle has arrived. It is about then Mark gets hold of another pilot on the radio to relay to the office the message: 'where's my transport to camp?' The office phones the camp operation, who radios the camp. "So sorry, there is no vehicle as they are short of them today; two have broken down and the clients are out with the rest." The immediate question is, 'Why wasn't the Air Charter Company told?' Again, "So sorry, we forgot: the pilot needs to wait." "What about sending the helicopter at the camp?" "No can do, we would need approval from the helicopter company's office." Ten minutes later - Ok we have approval but, guess what, after all this now it's too late as darkness has fallen and there is no night flying.

Meanwhile, Mark is still sitting at the airstrip unaware of all of this. He is a smoker, but he has only one cigarette remaining and no matches, you could say Mark is a disorganized smoker. He warms up the aircraft and then shuts down the engine, lighting the cigarette off the exhaust. He inhales - ah much better. Cigarette finished, he toys with the idea of making a fire as it's getting a bit cold. Mark should have thought of this before he finished the cigarette as, of course, he has no matches. Never mind, he's resourceful. He wonders how hard it can be to make a fire the old-fashioned way, like a Bushman does. He uses a glow stick to find a small piece of wood and some kindling. The time is now 1810 hours, the sun is down and being winter it is VERY COLD. Fast forward to 1945 hours on this moonless night and Mark's hands are sore from rubbing sticks and he is now freezing – still no fire - FAIL. He gives up on his masculine moment and retires to the back of the aircraft with his laptop. He is going to watch a movie to take his mind off his rumbling stomach. He presses play, the title rolls, the first scene is running, so he prepares to sit back and enjoy; this is about the time the battery dies. Except for the glow stick Mark is in the dark about his future.

About 2155 the camp vehicle finally arrives at the airstrip and Mark is driven back to camp, a 45 minute trip. From this day on, Mark carries a fire-starter and a pack of smokes with matches in his flight bag. Do you think maybe he will finally see the light?

I see wheely well, thanks

From time to time a pilot may have a problem, even an emergency; it's fine, as we are trained to deal with them. Occasionally, though, this training gets the better of a pilot and the 'emergency' is more of a perception than a reality. This is ok too: better an overly cautious pilot than a careless one.

Our friend Mick, who has now received his new Ray Bans and a Go Pro is on order, is today, flying a Cessna 210. The 210 has a streamlined fuselage and thinner wing than a Cessna 206 and doesn't have the lift struts. There is one other major difference, it has retractable landing gear. The landing gear folds away into the body of an aircraft, as happens in most airliners, so there is far less drag and the aircraft is much quicker.

When a pilot flies an aircraft with retractable gear there is always the possibility he or she may forget to extend the gear before landing and so we have procedures to ensure this does not happen. For the Cessna 210 you have a yellow light, gear up, and a green light, gear down. Once you have checked your green light you look out the left window where you can see the left main gear to verify it is down. Then, as the right main gear and nose wheel are not visible, Cessna has thoughtfully provided a small mirror, which is mounted halfway down the right wing which allows you to see said right main gear and the nose wheel. You should undertake this procedure at least twice, just to be safe.

It's a great system

Mick is in the midst of this procedure when he realizes he cannot see the nose wheel at all. Everything is showing the gear is down and locked – green light and all! Mick looks carefully again: No, the nose wheel is definitely not there! He even asks the passengers if they can see it – no they can't either. He declares a MAYDAY contacts the office through another aircraft and reports the emergency, saying he will divert back to Maun with the passengers he has. As it is a weekend both the Safety Officer and the Operations Manager have to be called in from their day off; the Chief Pilot is on leave. He explains the matter to the people on board and they are fine about the whole thing.

He flies the 40 minutes back to where his company is based. He speaks to ATC and Mick informs them he may have a gear problem and he will need fly by the tower a few times so someone can visually inspect and confirm the nose wheel is down. He re-declares the MAYDAY, which means a slew of other parties become involved, including airport fire services, there will also be a host of paperwork to go through after landing – if he makes it without destroying himself and the aircraft.

As the tower looks on so do several members of Mick's company who are standing close to the runway with binoculars. Mick is told it all looks good; the nose wheel is down therefore it's back to him, *it's his decision.*

Mick touches down ever so gently and, lo and behold, the gear is not only down, it is locked – the aircraft is safe on the ground. To be on the cautious side, the aircraft stops right there on the runway and the maintenance engineers come out to give it the once over while other aircraft circle above waiting their turn. No immediate problem having been found, the 210 is towed to the hanger for a full inspection.

An hour later the engineers have jacked the aircraft up, run the gear several times, the electrics guys have looked through the system and they can't find anything. Finally something catches a senior engineer's eye and because the aircraft is on jacks he gets a small ladder, which he climbs to inspect the little mirror on the wing. There is a small splash of mud, almost white in colour, covering one corner of the mirror. The engineer has an idea: he lowers the aircraft off the jacks and has it wheeled outside. He then asks one of the company pilots to get in and look in the mirror so the pilot sits where he would normally be when flying and looks over. He can't see the nose wheel and so leans back a little. Ah there it is! He leans forward. Ah, the nose wheel has vanished again. The engineer then wipes away the offending mud splatter and the pilot can see the nose wheel from any position. At this point Mick shows up and one of the engineers asks him what he's doing there. Mick says he doesn't understand.

"We don't do eye tests here", quips the engineer. "You need the doctor's office for that."

Mick is a little upset at being mocked and even more so at the fact after his Mayday call he needs to fill out a mountain of paperwork for what was no more than a bit of mud.

After this the company adopted a new procedure of giving the mirror a wipe after every landing just in case it got contaminated and required another pilot to undergo an eye exam.

PS: Although kind of funny I respect a careful pilot more than a careless one. Mick did it right!

Swapping Guests

Today Kenny has a very simple schedule he is to collect two couples off their international flight and fly them to their respective camps. He has greeted them, explained what is going to happen and loaded them in the aircraft.

The first couple, who we will call Jones x2 are only flying 10 minutesfrom Maun to Stanley's airstrip and will be spending two days in thevery lovely Baines Camp run by Sanctuary Lodges Botswana. The Jonesparty safely off the aircraft Kenny flies on to Omdop airstrip to deliver the remaining two people who we will call the Smith's to their Lodge called Duba Plains run by Great Plains.

Lucky for Kenny he is overnighting at the Duba Lodge and as he is arrivingjust at Afternoon Tea time, he has a few snacks and decides he will join his guests on their first Game Drive. All of this seems quite normal.

Meanwhile in another realm things are quickly unraveling. It seems theManager at Baines Camp has been on to the Air Charter Operator who delivered Jones x2 - seems the Jones' made it as far as the Lodge before it was discovered they were meant to be in Duba Plains not at Baines Camp.

After contacting Duba Plains the pilot came on the radio in the Game Vehicle and the problem was explained. He had dropped each couple to thewrong Lodge. He needed to return in the Game Drive vehicle to the Lodgewith Smith x2 to fly them back to Baines. Small problem, the Smiths, it seems were fed up with travelling.They have been on the go for 17 hours and they rather like Duba Plains. They are refusing to leave the Lodge.

So Kenny was instructed to get airborne from Omdop, and fly empty to Stanley's and collect the Jones party and deliver them to their correct Lodge - Duba Plains. As it was neither the Smiths fault, nor the Lodges fault it was the Air Charter Company had to pay for the Smiths one night in camp.

Oh, Kenny, he had to stay in the Lodge with all four of them, rather embarrassing for him. The key to this story: always READ YOUR SCHEDULE and RECONFIRM NAMES WITH THE GUESTS AT EVERY DESTINATION.

A call in the wild

Now strictly speaking, the use of a Mobile or Cell phone while flying is not something we pilots generally do. After all phone calls are for less intensive work periods. But it is Africa which is a vast continent, with some countries covering enormous areas. Flying here means you are often not under the control of any form of ATS and therefore communicate by making position reports so other aircraft know where you are. This said, if you have cell phone signal and there is an emergency, maybe your radio has stopped working, you can call an ATS station and let them know what is going on. In this respect using a cell phone becomes a safety option for the aircraft and its passengers. It is rare these things happen but it is nice to know someone can think outside the box and solve a problem.

Today, Paddy is flying through Tanzania to an airstrip called Mwanza which is an airport surrounded by a low set of hills, much like a shallow fruit bowl. Unfortunately this fruit bowl is missing one side which borders a large lake. As Paddy flies along his Mobile phone starts ringing; he ignores it. But the caller is persistent and a further three calls are made before Paddy looks at the number, it's the Office calling. Obviously they know where he and his aircraft are, so he relents and answers the call.

"Paddy where are you right now?"
"You know where I am, I am about 30 minutes out of Mwanza, what's the problem?"
"Whatever you do don't go to Mwanza, there is a big storm there. Make sure you divert now and give us a call on the ground, we'll let you know when it passes."

With this the Office hangs up. Roughly two hours later he is given the all clear to proceed on with his flight to Mwanza where he gets the full appreciation of how bad the situation was. Mwanza is a sealed runway which accepts some reasonably sized aircraft. The storm had appeared and basically parked itself over the airport and surrounding hills which is the fore mentioned three sided bowl. The rain bucketed down the hillsides and had nowhere else to go but the through the large flat spaces of the airport before it headed off to the lake. In essence the airport looked as if someone had taken any number of aircraft and tossed them into a swimming pool. The following are the pictures from pilots who were on the ground at the time standing in the Terminal.

Sorry, for the poor quality, the photo was taken from a screen capture off a video.

Always check who's calling while you are flying as you never know how helpful it might be.

INTEGRITY

In any business, when you hire a human being you can't immediately gauge their degree of integrity or honesty; this may sound sad but these days it is a stark reality. For aviation and as a brief summary, the work requirements for pilots vary from company to company but they are all fairly straightforward. The basics are: follow the rules, operate the equipment/aircraft as the company wishes, you need to show up in a fit state to work and on time, treat the clients properly: plain common sense.

From time to time *a Player* rolls through. You know the type; someone who sees a system, immediately dissects it, and then re-forms it in their head with all the exploitable angles. You will never get rid of them but the trick is to spot them before the damage starts. One irritating, but not harmful, example of this is the pilot who does just enough - you know the bare minimum of his or her work responsibilities.

A lot of the charter companies work on a system whereby once your scheduled flying is finished for the day, many of us only fly daylight hours, you can disappear home but you are required to remain on call, which means if you're needed you must return to fly. Some companies, however, will just assign the flight to the pilot sitting right there in the office rather than call a pilot back in. So the craftier ones get out of the office as soon as they possibly can to avoid being saddled with more work.

Another ploy is the: *I'm not well* or *I slept badly last night*. So if a flight does show up this thought is in the back of the manager's head and they are even less likely to be called in. Just so you understand I am not a heartless, callous bastard: peopledo have problems and medical issues, but patterns evolve and most people in this industry are not idiots either; although my ex-wife might differ regarding anything to do with me. These *Players* are mostly amateurs and it is the professionals we are going to deal with in the next stories.

Welcome to Zambia! I gotta go...

The Canadian pilot in this story used to fly passengers from north-east Botswana either dropping at, or collecting from, the airports of Livingstone (Zambia) or Victoria Falls (Zimbabwe). On his way to and fro he used to fly over Victoria Falls, a beautiful southern African landmark, well worth a view from the air. Whenever this pilot briefed his passengers regarding their departure or arrival he would hint at the possibility of a quick glimpse of the Falls from the air. The idea appealed to most and they were more than willing to assist him in paying US$20 to the poor African air traffic controller whose cooperation he would need to make the event happen.

Needless to say the 'poor African' controller had no knowledge of this and neither did this *Player's* company until a guest happened to mention to one of the lodge managers how lucky they were to have seen the wonderful Falls and how helpful the pilot was. This is when the proverbial shit hit the fan. The pilot was called in on the mat regarding his little side business. He was told he would be kept on for as long as it took him to pay all of the estimated monies back – this time to a local charity – after this they would decide if he stayed longer.

His final departure from the company involved dropping two guests off at Livingstone Airport, tossing the keys of his aircraft, which he was meant to fly back to Botswana to one of the ground staff and announcing he was quitting. An hour and a half later he got on the British Airways flight to Johannesburg.

As a parting comment he did offer up a storm was coming and maybe they should think about tying the aircraft down – you know good Airmanship.

This is the view returning up the Zambezi River from Livingston (Zambia) to Kasane (Botswana). A view our friend above never managed to see due to his sudden departure from the Company.

Not now, I'm all tied up

Not all perceived ethics issues are confined to pilots. A camp manager greeted a newly-arrived guest at his camp and the single young lady took an instant liking to the strong, sexy, wild man who worked in such a remote place. In the manager's defence the lady was hard to resist and after dinner on the first evening, when all the other guests had retired for the night, the manager accompanied the lady back to her tent for a night of passion. Surely not part of his job description, but hell I didn't see the contract - maybe it was in the fine print.

The following day when the lady returned from her game drive she went in immediate search of lover-boy. All the staff had been instructed to tell her he was away attending to someone else - wow, what a contract - which news did not please her at all. She stormed off to her tent in a rage. But all was quickly forgiven when she saw what was waiting for her – the manager had snuck into her room, stripped off and tied himself to her bed. His extracurricular duties resumed until her departure. There were a few of us who would have loved to see the comments card regarding the service she received during her stay.

It should be safe: just flip it over.

In all places on the planet you have people who are, there's no polite way of saying this, just plain stupid. For us some of them come and visit but we do have some home-grown talent. Enter Motusei (pronounced 'Moe-too-see', though this is not his real name), a camp hand at X Lodge. The consumption policy regarding alcohol in this lodge is staff may have a *couple* of drinks in the evening and absolutely no more, not even in the staff village which is their own area in the camp. It's not difficult to stick to this regulation, more common sense really, which seems to be pretty uncommon at times.

On this particular evening Motusei has had more than a couple of drinks - in fact he is well on his way to this month's alcohol quota, possibly even into next month's. As many of us have had the misfortune to experience first-hand, this is when a lot of people, mostly men, come up with *that one seemingly brilliant idea*; and Motusei's no exception. He has formulated the greatest idea ever! It involves the Lodge's office safe, a unit he is convinced holds enough money for him to retire – you know, buy a nice house, get a couple of lovely girlfriends and a blazer for his Saturday nights out.

The plan revolves around Motusei removing the roughly half metre-high safe from the lodge office and taking it to a place where he can work on it undisturbed. At 3 a.m., when he has run out of beer, he stumbles through the darkened camp, grabs the heavy safe, which was not secured to the ground - rookie mistake for the lodge, but finds he's unable to lift it; second flaw in the plan – yes, the first flaw was the plan itself. So he wraps a vehicle tow rope around the safe and slowly drags it through the bush some 200 to 300 metres. Now he gets to work on the unit; for this he has brought a small hammer and a spatula, more at home in the kitchen I guess. After a half hour or so of tiring work, Motusei needs a rest so he lies down, just for a minute...*Zzzzzzzzzzzzzzzz.*

It is about 0515 when he is rudely awakened by the camp manager who has not had too much trouble locating him, as the drag marks on the ground made following his safe very easy. There is a bewildered and awkward conversation which includes the trusty, ' I don't know how I got here' and 'I've been framed!'

Unfortunately for Motusei, the police found his defence unconvincing and shortly after this a job ad went into the local press: "Camp Hand Needed".

Rating your employment

Just as many automobiles are, aircraft are all different as well. Unlike cars, as a pilot, you can't just jump in any aircraft you like and start flying it around. In most countries you usually need what is known as a Type Rating.

This involves the pilot attending a ground course to understand the aircraft manuals and other written documentation, systems, etc. After which they are required to pass a written exam, before they undertake flight training in the aircraft, or Simulator and then finally a Flight Test with a qualified testing officer. Of course because it's aviation all of this costs money - often a lot of it.

Enter a guy we will call Cameron, who has flown in Botswana as his first piloting job before going overseas to gain yet more experience. It has been three years and he has now returned and is working for a company in the country's capital Gaborone having been back about a year. As is common, pilots move on and as they do more junior pilots are promoted. Cameron has been asked to fly the company's Dassault Falcon a beautifully streamlined private jet which goes, for want of a better description, very, very fast. For this he needs the previously mentioned Type Rating. Not a problem the company will pay for Cameron's Rating, as he cannot afford it himself, and in return he must agree to remain employed for a further two years. Essentially I pay for the rating, which he can use at the next job, but you need to work for me for a prescribed time so I can make some money out of my investment – everyone gets something and all is fair. For those of you not familiar with aviation this is commonly referred to as being *bonded*.

Cameron is an experienced pilot and moves quickly through the Ground course, the exam, the flight training and finally the Flight Test. This satisfies the legal requirements but these days the Insurance Company has the final say. They require the newly rated pilot complete a requisite number of operational flight hours under the supervision of a more experienced pilot. Cameron completes the stipulated time and the supervisory pilot is more than happy with what he has observed and signs Cameron out on the aircraft.

Three days later Cameron does not appear at work and nobody knows where he is; they visit his flat and it is empty. One month goes by and still no news of the missing pilot. In time it is discovered Cameron has absconded with his new Falcon Rating to a job in Georgia – no, the one in Russia.

It takes a full four months for the entire story to come out. Seemingly Cameron had been speaking to this company for over six months prior to even starting his training but the Russian company had only one stipulation - 'they would only hire him if he had a Type Rating on their aircraft' – which was, yes, a Falcon! So Cameron had a think about it and came up with a simple solution – *I'll just get someone else to pay for it*. He then simply breached his contract and bond to remain flying with the company and disappeared – not to worry it was only his word!

It is these sorts of dick moves which screw it up for the pilots who have some measure of integrity. Companies now don't trust pilots and as such are now making them pay for their own ratings – something a lot of us are not in a position to do – seemingly this includes Cameron. Just goes to show you the list for people with *Integrity* is getting smaller each day – thanks to all you wankers practising this sort of thinking!

I have to go to a funeral

One pilot from an unnamed African country whose father passed away was given compassionate leave - as is fair. A parent passing-on is hard for anyone but it is particularly difficult for an African, as tradition often requires the first born son assume responsibility for the whole family. After one month's fully-paid compassionate leave the pilot in question was asked when he might be ready to come back to work. He indicated he needed more time and more time was given, although this time it would need to be unpaid.

African aviation is a small arena so when a few days later someone called this pilot's company and asked if he still worked there, the chief pilot's reply was an emphatic "Yes" because as far as the company was concerned he was still working for them, he was just away on personal time. The call was very long distance, another country, and the inquiry involved a pilot with the exact same name applying for a job and claiming to have worked for this charter company. This was news to the previous, or should I say current, employer. The pilot was immediately contacted and asked what was going on. His response

'What I do during my time off is my business.'

And this was the last the company ever heard from him! No resignation letter ergo no notice period therefore under Labour Law he owes the company one month's salary. He also still owes the company money having borrowed some from them – a refusal to pay or acknowledge he will pay the debt amounts to *theft* - and the company has yet to ascertain if anyone actually passed away. Based upon his behaviour there were doubts from some. *If no one died*, well this could amount to a criminal offence as making a false statement in order to collect your salary is called *fraud*. Yeah, I know you are reading this, so have a think about it Einstein!

A bitter lesson for the charter company, left high and dry, and out of pocket by a self-centred pilot. Integrity, yeah I am pretty sure this doesn't come from your genes.

I need the sheets clean

Theft is not confined to your common man, sorry person. Guests have varying degrees of Integrity when it comes to what is their property and what is someone else's.

Each Lodge normally offers a laundry service, which is another reason Guests should hold off on bringing half their wardrobes. In 2013 a Lodge operator had a rather unusual set of items placed in the room laundry basket, so unusual the housekeeping staff brought to the attention of management – a full set of sheets, with pillow cases, and throw pillow covers. None of it was new and clearly looked as if it had been stuffed into something for transportation. As you might have guessed, and much like a hotel, you are not required to make your beds or strip them once used. This set of bedding had come from the previous

Lodge these two guests had stayed in. Am I sure, pretty sure, as the previous Lodge operator had monogrammed much of the linen.

Management contacted the previous Lodge who acknowledged they were missing some bedding. The current Lodge had a quick think about it and decided to lose the stolen Bedding during the Laundry service and the guests even made enquiries, if you can believe it as to where it had gone. The Manager shrewdly asked very leading questions until she finished with: "The only bedding which we have is marked with the name of our Lodge on it. I haven't *seen* anything other than this. Did yours have any markings"?The guests realized they could go no further and dropped the subject. Guys, maybe look up the legal definition of theft - we have Laws here as well.

Can I have the Paper?

Now, before starting this story I would like to tell you how embarrassed many of us are regarding the behaviour of these very few pilots. There is very little of this level of theft, yes there is no other word for it, and it paints the rest of us who do not do this very badly, but some people just don't get it, and never will.

As was discussed we have all removed something from a hotel from time to time: soap, hand cream etc. When we found out a few of the pilots were taking rolls of toilet paper from the Lodge's they were overnighting in there was a very serious discussion amongst all of us. WTF – Toilet Paper. One pilot was even taking empty rolls from his house in his bag and then collecting the full ones and leaving these behind so they couldn't prove he had taken their ass paper. If you are going to stoop this low you need to think about getting some professional help – Really!!

DRIVING PROBLEMS

Alcohol has contributed to a number of traffic-related incidents over the years. From time to time, pilots have been known to tip back a few more than they should. Most of us don't subscribe to this sort of behaviour but for some once in an inebriated state this form of rational thought is not always there.

Conversely on the non-alcohol side there is always the question as to whether an individual should actually hold a driving license based upon their behaviour behind the wheel or their level of intelligence.

A River of vehicles

In 2009 two pilots were on their way home, about 2am, in this unnamed African town and for the sake of a better description they were completely trashed. One was driving and the other one was keeping him awake. "Tell me where to turn", the driver asked his passenger who said, "It's just up here on the left". The driver apparently only heard the word *left*, so he turned. A few seconds later they were inside the vehicle as water filled the cab; about three meters into a river. It wasn't sinking but it also wasn't going anywhere either.

It was however, winter and the water was cold so the passenger made a hasty exit through the window and stood on the bonnet (hood) of the vehicle; even there he was ankle-deep in water. The driver opened the door, which took him a good ten seconds as he pushed against the water and he then pushed hard to close the door, in case of thieves, I guess. This was when he noticed his passenger standing on his bonnet he became quite agitated. "Get the fuck off my car! Are you crazy? You are going to damage it you fuckwit!"

Being as lubricated as he was he obviously did not realize he now owned a submarine. The vehicle was eventually towed out and it needed considerable work before it was back on the road. Anyone want to go for a drive with this guy, don't forget to bring your trunks!

Unlike our two friends in the above story these guys pre-planned their trip through the water. We drive a lot of places which vehicles normally wouldn't go, but alas we still need to get there.

You cheap bastard, pay your electricity bill!

A couple of the pilots went out one evening and after a few drinks decided to change venues. Kris (not real) a brash young Scandinavian and Paddy decided to drive over to a local watering hole which is more remote. It is a backpacker's establishment and a popular place among those on budget travels through Maun, it also has a loyal local clientele which include some pilots.

On the way down the road to the establishment Kris, who was driving a little fast, lost control of the vehicle which started fishtailing; then there was a loud bang and the sound of glass shattering. The two sat in the vehicle for a second assessing if they were both okay before getting out to have a look at the vehicle; it was a moonless night and therefore difficult to see. Seems they had hit a traffic sign and the car was going to need some panel beating, but no real harm done. They continued on their mission.

They arrived at their chosen drinking establishment but were having a little trouble finding the bar as everything was in complete darkness. Kris wasn't happy with the ambience and started ranting. "Who's forgotten to pay the electricity bill? Look across the river, they all have power! You lot are useless – we're going somewhere else."

Fast-forward to the following morning. Paddy is called into the boss's office; there had been a complaint from the Backpackers. "Yes, we were there last night," admitted Paddy, "And yes, we did run into something, but it was a traffic sign." The boss indicated it might have been more than a traffic sign. Paddy was emphatic "it was just a traffic sign".

The conversation had left Paddy wondering so he returned to the scene with Kris. There was the traffic sign all right. But wait, what was just behind it? Ah, the power pole which supplies electricity to the whole area. They looked from the pole to the vehicle and the penny dropped. The power had been out all night and the so-called 'useless' owners of the bar, which was also a restaurant, had lost all the meat in their fridges and freezers. At this point out came Kris' credit card and he ended up shelling out rather a lot more than he had initially been willing to spend on a drink.

RELIGION

Before some of you go off and start yelling 'blasphemy' or 'sinner' etc., try to remember God and Religion relate to each other much like Gin and Tonic do – it's obvious who's in charge, the people are just there as the mixer.

It could be said that religion is *Man's* interpretation of God (okay now you can start yelling) – this is provable in the fact we have so many religions. If God were really upset about the whole setup, well, I am sure he would have struck a couple of these belief systems (and their followers) off the planet by now. This also proves not only did God give us a sense of humour – he has one as well, so let's not lose it now.

Ponchos Pilot

One pilot flying in Botswana in 2008 was undertaking his orientation training. This is the training most companies do when a new pilot joins them. For us it is done so the pilot can learn the various destinations we fly to, general company procedures regarding aircraft operation, and teach them customer service, etc.

This is also the time the company training staff assess if they are happy with their new acquisition. Many things can lead to a pilot being unemployed from a company. Maybe the new pilot has time management issues; for aviation running on time is paramount and some new pilots just do not understand getting airborne to fly a five hour day at 0630 hours means just this. Yes, it does stagger the mind they have made it this far.

In other cases it is personal appearance issue regarding; hair length, their inability to stand near enough to a razor or even own one, and even the pilot's *musk* - if I can phrase it this way. Then there are those pilots who just do not play well with others – shout all of the time, and generally interact in socially inept ways. Needless to say this sort of behaviour causes day to day issues with the remainder of the staff – so the best solution is to bid these types of pilots goodbye if they can't get their shit together.

Today we have a new pilot flying with a Training Captain Andre. This new pilot has none of the above mentioned issues and his training is going fairly well. Andre has climbed in to the Co-pilots seat and our new pilot has briefed the passengers, jumped into the front and belted himself in. Andre is staring out the window and has his notepad out when out of the corner of his eye he sees an unusual movement. He looks at the pilot but was not quick enough as what he thought he had seen was now finished.

They fly 15 minutes to their first stop, the clients get out and a new set of clients get in. The whole process repeats itself but this time Andre is watching the pilot and just before starting the engine he pushes the fingers together of his right hand and touches his forehead, the centre of his chest and then his left and right shoulders – yes, he crosses himself as many Christians do when taking mass.

Now you religious types reading this - if there are any left at this point - don't get me wrong. I am very much a believer in 'to each their own', but I am also a big believer in 'there is a time and a place for everything'. I think this is a little inappropriate and passengers don't really need to see this from their pilot. It is my opinion we should avoid bringing our beliefs to work, openly if you see what I mean. Let's face it guys it does make we heathens a little uncomfortable. I can see some of you telling me to get over my issues with Religion. So let's paint a rather bigoted picture of a religious moment in aviation and I would like to apologize in advance to the religion I am going to use to demonstrate this awkwardness.

You have decided it is time to see the Pyramids, have obviously booked a flight and have chosen to treat yourself to First Class. The day has finally come, you have boarded your flight to Cairo and are sitting comfortably in your First Class seat. The Captain and the First Officer enter, bid the cabin all a good evening before placing their Prayer Matts in front of the cockpit door - obviously facing in the correct direction. They then spend a respectful amount of time practising their right to a religious moment. Wow, I am feeling some of you are maybe a little less tolerant too including this as one of your holiday memories. They call these moments 'the shoe is on the other foot'.

Now for the multitude of Muslims around the world, I apologize again. This was not written to upset you but more to weed out intolerances amongst others from different belief systems. I know several people who are Muslim and am grateful for the time they have taken to explain questions I have had.

No, the reason I have painted this picture and more importantly is to point out the *'time and place for everything'* argument; so we pilots, let's just keep those prayer moments to ourselves.

I believe in nothing

One domestic pilot, who we shall call Tommy, was finished flying in Maun and was hoping to move up in his career and fly bigger aircraft with more powerful engines. One operation in Botswana was hiring and seemed to meet all of Tommy's requirements. From the company's point of view Tommy was perfect; he had the experience, good references and was a local pilot, which meant no labour issues. Tommy went for the interview and, having passed the technical part, the interviewers moved on to discuss a very important company dynamic or programme.

Each Sunday was when church services were held, and during the week they had a couple informal prayer meetings if he so chose to come to at least one of them this was fine as they were not fanatics. Always makes me nervous when someone who goes on about religion uses the word <u>fanatic</u> in any context. Yes, theirs was a Christian operation; these guys were bible bashers, here to spread the word of God and save the heathen African from himself. Sorry, it's my upbringing – no a Priest did not touch me, we were just friends with secrets.

Tommy has a small problem, he is not Christian; does not go to church, in fact he avoids the place. In their view he is worse than me, as I actually believe in God; Tommy is an *atheist*. Needless to say this confession caused a little stir in the interview room.

"But surely you know we are an Aviation Mission Service" is the question; Tommy's reply:

"You need people to fly aircraft, transport people, books, this I can do. I don't need to go to Church or believe in any of the other rubbish to do it".

Okay maybe not the most diplomatic way to respond, but his thinking was they needed to urgently understand Tommy's commitment to his atheism. Eventually, they did hire him, probably grudgingly. But as he put it they had to or they would have been overlooking a local pilot who needed employment based upon his religious beliefs.Remember not believing in God is a belief system!

Crucifixion

One foreign pilot did not have any such luck. His current contract was nearing an end and he was in email contact with the above-mentioned company. He was hugely experienced having flown not only in Botswana but having also done contract work for the U.N. in Central Africa. He was just what the company was looking for: they were impressed with his CV and things were moving towards the interview stage. Before they set a date, however, they needed to know his depth of commitment to the Christian faith - the number of visits to church per week, prayer meetings and so forth.

He emailed back telling them he was, in fact, Jewish. To this he received no answer so he emailed again to check when the interview was going to be. Still no answer. A further five emails were sent before he finally gave up.

Obviously not one of *the chosen ones* in this case!

We do like to have fun at work but Christmas is in our summer (40+C) and so is probably not the best time for this clothing.

Don't pray on me

People who know me may be aware although I am a Christian I don't visit churches often. Years ago a priest told me god is everywhere, so my thinking is I can pray and pay my respects in my own way and in my own time and, more importantly, from my own location. This system has worked well for me although from time to time it raises a few eyebrows among the zealots. No problem – each to his own, I say.

In 2009 I was in what some would term a management position and was approached by one of the older members of staff, a woman, who announced the staff in the office had decided to start conducting morning prayers. Cynical me, smelled a rat and I said it would be fine but to bear in mind work was not to be interrupted and the time before 08:00, still constituted morning. She said she understood and added the prayers would start immediately. I was a little taken aback but told her to go for it and went on with what I was doing. A moment later she poked her head around the partition and looking at me said, "Well, we're waiting."

"What for?" I asked.

"You," she said.

"Ah no," I replied. "You misunderstood, you can pray but I won't be there."

She insisted, and I insisted back. She then pulled a chair over and sat down - I could feel a lecture coming on so I held up my hand. "Laurie" (not real), I said,

"How would you feel if I forbade you from having your prayer group here in the office?"

She was more than a little indignant.

"You can't do that! You can't tell me I cannot pray."

"And you, little lady, can't tell me I *have to pray* so if you want this religious moment to continue you'd better come to terms with the fact it will not be involving me. Am I making myself clear?"

Apparently I was, for the subject was never brought up again. But they did used to pray awfully loud, so I took this time to go over the road for a coffee.

This was a terrible accident involved a Namibian Private Flyer in a Cessna 172. Everyone was alright – well, except the Giraffe – let us pray!

Prayer meetings

My heathen ways were not common knowledge but it did seem with each passing day a little more information concerning me leaked out. One day I was attending an airport operations meeting; these traditionally started with a prayer, which was a good time for me to check my shoes were clean and undamaged by previous days' work, but apparently not on this day.

The airport manager singled me out to lead the prayer for the group of roughly a dozen people who were in the room. I politely declined, but the airport manager, who was unaccustomed to being turned down, pushed a little harder. As I could see where this was going I told him,

"While I am flattered you have considered me for this task, I would also like to point out it is hugely important the prayer be well received or actually even reach the intended audience. Lately, in both these areas I have been sadly lacking, so for the good of all assembled it would be best if someone else stepped forward."

I received a very cold stare and another person assumed my duties.

PS - My shoes were fine.

The naked truth

When you visit other people's countries you should be sensitive to their Culture and/or Religion, after all they have developed these practices over thousands of years and many of these people are committed to their beliefs. So while I know it is difficult to watch someone having their hands chopped off for stealing food or enduring a court case of a woman accused of having sexual relations outside of marriage, when she was in fact raped; these are the Customs of the land; however different they might be. You may not agree with them but what can you do?

Having said this some of these Religious Customs are easier to adhere too than you might think and often correspond to Laws we have in our own countries. Making racial comments is considered bad form in most western countries and in many African ones it is actually an offense.

In many countries on this continent you cannot swear and if you do so, you may be fined and/or depending on the severity taken to the Tribal court; the outcome of which most often involves being caned – yes physically struck and none of this school shit, properly damaged. Usually from the Tribal Court you will then proceed to the hospital to start repairing the injury done by your traditional sentence. Don't worry none of this is done lightly and is an important part of the redress system of the people of these lands.

Appearing in public naked is also not considered socially acceptable. When this pilot who we shall call Thomas (more about him later in Special Cases) decided to do this he did so at an outdoor shopping centre, on a Thursday night. He jumped into a water feature (just as a joke) which everyone throws coins into; oh and it was in Dar Es Salam, Tanzania - a heavily Muslim country. Now as is Muslim custom showing your body is not in keeping with their faith – fine no harm no foul. In Tanzania they grudgingly accept other faith's which allow people to wear more revealing clothing. What they have a little trouble with is a 20 something year old pilot from South Africa with pasty white skin completely naked in their Wishing Well.

Nope, wasn't there, this moron posted it on Facebook – probably to offend everyone rather than just the hundred or so people who were eyewitnesses in his country of employment. Probably not well thought through which was communicated to Thomas and he quickly removed the offending post. Thomas, don't look now but your ass is showing!

RACISM AND OTHER PREJUDICES

This is one of my favourite subjects – but maybe not for reasons you may think. There are any number of bigots in the world, so as an introduction to this subject I have the following to say.

In a perfect world bigotry wouldn't exist but unfortunately for us we live here on Earth. To sum our situation up; there is always at least one *complete asshole* out there training the *next asshole* to take over should he suddenly die and be unable to continue carrying *the gauntlet* of their prejudice.

In my view the most common of these categories is Racism. In this spirit, in the following stories I have tried to maintain equality by including as many skin colours of the racial spectrum as possible, which seems fair and regrettably was not very difficult.

The wonderful thing about racism is it always takes the devote racist down a road which will inevitably reach an illogical decision-making paradigm. By the time the racist has figured this out he has usually screwed himself and has to follow through on the stupidity he started for fear he will be ousted by his brethren for not standing up for *the cause*. My goal in life is to be there for *that moment* so I can rub my hands together as I watch the egg run down the their face.

I have lived in five countries and visited many more which could be labelled 'third world'. Never-the-less some of the worst examples of racism I have ever been exposed to took place in 'first world' nations, which might give people some pause. Aren't we the countries who are supposed to be encouraging the 'let's all work together for he is your fellow man' or 'she is your kindred Christian soul' mentality? Of course, the third world itself is not off the hook and if I hear one more person use the phrase 'but that's just reverse racism' I am going to lose it. There is no such thing as reverse of anything: racism is racism whoever is dispensing it.

As an example, the current BEE (Black Economic Empowerment) programme which is ongoing in South Africa at governmental level in order *to right the wrongs of so many years of white oppression* is a form of institutional racial discrimination. Any time you make a differentiation regarding a person based upon their skin colour, gender, age, tribe, religion, even sexual preference you are practising bigotry. So if the treatment is based on skin colour it is Racism; it was no different when it was called Apartheid, so maybe some of the people who have instituted this BEE system, the ones who these days so often yell about racism might take the time to wake up to what their current *right of redress system* is – its bullshit and illegal. Oh, sorry you passed BEE through Parliament, my mistake – but hey, didn't they pass Apartheid through Parliament as well – I'm confused?

█████████ shared his post.
3 hrs · 🌐

Stop fucking cutting our animals hobbles you racist fucks. Dont stick your long pointy honkey noses in other peoples shit. If you cant live with us trace your roots and go the fuck back to where you belong.

████████████s
1 Jul at 2:42a.m. · 🌐

Please tell your crazy white buddies that its totally not coop at all to go around cutting off ropes tired on our donkeys and horses front legs. We work hard to own those animals and to keep them close as they are our transport so please.... Keep you filthy rich " conciderate animal loving" hearts to yourself. You dont see us coming to maws and opening you gates to set your horses and shit free. Please mind your own business.

👍 Like   💬 Comment

No matter who is dispensing it there is never a justification for Racism!
Approach it this way – target the Book not the Cover.

Having said this I believe we have all been guilty of some form of bigotry at some time in our lives – honestly is there anyone on the planet who can claim they have never said, 'Oh typical Nigerian' or 'There's another Asian driver' or 'what do you expect from a woman or a man'. But these rather small closet prejudices are not what I am referring to in this section: this section concerns people who *live their bigotry,* behaving and announcing it for all, doing so regularly and more often than not oblivious to the social or legal implications. This is when you start looking at them and thinking "Wow! I wonder what it is like in your world". Still it doesn't mean we can't have a laugh at their intolerances.

Get the bags

Let's start with a guest as we seem to have so many of those. There was a pilot undertaking what is known as Conversion Training. This is when a pilot is converting from one aircraft type to another and must undertake a requisite number of training hours with a qualified Training Captain; after which they may be let loose on their own. Happily for this story we do not need any phony names we are going to describe Conversion Training pilot as White guy and Training Captain as Black guy, accurate, easy, and neither is a slur, so get over it.

White guy is flying from the left hand, or Captain's seat and Black guy is in the right hand seat to oversee training and is ultimately Pilot In-Command of the aircraft for any of these flights. White guy wants to adjust his seat and asks Black guy to take over control of the aircraft; Black guy obliges, and there you have the whole sordid transgression - seems straightforward, right?

Now, one week later there is a terrible complaint letter from a client, apparently someone witnessed the entire event being seated just behind the two pilots (Cessna - please install a door, we beg you). The *indiscretion* which got everyone's attention was professionally detailed in the second paragraph of the letter where the client stated **'I saw it with my own eyes the pilot let the _porter_ fly the aircraft'.**

Okay so apparently there are no black pilots where this moron lives or maybe the door to the cockpit has always been closed. In addition our Black pilot's status in the company had been downgraded *by the client* from a Commercial Pilot and Training Captain to a porter; or should I say Black Porter, or is the word *black* unnecessary, the reader's individual bias will decide?

187

Now, one could almost believe a person being stupid enough to blurt this out in a moment of poor decision making. But this bigot actually took the time to sit down and write it out; I love these people because they can't deny it later and it can be used as evidence should it move to a legal issue.

Black pilot took it well, we white pilots all asked him to carry our bags for the next week, get us drinks you know the service related stuff porters are supposed to do. He is a great guy with a good sense of humor and apparently at least one idiot as a passenger.

Black is not my colour

Let's return to guests as they are our bread and butter. The thing about most of our guests is they are very, very wealthy and yet some of them have managed to get this way by sidelining large portions of the world community based upon skin color. You kind of wonder how much richer they would be if they weren't so bigoted.

In 2013 there was a female pilot who we will call Ms. Black (I like these new names), who flew some clients to Mombo Lodge, a very expensively swank Camp in the Delta. The flight was uneventful, as they all should be, and all arrived safe but apparently not happy. A message was received from the camp to the air charter operator. The guests have a request, they would like their next pilot *not be black* and preferably *not a woman*. Wow, these morons, Americans, were going all out on this one, racism and sexism in the same application.

The owner of the Charter Company apparently did not like this request and informed the camp the guests needed to speak to their agent as all future air movements would not be undertaken by any of his pilots or aircraft; Charter cancelled! This idiot turned out to be the worldwide head of a major U.S. Credit Card Company, now there are only three I can remember - you pick one.

I don't see your brand

Colour prejudices are not confined to white people; in my time on this continent I have unfortunately witnessed a lot of these, and some of my friends have been the brunt of

188

this. I see a person as a person, can recognise beauty when it is there, and there is no shortage of beauty among the African people. In my case, it is the African women who more often than not catch *my* eye; but essentially I will look at anyone. It also took many years for me to realize it is more about what is inside which counts – profound huh? Okay maybe not, maybe I am just a little slow.

On one occasion I was leaving a place called Bon Arriv'e, a local watering hole, with a black lady friend. I had had a drink or two, as had the man of local ethnicity who felt the need to get something off his chest. As I tried to pass him he grabbed my arm, and I mean grabbed hard, the legal term for this is assault. He pushed me back a little blocking my ability to exit the establishment. He then asked me 'what are you doing'? I said I didn't understand the question. I had a pretty good idea where this was going but playing dumb usually moves the conversation along.

"Where are you going with *the woman*"?

"Well, I was over here", I said pointing behind me, "and in a minute I will be over there. Then I will be gone from your sight, which will no doubt please us both". Then the chat went down the usual path.

"You fucking white people, you come over here, you disrespect our customs, you steal our women........," (blah, blah, blah).

The content varies slightly but the gist is the always the same and I had heard it all before. Unfortunately these encounters happen more frequently than you might think and my reaction is gauged on how drunk or sober the individual is. A sober person will get a very bad reaction from me as they should know better, but I give more sway to a drunk one, knowing from experience that one occasionally says things which are not well thought through. The young lady I was with was as smart as a whip, so I whispered to her and she quietly agreed to play along. After this I held her at arm's length, looked her up and down and said,

"So, this is one of yours? I am so terribly sorry for the confusion!"

I said this with genuine embarrassment but loudly enough for the other patrons to hear. You don't know when this will turn from a conversation to a boxing match. I gently raised her arms and checked under them, then peeped down the back of her dress, checked behind her ears, inspected her fingers and finally asked her to pop her mouth open and peered in there.

"Nope, sorry, you are mistaken, this one doesn't belong to you."

This guy looked at me as if I was out of my mind.

"What do you mean? I don't understand," he eventually slurred.

"Well, you described this woman as stolen property and I've looked all over her yet cannot find any brand anywhere; if she is *yours* you seriously need to put your mark in a more visible place to avoid this kind of misunderstanding".

The lady started to giggle but I winked at her and she regained her composure. I looked at the guy and went on.

"Now, you would be what? 35 years old?" - Always pick a higher age as it provokes a reaction.

"I am 27"; came an indignant response.

Now this is when you need to show genuine concern: a real 'hand on the shoulder' moment, so to speak.

"Jesus man, you're in bad shape for 27! You'd better start taking care of yourself or you won't last long. Maybe lay off the alcohol for a while. Anyway, what I was trying to say..."

Then get very serious and lean in, but you must keep the volume up for the potential court case.

"….as for me not respecting your customs try to remember I am almost twice your age and therefore your elder, so it is you who are not respecting your customs by speaking to me the way you did; also you swore at me, made a racial comment, grabbed my arm, interrupted my conversation with a lady and accused me of stealing your property, when it was not yours in the first place. Next time maybe think about all of this before you start. Now, am I making myself clear?"

Then you cheerfully bid the little idiot goodnight and walk away. If you are in any way impeded from doing so - plant the fucker into the bar – I have only had to do it once and it was hugely satisfying. Then there was black and blue, but not much white!

The root of the problem

These situations are borderline racist but my feeling is they are hugely disrespectful to the *true African people*, those who were born and raised here. Not the idiots claiming their heritage from 150 years ago. Like, I'm from originally from Ireland when their family has been living in another country for 97 years.

Guests sometimes come on Safari as a lifelong rite of passage. Some African American's are hilarious in this respect. They arrive, having stopped in Europe on the way and often intend to stop in Mauritius or the Seychelles on the way back. It's fine, not a problem, if I had the money I would too.

The guests are met off their international flights and we pilots are often the first people they see. They introduce themselves by announcing they have come to Africa to 'see my homeland' or 'get in touch with my roots' and 'to see the land their ancestors were taken from' - hence the proud label of African Americans. Wow, seems like quite a trip!

Now first, I am a little sketchy regarding the whole slave trade thing but when I read about it in school, it centered on the geographical areas which now house the countries of Sierra Leon, Ghana, Liberia, you know the section of this vast continent, sort of the Central western side of Africa. Zambia, Botswana, Kenya and Namibia weren't really mentioned in the American slave history I read about. But hey maybe I need to read some more or maybe I was misinformed.

So let's start with the 'get in touch with your roots'. But then if you were doing *the Roots thing* I don't think staying in a Lodge catering to foreign visitors which charges you anywhere from US$1000 - $3000 per night would be the way to go. The idea of the Lodge is to look at wildlife and be pampered like a 19th Century Prince of the European Court. Of course the camps have cultural activities but they amount to no more than me going to the Ocean and staring at the water for a few hours and then claiming to be in touch with its true beginnings. Plus most of these returning cultural voyagers, back on the continent to feel the soil, stay only four to six days and then jet away.

If you were really seeking out your cultural beginnings (probably go to the correct country would be a good start) and maybe stay for a year in a true rural environment. Live like the people of the country do, use their health care system, their schools. In some cases give up the Internet, Keeping up with the Kardashians, Starbucks, KFC, McDonalds', etc,. Too much, no can't bear it; sorry I was just thinking out loud?

When these visitors wax on about 'I have come to see my homeland'; the question I encourage pilots to ask is *'so where were you originally from before your ancestors were taken from Africa'?* Answers to this fluctuate but often involve the previously mentioned African nations who actually have a slaving history associated with the USA. The follow up question is *'so why didn't you go there'?* Answers usually come down to a perceived safety concern.

"Well I was watching Fox News about a year ago (I love current affairs) they said there was some trouble in Liberia between the Army and this one village."

"But didn't you say your family originally came from Ghana?"

"Yeah, but Liberia, that's like right next door, isn't it?"

Now I would like to congratulate these individuals regarding their geographical knowledge of the area. I am not being funny we do get a few people out here who simply could not point on a map to the country they were standing in if asked - Yes I have asked them with a map of Southern Africa – I've got to have some fun.

With regard to the Army and a problem with the local villagers yes, sadly, this sort of thing happens, it's really terrible; pretty sure there were similar problems during the Vietnam War and the Civil Rights movement involving the US National Guard. In 2015 there were riots in both Ferguson, Missouri, and Baltimore, Maryland concerning racial incidents involving the police and the black community.

As regards to right next door, I don't see Mexico as particularly safe, what with the drug cartels, murders, robberies, rapes, etc. Mexico is next door, are you planning on moving from your country of birth? YES that is where you were born – maybe own this as your legacy; and when you come here just enjoy your holiday rather than making a political or sociological statement about why you are taking it. Or just continue the way you're going – it's over to you. It certainly amuses most of us – however disrespectfully you are treating the TRUE Africans. These are the ones who don't address each other as Nigga and Hoe!

The little Dutch Boy – not enough fingers for this one

Our friend Steve was flying a CASA 212, which is a medium-sized high-wing twin turboprop aircraft. A lot of private companies are now using ex-military aircraft because, let's face it, the military make aircraft for difficult flying situations and we in the third world have plenty of these!

Today Steve was in the early days of conversion training on this aircraft type so he was sitting in the right hand seat as first officer and, according to Steve, a Kenyan pilot, as black as they come (it's relevant), was sitting as captain, or left hand seat. They were due to fly from Pointe Noire on the coast up to a small mining airstrip in the inner section of the Republic of Congo. This aircraft actually has a cockpit door, something many of us are working toward, but it was a hot day so the two pilots had left the door open along with the cockpit's storm windows, small windows which can be opened for ground ops, in an attempt to get a breeze going while everyone boarded.

"Captain?" Steve looks up at a man in the suit framing the doorway who turned out to be Dutch. Steve pointed with his pen to the Kenyan gentleman. Mr. Netherlands looks at Captain Kenya and then back at Steve, and then what was described as an obvious expression change crossed the Dutchman's face. There was an uncomfortable silence which Steve decided to break. "You wanted to speak to the Captain? Here he is - what

193

can he do for you?" More silence, and then the Dutchman continues: "But I thought you would be the captain."

Needless to say Steve is a little pissed off with this and the disrespect that is being shown to the aircraft commander.

"Why? Why would I have to be the Captain?"
"But he can't be! He's........NOT WHITE!"

Now you racists out there when you are practising your trade please at least have the balls to say what you mean – do not hedge on the opposing fact – a real egg on the face moment for our European friend. Steve said the Captain, who had overheard the entire exchange, just smiled, shook his head and went back to what he was doing.

Now the Dutchman suspected he had crossed some sort of line but he had also not reached his position as Chief Financial Officer of the large mining company's Congo project by being pushed around, especially by a mere pilot. Steve however, was having none of it. He instructed the gentleman their aircraft was no longer available to him and he needed to return to the Charter Company's offices across the apron and work it out with them – he then stood up and escorted the Dutch guy out of the aircraft. The guy didn't want to go but Steve told us he just kept moving forward basically forcing the guy to back up until he backed out of the aircraft.

On entering the office Mr. Netherlands demanded to see the Operations Manager (basically the guy who runs the company) and then explained the conversation verbatim – what an idiot – especially as the Ops Manager was black as well. The Operations Manager offered the gentleman a seat and then phoned the CEO of the mining company and explained that seemingly his CFO was uncomfortable flying in an aircraft commanded by a black man, he also went on to explain; "If this is the case," said the Ops manager politely, "I am afraid any future air charter work for your mining operation cannot be undertaken as our staff includes pilots of various skin colours. So just to clear up any confusion our position is – your company charters the aircraft and I assign the crew, do we understand each other?"

The CEO was hugely apologetic and asked the CFO be directed to return to their Pointe Noire offices, immediately! He was removed from the African project later in the day and sent back to their headquarters in Europe: he left one day later, wife and kids in tow. Bon voyage and good riddance!I wonder if he enquired about the Captain for the international flight as well.

Steve Hollingworth with some Himba's- Nambia 2004

Who said he was local?

Pilots are not immune to the bug of prejudice principally because they are human. Not long ago a pilot saw his schedule, which read 'pilot to share with guide'. The pilot asked what this meant. Just to explain a little, guests can often arrange for private guides to escort them throughout their entire holiday; it's a great idea if you can afford it and these private guides often have repeat business year after year. This was explained to the pilot;

the guide would be accompanying his guests and would be sharing a room with the pilot.

"I'm not sharing with a *local guide!*" blurted the pilot. What he meant was Black Guide!

Management quickly assessed what was happening and addressed the issue with a very western sounding name for the guide; the pilot then relaxed a little and said it would be fine. It was then pointed out to him management had absolutely no idea who the guide was but the obvious racist overtones were not appreciated. The pilot was reminded when the company asked him to overnight it was part of his contractual responsibility not a freedom of choice moment to exercise his narrow social views. You overnight and share where needed with anyone required. The pilot then slunk out of the office and although the subject was closed rest assured his original mind-set was probably intact.

I don't want to share with an indigenous bloke

A year earlier another pilot (pilot A) saw he was to overnight with a pilot from another company (B). Pilot B was from India, a Sikh, and as is their custom he wore a full turban. He is also an incredibly nice guy; is well-spoken, has excellent manners and is a thoroughly educated individual. Pilot A, however, saw none of these qualities (probably just another raghead to him) and said he was not comfortable *sharing with an indigenous person.*

Now when I was at school, 'indigenous' always meant someone from the country you are standing in or speaking about. So, apart from being a racist Pilot A does not have a complete grasp of the English language – add to this Pilot B is a work colleague, someone you trust won't taxi into your aircraft at an airstrip or fly into you in the air. So you trust him with your life but you can't share a room with him? I wondered if the root of the problem could be to do with some weird customs they might have in India but after scouring the internet I could find none – alas they all seemed quite normal to me.

Management made short shrift of pilot A's complaint, warned him never to raise such an issue again or there would be an official sanction, and booted him out of the office to go and fly.

A Marathon is a Race

One night about 10pm I was leaving *Sports Bar*, an establishment located in Maun which has very nice food and a reasonably sized bar. As I walked out to the road I decided tonight might be a good night to walk the 5 kilometres home. Maun is relatively safe and it's good exercise, a great chance to clear the head before sleeping.

On the road was a local lady in her forties, about five foot five and weighing in at what I estimated was 110 kilos. I had seen her many times before as she had been plying her trade around town for a few years now and here she was standing on the road waiting for a taxi. Also, I knew 'she wasn't quite all there', having seen any number of her outbursts over the same period. She greeted me and I greeted her back but kept walking.

"Where are you going?"

"Home".

"Can I come?"

"Ah, sorry no".

"Are you walking?"

"Yes".

"Can I walk with you?"

I thought for a second

"Look, I walk really fast, so you'll have a hard time keeping up".

"I will, don't worry".

I hesitated and then gave in - *my first mistake.*

"Ok, just so we understand each other, we go at my speed and I'm not slowing down."

She agreed and with it all sorted, we set off. She actually surprised me! She was keeping up, even with all her girth. We hit the 2km mark and then it seemed marathon girl wasn't going to make it after all.

"Can you slow down?"

"No, I can't".

"But…"

"Look, we discussed this already."

I kept walking and she had dropped back ten metres or so when we were approaching a small club called Rhino Bar. There were thirty or so local people standing outside and this was when she started shouting at me.

"You're a racist!"

"Excuse me? I am a racist because I walk fast?"

"Yes".

I didn't reply, just continued on my way. I heard her stop walking: good, problem solved.

"You fucking racist, you can't speak to me that way, RACIST, RACIST, FUCKING RACIST!" She was screaming now. Okay, so the problem wasn't solved after all. I stopped walking and looked back at her. It was then I realized I had a bigger issue; the roughly thirty black people outside Rhino Bar who were currently staring at me and wondering how I had offended this woman. Fortune favours the bold so I headed straight for them and politely greeted them as I made my way to the entrance, nodded at the security guy and I went in: *second mistake*. I went to the bar and got a drink. It was so noisy I didn't hear Marathon girl move in behind me at the bar; she scared the shit out of me!

"Where's my drink?" she asked.

"Just over there," I replied, "in one of those glass cabinets behind the counter. All you have to do is pay for it and it's all yours".

I actually couldn't figure out why was I still speaking to her?

"So you're not buying me a drink?"

All that came to my mind was, only some kind of masochist would put up with insults, run the risk of getting beaten up by a mob and, on top of this, pay for your drinks.

"That'd be a no and the conversation's finished as well."

I moved to a table with a dozen or so young ladies and a couple of guys, thinking it would be the end of it. The manager appeared a few minutes later:

"Look, you have to do something about your girlfriend."

I raised my eyebrows: "I don't have a girlfriend."

"Yes, you do," insisted the manager. "The one you arrived with."

I explained we had entered at the same time but we had nothing to do with each other. I

198

also warned him she may have a screw loose. At this precise moment we heard the sound of breaking glass and both turned to see her brandishing the remains of a bottle at some poor young girl on the other side of the room. Funnily enough, my only thought was the pressure was off me now. Selfish, I know, but sometimes you should go with your gut feeling.

Security threw her out but the respite was short-lived. Fifteen minutes later, she had somehow convinced the manager she was able to behave, and she was in again. Shortly after this she threw a glass at one of the security staff. Mercifully, this was the end of her and I was free to leave this bar I had never wanted to be in in the first place.

Now my problem was I needed to escape and she was loitering outside in the hope of being allowed back in. As luck would have it, when I stepped outside I saw a Mercedes about to leave. I knocked on the window and it opened to reveal two beautiful Motswana girls. I explained my predicament, which they found amusing, and they agreed to whisk me out of there. Thanks ladies, never did get your names!

Get the sleeping arrangements right!

Bigots will always rationalize their behaviour in any attempt to show *logic* for thinking the way they do. As examples; on the racist side some White people have suggested in the past (and unfortunately in the present) that 'Blacks are inferior and are unable to develop *the cognitive ability to do the same work'* – therefore they should get treated differently. Wow, your skin colour determines how well you process information and make decisions; this makes the same sense as your Ferrari won't go fast because it is yellow.

For the gender bigot: 'She is a weaker woman therefore shouldn't have the job.' No argument, a lot of women are physically weaker than men and if the job was an NFL Line-backer or Rugby League player I could see the point but most often the people making these statements are not speaking of these particular jobs. People who argue with line of thinking are more often afraid of the female job seeker seeing them as more qualified. This female job seeker is now standing next to their less productive male ass so their job is under threat for nothing more than the bigot's inability to pick up his game.

None of these examples makes any sense and anyone who utilizes them could not produce a thread of proof holding each rational together. This was a conversation I had with another pilot in 2008.

As I have said in our off time we sometimes socialize. On this particular day we sat in a bar having a few beers and my new girlfriend was sitting with me, yes she was Black. We had only been going out a couple of months and were still in the *getting to know each other phase* - but so far all had gone well.

As we are more or less a community of pilots we often all sit and drink together in groups after work – regardless of which company the pilot works for. I was sitting with a half a dozen or so guys, it was mostly guys but these days the ladies are making their way further into the industry in numbers. I had noticed one guy who I will call Brian for the sake of a better name. Brian is white and from South Africa and unfortunately he is also a racist. Now before you all go off on a tangent about *white South Africans and racism* you need to hold your own bigotry in check. If you are even remotely thinking in this direction please immediately re-read every story in this section and try to remember, other than this one, not one of them involves a *white South African.*

While bigotry involves skin colour and gender, it also involves nationality – it's called Xenophobia and not all South African white people are racists – so if you are generalizing like this wake up and stop being a moron. Racism is not a White person's disease it is a wiring problem in a racist's head – and the wiring issue exists no matter what their skin colour is; so you *non-white racists* need to wake up as well! Unfortunately for this story South African Brian is a racist; not a *burn cross kind*; but still a racist.

I had noted several times during the evening him staring at my girlfriend and then me. Just passing glances, nothing mean, just a *certainlook*. She had just gone to the other side of the bar to speak to a friend and at that moment everyone went off to get drinks – so we were effectively alone. I believed I had seen this look before and decided to explore his thinking.

"Something on your mind?"
"Not really."

A few seconds went by and I dove in.

"I may be reading this wrong but you don't approve of my relationship do you?"

He smiled and didn't say anything for a few seconds more.

"I guess it's just not the way I was brought up."

Now people if you are going to continue a conversation like this there are fundamental rules which should be followed. Rule one: Please understand regardless of which side you are approaching the race subject the other person has an opinion even if you think it is wrong. Rule two: DO NOT yell or get belligerent at them for not accepting your side – it's a discussion. Rule three: If the other person behaves this way, walk away – you cannot change a person's mind, you can only present *yourfacts* and one day they may change their own mind – if they choose to do so. I have had people from time to time attempt to physically prevent me from leaving during such conversations until they got their point across – at this stage all bets are off – they get a warning to stand aside and then diplomacy goes out the window, as well as their teeth. Luckily for me Brian was a conversationalist on the subject.

"What *way* was that?"

At this point I decided I am actually interested to find out how this thinking works, I am not looking to convert, just gathering information. It seemed, today, Brian was going to help me with my research. He turned square and faced me across the table.

"When I was growing up we were taught about the animals. We were taught the Lions they sleep with the Lions and the Giraffe spend time with the Giraffe, the Zebra lay down with the Zebra. BUT, and this is the important bit - you never see a Lion lying down with a Giraffe or Zebra."

With this he stopped speaking and continued to look me in the eye. I could see he was completely serious – I burst out laughing. Initially his facial expression reflected he was a little upset, but then he seemed to relax. I shook my head as I didn't have much to say to the analogy. I guess in the end we can safely say; *each to their own; until they decide to come to their senses* - a thought I am sure both sides will agree upon.

Genderless

Women in aviation – a subject some male pilots can have some quite expressive views on! Now ladies, hear me out as you may be surprised to know there are quite a few male pilots who don't have an issue with women flying. My attitude extends from the Race issue. Skin colour is not a problem for me, so why would I now start with gender or even sexual preference. My entire concern is can *apilot* operate the aircraft safely, treat the guests properly, follow the rules, etc?

Now having said this I also don't tolerate the *little games* a few very select women pilots attempt to play. "Oh can you do my paperwork" or "pre-flight my aircraft", all while batting their eyes at some male pilot. One of my favourites is "I was late because I was doing my make-up". I am truly not interested, get out of bed earlier and show up on time. Imagine I told you I was late because I was shaving; it doesn't sound any less ridiculous.

When I arrived in Maun there were very few woman pilots, but these days they are much more common. Of course the guests being as observant as they are have also noticed this – with this observation comes the obvious comments which pretty much all come from other women. Don't worry ladies about 98% of these comments come from American women! So the rest of the ladies around the world relax as I am targeting in on this demographic. One of my least favourite comments goes something like this:

"Oh good, look girls - *speaking to the other women in the group* - finally we get a woman pilot. It's nice to see We Females pushing into this industry to carry the flame for the rest of us".

Okay, first it's not the fucking Olympics so I don't know why they reference this dribble. Secondly, I realize the good old' US of A isn't exactly user friendly when it comes to women's issues; but maybe do some research as there are a lot, and I mean a lot of women flying commercially in the United States. Maybe you just haven't bothered to check behind the cockpit door to see who is actually operating the airliner you are jetting to Hawaii in.

In addition, and this is very important, try to remember companies are looking to employ *a pilot* not a person who is on a coast to coast march for gender equality. If you come across this way - you know make sure you stand out on the issue - it really sort of defeats the purpose of *equality*.

Okay so why did I bring this up. Well you feminists; can't think of what else you would be, who make these comments are not only embarrassing the female pilot you are also being condescending regarding her gender. Yes, you are, so wake up!

To illustrate this point picture this; I am a Black man, mid to late forties and while wandering through JFK with some friends and I spot another black man wearing his Captain's uniform for an airline. What would you think if I approached him and said?

"Hey man, it's great to finally see a Black pilot. Thank god you are out there helping us push the race issue through this Industry".

This is condescending and is no less so when it is done on a gender basis. Every single female pilot I have ever worked with says emphatically how they hate when women guests make these comments. You want this very male dominated industry to treat female pilots equally, not as a woman, but as a pilot. So we do this and along you come and single out her gender in a very public way – not very bright is it? Maybe have a more discreet conversation or don't have any and get in the aircraft and enjoy the ride and leave the politics out of it.

Old Age vs. Youth

Okay, unfortunately we are not finished with singling people out. Ageism is a form of prejudice and crops its head up regularly in Charter operations. It is a subject I noticed gained a lot of traction in the early 1990's, especially in the United States; I noticed this for family reasons.

Seemingly, during this period, older people were being rejected for jobs they applied for or were being pushed out of the ones they had, based upon their age. Age had never been an issue before, because older people retired to enjoy a well-deserved rest. However, now because of Reganomics, the aftermath of the Savings & Loan crisis and several other areas of the U.S. economy, old people could not afford to retire - they had to keep working.

This period also coincided with a technology change – a *bigincrease* in the use of office computers. I know they were there before but now management was looking at what was coming and probably thought Grand-pa couldn't handle it. It was a difficult time for many, my father included, as he lived in the country. So what has this got to do with flying?

Everyone likes to think of Pilots as *old guys* butthis is very much a thing of the past. These days even Airline pilots are much younger than you might expect. Technology, once again, has played a major role in this as well as an ever expanding industry. Add to this the 'Everyone has to start somewhere' concept and the Charter Industry is where most young budding aviators go to build their flying hours or experience.

Along come more Americans, sorry, but if some of you would just shut up I literally would have nothing to write about, who are very old and they meet the Charter Pilot for their flight to the Lodge:"How old are you. Are you old enough to fly?"

Those two questions usually come as a single sentence. Now let's have a look at these rather inappropriate questions, especially as you Old Farts would form part of my Father's generation. The same idiots who were screaming about being unemployed in the 1990's based upon your age; and are now doing the Ageism thing in reverse.

There are regular requests, in some cases demands, for the twenty something year old pilot to produce his Commercial License to prove himself. One idiot in 2016 demanded one of the pilots show him his Commercial License and when the pilot declined, the guest reinforced his request by informing the pilot he was a Lawyer in New York City. Yes, you are also a moron because you were standing in Zambia when this conversation took place. Pretty sure you haven't passed the Bar exam in Lusaka, not that in doing so it grants you any special privileges. If you and your pilot were in New York this would sound strangely like *coercion* – which having passed the Bar you would know to be illegal.

Company policy for such situations is we do not show clients our Licenses. You have paid for a seat on the aircraft, not the right to conduct a rectal exam of the person's professional credentials. The individual company and the Civil Aviation Authority are responsible for these documents and their legality. You know, to ensure your pilot Fred hasn't just woken up one morning decided he has logged enough Microsoft Flight Sim hours and is going to grab an aircraft and fly guests for a Charter Company.

Also with Age there is supposed to be wisdom, apparently not for people who make demands like this. Maybe next time Grandpa can produce his Driver's License – just to make sure you're not too old to get behind the wheel.

CELEBRITIES

From time to time we have some well-known people visiting this corner of the planet; actors, politicians, former heads of state, royalty and big fish in the business world. However, apparently we don't always appear to be up-to-date with current events or people don't think we are.

In Liu of knowledge

One pilot flew the very beautiful Lucy Liu off to a camp in Botswana and of course many of the other male pilots were a little jealous and jumped on the company chat frequency shortly after the flight was airborne to speak with the lucky aviator, shooting questions at him: "So what's she like? Is she as hot off screen as well? Where and when is she flying next?"

Puzzled, this pilot asked what they were on about. "Dude, you are flying Lucy Liu!" to which he replied, "Who the fuck is Lucy Liu"? Don't worry, Lucy, he's led a sheltered life!

Having a Hardy time putting name to face.

Andre was told he had a 'pilot-to-wait' with a passenger at Abu camp. This means you fly the passenger out to the camp and wait around until the person is ready to leave. It can make for a pleasant day provided it does not happen too often – we are here to fly remember, you know build hours?

Pilot and passenger hit it off on the way out: Andre was French and since his passenger Tom spoke the language they chatted away all the way there and Andre was invited for lunch as well. Tom was scheduled to fly back in another aircraft but requested to return with Andre so they could continue their conversation. And so it was. Back at the airport, Andre popped into the local for a pint with his fellow pilots. He recounted the day's events, adding that his passenger, some radio personality, had been a really nice guy.

"What was his name?" someone asked.
"Tom Hardy." The guys laughed.

"You flew Tom Hardy, spent the day and managed to have lunch with him, then flew him back?"

"Yeah, so what? Who is he?"

The group then started naming his movies, most of which Andre had actually seen and only then did he put face to name. Better late than never, I suppose!

The Royal blush

Several members of royal households from Europe, the Middle East and Asia have passed through on their way to view wildlife.

By far the most interesting and more regular of visitors are both English princes. Harry sponsors different projects here and is truly passionate about them and William enjoys the solitude; but we should always remember they are both fun-loving young men at heart.

The King of Spain, the previous one anyway, appeared for long enough to break his foot on a hunting trip. This injury made it into the Spanish papers and suddenly everyone was aware of this little holiday and it did not go down at all well with his subjects. The country was going through a rough financial patch and it was felt this was time and money not well spent. The whole thing became a bit of a political flap at home and shortly after this his son took over as monarch.

We have had a prince of the Saudi household who rented an entire camp *for his staff*; for himself he built his own Bedouin style set-up nearby where he enjoyed his two-week holiday with the family. He had all his food flown in when he arrived, along with a sizeable security detachment – just in case the animals got out of order. He arrived in a C130, nicely kitted out just like a private business jet and complete with gold fittings throughout for his comfort. The thing was so heavy it used the whole runway when it took off.

I love the Hue

One of our pilots had the pleasure of Hugh Laurie's (Black Adder, House) company here in 2005-2006 or thereabouts. After flying him around for a bit Steve suggested a beer in one of our numerous local taverns – Bon Arriv'e, yes we have to do something in our spare time; not all of us write.

Bon Arriv'e

Anyone who has ever been to Maun has had the opportunity to eat or drink at Bon Arrive' which is directly across the street from our somewhat dated Terminal; alas The Bon recently closed and is no more.

To give you an idea of its former ambiance, the place is decked out with most things aviation. Old aircraft wings used to hang over the bar, there were several clocks to give you an idea of time in the rest of the world. The Maun clock spent a period of time with only the big hand to signify time has stopped – it does most days. There was also any number of pictures of aircraft old and new, of times gone by.

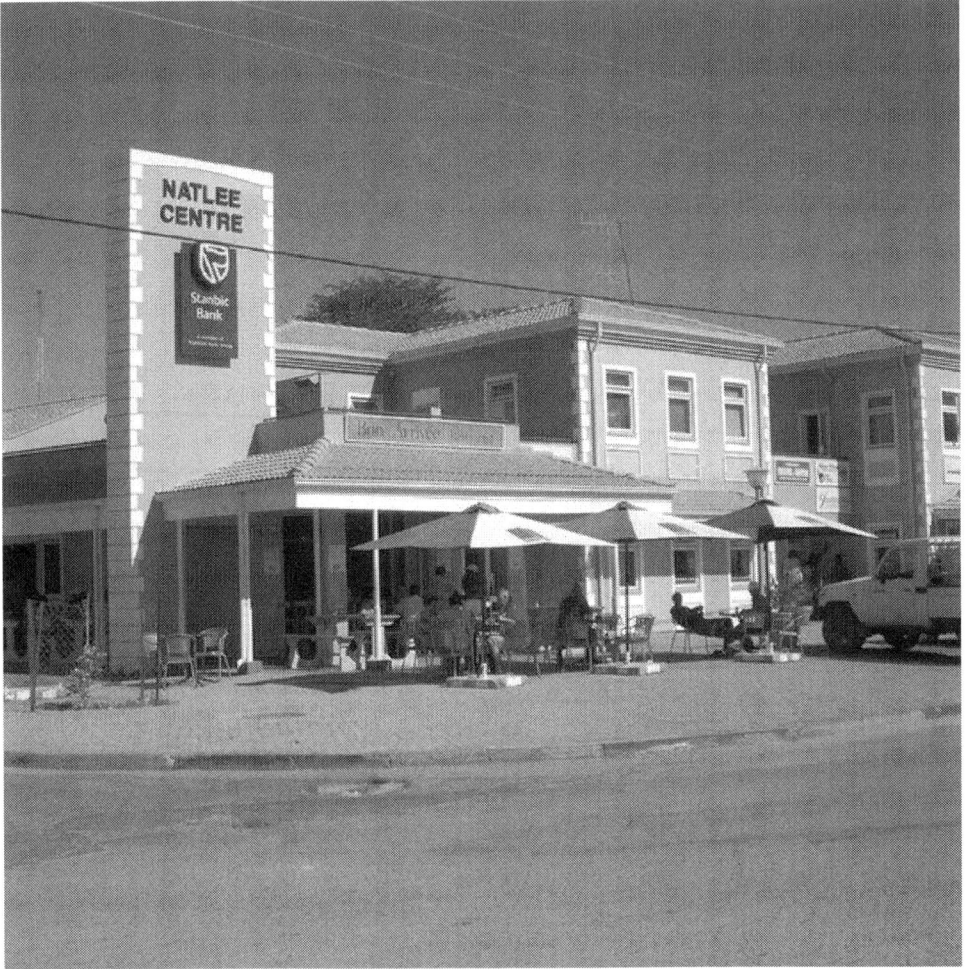

As Steve and Hugh wandered into the bar, he was given one of those group introductions to the half a dozen or so Maunites sitting there; they all waved and then went back to their chat. Steve and Hugh departed to the upstairs area and Hugh commented it was kind of fun as no one seemed to know who he was. I guess he was more used to people following him, taking his picture, paparazzi moments. Steve merely said:

"Oh, they know who you are all right; they just don't feel the need to bother you."

Yes people, we get a lot of celebrities through here and we know you are having some ME time, so we tend to leave you alone.

Look at the state of it!

Politicians are also allowed ME time. After all, they need to get away from whatever it is that politicians do: kissing babies, getting caught with hookers, appearing before Congress for getting sexual favours from members of staff, but strangely enough, not appearing anywhere accountable for invading a country based upon doctored intelligence. Sorry I digress - again.

This politician was a mere United States Senator when he showed up at the Maun Airport metal detector trying to board his international flight. Our pilot Frank was attempting to make it through the birthing machine as well, one of his thirty odd trips a day when the person in front caused the contraption to go off. Frank was a little quick off the blocks and he and the gentleman met half way through the machine, colliding.

"Sorry Senator Kerry"
"You know who I am"?

Now Frank felt a little insulted, so unfortunately he responded in this spirit.

"Yes, we have one of those new TV box things in town at the general store. Occasionally I stop by to stare at it through the window."

Apparently Senator Kerry looked at Frank twice before removing his offending watch and the metal detector became cooperative; eventually Frank got to work.

JUST LET ME FLY

This section deals with those people who feel they have *the right* to operate your aircraft. Lets just say you came to collect me in your car and the first thing I said was, "I have a driver's license - can I drive?" Would you like this? No, I didn't think so. In some cases we deal with people who expect to be allowed to sit in a pilot's seat, purport to know more about your aircraft than you do, or are not happy with the pilot who is there and openly comment on this. Sort of like me showing up for a United Airlines flight, glancing through the cockpit door and announcing "well I'm not happy with this".

A beautiful heard of Elephant crossing a river system in the Moremi Game Reserve - Botswana

Look but don't touch

Steve flew a family of four to Xakanaka airstrip in the Moremi Game Reserve in the Okavango Delta in late 2003. He said they seemed like nice people even though the father had already announced *I have my pilot's license and I was going to fly the aircraft* – yes a statement, not a request.

They all boarded and as expected Dad ended up in the front, or co-pilot seat, next to

Steve. He immediately grabbed the flight controls and did a full and free movement check. This is done by pilots to check there nothing is interfering with our ability to control the aircraft prior to leaving the ground – put another way you do it so you don't find out you have a problem while in the air.

Steve dispensed the required emergency briefing and then specifically instructed dear old Dad that although he had his license he could not touch the controls *while they were flying* – first mistake. Dad looked disappointed and asked:

"Are you serious?"

"Yes I am" was Steve's very succinct reply.

The aircraft started to taxi for take-off and Dad started grabbing the controls.

"Excuse me, but what are you doing?" asked a surprised Steve.

"But we're not flying yet: you said *while we were flying.*"

Seems Steve had not been quite specific enough so he reinforced his statement with his second mistake:"In the interest of safety I must ask you not to touch *the controls* at all, ok?"

Dad looked like someone who's weekend golf trip with the boy's had just been cancelled but he said, "ok". The aircraft got airborne and was about fifteen minutes into a 25-minute flight when Dad felt the need to play with the GPS, which, when all is said and done, is not a *flight control,* is it? Steve could see this guy had some kind of indefinable problem, you know he just had to be involved with the flight somehow; he could also feel himself coming to the end of his tether. Dad managed to press three buttons before Steve spoke again:

"Sir, what are you doing?"

"Just looking at the GPS."

Steve told us he just smiled his special smile. This is the smile which used to make his friends tremble when we saw it: his is the smile of Steve running out of patience.

"Ok, watch me." he said to Dad. He turned and looked at this guy's wife who was sitting behind them and just stared at her, he said she was really quite lovely. She, of course, was wondering what was going on. He told us he continued to stare at her to the point it started to look a little creepy to anyone else watching.

Steve turned back to Dad. "And there you go."

Dad apparently looked a bit perplexed. "I don't understand."

"What I did constitutes *justlooking* but by your definition I should be poking and prodding your wife."

At this point he said a little colour flushed through Dad's face; but Steve wasn't finished just yet.

"What do you do for a living?"

"I'm a surgeon."

"Good, how would you feel if I joined you in the operating room, grabbed the scalpel and made a few incisions? I once dissected a frog in high school, you know"

Dad just stared at him, speechless.

"So let's have an understanding; I won't mess with your work and you don't mess with mine, ok?"

They flew on another five minutes, landed, and the passengers disappeared never to be seen again, much to Steve's relief.

Are you alright?

It is late in 2007 and I have been flying steadily for the company since February, with a short break to bury my father: not to worry, he *was* dead at the time. He would have appreciated the dark humour and this story continues in this vein.

As mentioned, holders of a private pilot's license often ask to sit up front so we are perfectly used to this request. However, I was rather taken aback one day when a woman from Illinois said to me, "My husband is a pilot so I'd like him to sit up front just in case you have a heart attack and then he can take over and save us."

Now, people who know me will vouch for the fact I am usually capable of giving a witty comeback but on this day I was speechless! What was odd is I was asked the same question the following week and later in the month once more. Over a few beers my friends started to jokingly hint maybe these guests could see something we couldn't; maybe it was my time to go, to move off the planet. The conversation gave me an idea. The next time I was asked this question I pretended to look completely shocked, stunned actually, and said:

"Have you been you been speaking to my doctor, because that information is supposed to be confidential"?

A few seconds went by as this sunk in. Then the guest got very angry. "That's not funny! Don't you joke like that?"

"Madam, you started it", I replied.

I refused to let her husband sit in the front for every flight I did with them.

It's child's play

Most GA aircraft (General Aviation or small) don't lock. They may have started out with a locking system and it has rusted over time, or there never was one in the first place. Thomas, featured in our Special Cases section, was flying a Cessna 210 working for *a Zambian company* and staying the night in Lusaka, Zambia's Capital. When he returned to the airport in the morning he was promptly arrested.

Early morning, about 0630, a fourteen-year-old had made his way onto the apron of the Kenneth Kaunda Airport International airport. In most countries big airports are secure areas, certainly not places one might normally find a teenager wandering around, and this airport is no different. He found Thomas' aircraft parked there, opened the door and got in, he then located the keys, well hidden in the aircraft – which is not uncommon practice. He then started the engine and the aircraft started taxiing around. Eventually some airport ground staff jumped in and shut the engine off and pulled the budding teenage aviator out – luckily no damage to the aircraft or any people.

So why was Thomas arrested? Well, no one was willing to blame the kid as he just came to work with his Dad and got a bit bored. What about Dad, maybe he should have taken responsibility. No, it wasn't Dad's fault either as who from airport management would blame the Deputy Air Commodore for the entire Zambian Air Force? But as is society today, someone had to take the fall - this left Thomas. There was a three-hour interrogation before the whole matter was finally dropped. Reckon Thomas ought to take the key next time!

Your son is in my seat

Passengers like to let us know they have flying experience and one such tourist took it a step further. He was a former airline pilot and he sent a copy of his ATPL (Airline Transport Pilot's Licence) along with his booking information – after all written confirmation of his piloting skills is better than verbal isn't it?

So you understand the ATPL is the highest licence you can get in commercial aviation, short of being a Test Pilot. The age on his licence clearly reflected he was retired (he was 78). Sorry, aviation is just like Disneyland; there are age limits for the rides. His suggestion was he wanted to be permitted to sit in the co-pilot's seat throughout his travels with us as he could help spot birds and other aircraft: a safety pilot, if you will.

Along comes Chris flying a Cessna Grand Caravan and today a female pilot we shall call Harriet has joined him and who is sitting in the right hand, or co-pilot's seat. Although Chris has seen a copy of the license floating around the office he does not know Mr. ATPL, an American, is about to board his aircraft. The man enters through the rear door and marches up the aisle of the small cabin, Chris said in hindsight he looked more imposing on his licence; he then sits down in the seat immediately behind the co-pilot's, points at Harriet's seat and asks, "Is this seat taken?"

Since Harriet is actually sitting in the seat it seems a redundant question, but Chris answers as best he can: "I am sorry, but as you can see the seat is taken." He introduces Harriet, a pilot who has just joined the company and feels this information should settle any further seating issues. But ATPL needs to make quite sure.
"So I can't sit next to you?"
"No, I am sorry, you cannot," replies Chris slowly. He goes on:
"But as a consolation prize we have this lovely seat right here".
Chris points to the seat Mr. ATPL is currently on the edge of awaiting the 'GO' order to

move forward. There is hesitation and then ATPL realizes he's not going to get his way, so he sits back in the seat. Unfortunately pilot and co-pilot have not had their fair share of idiotic behaviour as the next passenger to come in, a British gentleman, sits down behind Chris and says:

"Morning guys! What is it, father and son day? Bring your boy to work?"

"Morning to you too and no, no it's not father and son day. Let me introduce you to Harriet, another commercial pilot and a woman."

The Brit looks from Chris to Harriet and back to Chris before he sits back in his seat mumbling, "Sorry." Chris assumed the mumbling was because he had his foot in his mouth. The rest of the flight was surprisingly quiet.

SPECIAL CASES

In every avenue of avenue of life you have some really good people with good hearts and a great sense of humour; commonly referred to as the 'salt of the earth crowd' and they are truly memorable. In aviation these are the ones whose professional contributions far outweigh anything most of us mere pilots offer. Their attention to detail, knowledge of regulations, common sense, and ability to remember we in the end are all human beings with feelings and emotions make them truly *special*! These are the same people who often suffer personally when they have made a mistake for fear of having let down those they are mentoring. These feelings are amplified when their actions have involved other parties and maybe got them into trouble or endangered them.

Then there are others who also belong to the 'special' category for entirely different reasons. As has been shown in the previous anecdotes, no one in aviation is perfect; this industry attracts the same human giants and epic fails which other industries do. Rest assured our epic fails don't tend last too long as we have so many rules and regulations it is only a matter of time before the individual crosses a line and is thereby relieved of their responsibility/authority – remember it's not always a pilot.

Still others can enter the Epic Fail category for a simple lack of social skills or etiquette. Some of these types of people rarely give workmates or colleagues a second thought and seem inured to others feelings, and can best be summed up with – *'the world revolves around me'* mentality.

Then there are the ones who have different perceptions as to what is socially acceptable.

Am I really undesirable?

Being desirable is a quality many of us on the planet strive for. We want people to look at us, want us, need us, because for many human beings it feeds our ego and makes us feel better about ourselves. For Paddy his needs are a little simpler.

So it's 2016 and Paddy is visiting South Africa to renew his Commercial Pilot's Licence (CPL). It is common these days for many of the world's pilots hold more than one Commercial License – Paddy has three, which correspond to many of the countries he has worked in. He hasn't worked in South Africa but did get a CPL there some time back as this License assists with gaining employment with SA companies who work elsewhere on the continent. Paddy is back to undertake a few exams and time permitting a flight test.

Paddy's birthday is also coming up and he has decided to spend it with his brother in the United States so he books a ticket and continues preparing for his exams. Closer to the day Paddy reconfirms his airline ticket and just double checks his passport – it is only then he realizes his South African entry visa will expire three days before he departs for America. No problem, he telephones the Home Affairs Department and discusses the problem with them. They say it will be fine, just discuss it with the Immigration Officer on the day of departure – mention this conversation! Unfortunately for Paddy he does not get the name of the person he spoke to.

Paddy has checked in, and is proceeding through Immigration when the officer quickly notes the three day breach and states "oh you have overstayed" and before Paddy can say anything the officer grabs a special stamp and promptly brands poor Paddy's passport. "Go and see the Officer over there."

Paddy wanders over and is rudely told to go in to a small interview room. All civility aside the officer just starts in on 'people like Paddy who come to this country and break the law'. Then the officer starts filling out a two page form – Paddy tries to ask a couple of questions and even explain about his call to Home Affairs – he is ignored. The officer hands Paddy the form which he begins to read; the officer gets upset "Just sign it." Paddy says he needs to read the form before he signs it. The officer stands up and says he will be back in a minute and 'you had better have signed it'. Paddy continues to peruse the document and phrases like 'breached the immigration act'; 'overstayed'; 'committed an offense'; and finally 'South Africa considers you an *undesirable* person.' Jump out at him while he reads.

When the officer returns two minutes later Paddy proffers the document with a question regarding the wording. The officer who could see he hadn't signed grabs the paper from him – "so you have refused to sign" and scribbles the same on the signature section and quickly stamps the form, seems getting a stamp at the SA Immigration is done at the same speed a Formula One car travels. Paddy is now getting upset, as he says he did not refuse to sign he was just asking a question. For the first time the officer relaxes and says he is sorry, he misunderstood. Paddy asks the question and satisfied with his answer requests to be allowed to sign.

"Sorry I have already recorded you have refused to sign. Furthermore you are banned from entering South Africa for one year – you may go."

Apparently this is a new system which was developed recently when the old one which involved fines was decided to be outdated. Now Paddy only wants to be desirable in one country – the overriding problem is he just can't get in there for a year.

Seeing double

Nick arrived from an EU country which will remain unnamed and who was at the time looking for work in Tanzania. Whilst doing so he was also having a small problem; he held dual nationality but one of his passports was about to expire.

On this particular day another pilot, who we'll call Rick noticed Nick had something on his mind – he actually looked like he had just lost his niece at the shopping mall and wasn't sure how to call his sister and break the news. Being somewhat concerned, or maybe nosey, Rick asked if there was anything he could help with. Nick explained the problem and added the closest place he could have renewed the passport was in another country, which was not only a long way but an expensive trip. So, for these reasons he had cooked up a plan...

"You know I told you I have a twin brother at home?" (Actually he is an identical twin)

"Yessssss," Rick cautiously replied. Wow Nick was really wound up!

"Well, I sort of ......, I asked him to.........., I don't know what to do!"

Nick then stopped speaking and looked at Rick pleadingly, as if he could hardly bear to continue. Rick just stared at him for a while and then the penny dropped.

"NO! You didn't, why would you do that?"

"Yeah, but it worked before."

"What do you mean?"

"Well a couple of years back he did it for my driver's licence".

"Your fucking driver's licence, are you kidding? You sent your twin brother to a passport office in a European country, post 9/11, and asked him to get you a replacement passport so you wouldn't have to go to the country next door? Are you out of your fucking mind? You didn't think this whole thing might raise a few alarm bells, with him being, well.......not really you?"

Apparently everything regarding the application had gone without a hitch until it came to the fingerprint part of the renewal, which both of them had totally forgotten about. Brother dearest was sitting across the table from the immigration officer when the man's face completely changed shade and a quizzical look passed across it; something must have come up on his computer screen.

The officer quickly got up and said he needed to consult a supervisor. Brother dearest knew the gig was up and came clean and was promptly led off to a police cell. Nick had received this information about twenty minutes before Rick ran into him and was beside himself with worry and a fair degree of remorse for having come up with the rather stupid idea.

The upshot was, while a lawyer friend tried to clear up the – let's call it a 'misunderstanding', Nick's brother spent two nights in a cell. The parents weren't told until after the fact – just as well, as the prosecutor was asking for 18 months jail-time.

During the 48 hours Nick's brother gave his fellow inmates (mostly small-time drug-dealers and pimps) the low-down on how to make home-brew beer and so managed to avoid becoming anyone's bitch. Anyway, now they know about yeast so when they get out of prison maybe they can rise above their past.

What are you Russian for?

When I first came looking for work in Maun, Botswana, having just obtained the coveted CPL or Commercial Pilots License, it was late 2006. I was eager for my first flying job, to finally become a real pilot, paid to do the work. In places such as Maun, these jobs are considered entry level and, while I know this doesn't sound great, everyone has to start somewhere, right?

A lot of my fellow job-seekers were in the same boat: the difference was they had matured to the 19 to 24 year old category, with the occasional really old one at 30. I appeared at the tender age of 44, so no spring chicken.

Some professions prefer to get their candidates from a young age when they have not yet acquired any bad habits, and then mould them. At this time there was a bit of age discrimination going on and no one was really taking me seriously, which was frustrating. I had just enough money to make it through four months in town doing what all other hopefuls do, which is wander from company to company trying to get someone interested. If at the end of the four months there was no job then I would have to return home, broke, and rethink my plan.

Then, all of a sudden, there was one company in town which looked like a possibility. They had three Cessna 206 aircraft - pilot plus five passengers for size appreciation - and one position vacant as a pilot of theirs was moving on. The best part was they seemed to prefer to hire older pilots, as the chief pilot and operations manager were in their forties and fifties respectively. This was how I met Steve Hollingworth who was more affectionately known as *Steve the Pilot*.

Steve was born in 1962 in England and when I knew him he had been flying for only eight or so years, another late starter to the profession, and had accumulated some 2,500 flying hours. Those who understand aviation know the measurement of a pilot's ability starts with their accumulated flying hours before descending into a dissection of how each hour was flown (multi-engine, instrument, night, jet – and all this depends on the job you are after). Steve had already done agriculture flying as well as flying medium-sized multi-engine turbine aircraft, something most of us had only dreamt about. So he was what the new pilots would call *experienced*.

Sorely missed by a great many people Steve Hollingworth (1962-2010) with his Vladimir badge on the left shirt pocket - he had the six bars made just for fun.

During the second week which I was flying with Steve and getting familiar with the area we were dispatched to an airstrip called Xakanaka to collect two guests and take them to Kanana, another airstrip for yet another Lodge. About 3 minutes (approximately 5 miles) from landing in Xakanaka Steve reached into his bag, pulled out a small name tag, much like a store employee would wear, and put it on his left shirt pocket. With my position beside him I couldn't read the badge but had noticed it was on upside down. When I mentioned this he just replied, "I know". I thought he may not have heard correctly and repeated what I had said. "Yes," he replied somewhat impatiently, "I heard you the first time". *Okay enough said by me!*

We landed at the airstrip and Steve turned to me and said, "You need to do only two things during this stop: do not laugh and do not call me Steve - my name is Vladimir."

Before I could say anything he was out of the aircraft and greeting the clients in a thick Russian accent with his hands above his head, feet together flat, positioned rather like a ballerina does, and a big smile.

"Helloooooo, Me Vladimir, non Engris *spek*, today *you* pilot, come, come, sit plane.....*pease* come."

Now, for any of you reading this and thinking I need *spell check* don't worry, it is exactly as it's supposed to be. The clients turned out to be a lovely older couple from somewhere in the mid-West United States. He was about six foot five and a solid man who towered above his petite wife. Both were a little overdressed for the bush but as I learn much later it is also nice to transport people who are not in track suits or Spandex all the time – especially as many of them have chosen a size too small. Just as an aside, you people know you can't squeeze the fat out of your body – right?

Anyway, Steve had started running around grabbing their luggage and cramming it into the aircraft; all the while the Americans had not moved a muscle or said a word. After a minute of relative silence (Vladimir was talking to himself about various things while loading the luggage) the husband found his tongue and started babbling to his wife.

"Honey, I *aint* sure, but I think the pilot is a *Soviet*."

223

Soviet, yes I was having a little trouble rationalizing this statement as well –roughly 18 years after the collapse of the USSR – yet seemingly some people still live in their own little world. I was thinking at the time they probably own a bomb shelter and run drills before dinner on Saturdays.

With this information from her husband the wife went slightly pale and they looked at each other with something akin to serious concern about whether they should get in the aircraft and allow Vladimir to fly them. Seeing their reluctance Steve (or I should say Vladimir) raced over, and gently grabbed the wife by the arm. Nothing violent, but with one hand on her elbow and the other on her wrist, and he just started slowly walking and repeated softly;

"Come, come, we fly now – go to camp, *dink, luk* animals."

This was enough to get her moving and move she did, straight into the aircraft. The husband saw his wife get and still babbling he sort of gave up and joined her. I had remained in the aircraft while all this was going on; but 30 seconds after Vladimir's introduction I had started to pinch the back of my leg really hard to prevent myself from laughing, which of course I had been forbidden to do.

The Emergency Briefing, which was circumspect on a normal day was now undertaken in its entirety, together with sound effects. 'Vladimir' stood at the door, with a silly grin on his face then there were several seconds of expectant silence. His lack of English was more than made up for by wild pointing and unusual noises.

"Exits... 2 and 1" he pointed. "FIRE" was shouted as if there had just been one and his hands blossomed in more ballet moves. "Shusssssssssh", gushed from his mouth to illustrate the operation of the fire extinguisher which he then pointed at. He then grabbed a sick bag, opened it and made realistic vomiting sounds before refolding the sack and placing it back where he found it. He gently took hold of the husband's arm, ran his finger across it to simulate a cut and then mimed bandaging the wound. Then he air-drew a box and pointed to the back of the aircraft to signify the First Aid kit.

Finally he clapped his hands together and displayed all ten digits, then repeated the gesture and pointed at his watch, making a flying noise with his arms out (like kids do) to signify the time of the flight. I couldn't resist getting a look at the passengers' faces whose attention was quite rightly glued to Vladimir and his performance. I just managed to squeeze out a "Hi" before quickly turning to face the front again. Vladimir jumped in beside me and we were off.After 20 minutes we touched down at Kanana and let the guests off. As the guests left and we were about to taxi I immediately asked why he had pretended to be a Russian pilot.

"Oh, it's just for a laugh. You need to have fun at work" he said, "As you can see the clients really don't know what to do when I behave this way".

The reason he put the name tag on upside down is it said exactly 'Me Vladimir – *non*Engris*spek*' (purposely misspelled). On some occasions he would look down at the tag and read it to the clients by way of an introduction.

The Vlad Badge

Two days later Steve and I landed again at Kanana and as I looked over at the game vehicle I saw the same two Americans and thought, 'Oh god, here we go again!' They initiated the conversation.

"Hi Vladimir!" the husband, called out.

"No, my name's Steve," was the response

The clients looked confused. "Oh, I understand!" Steve went on. "You must have met Vladimir – people say we look a lot alike." Now both guests looked really confused, probably as confused as me. They turned to their guide and said "Who's that?"

"Why, that's Steve the pilot" replied the guide. Which of course, it was!

The guests flew back in total silence, unsure about what to make of the situation, and departed on their international flight. After they left I asked why the personality change - back to Steve.

"I like to mess with people's minds, it's all rather harmless. Besides they have a long flight home and this will probably give them something to talk about."

Later, over a beer, I mentioned Vladimir to the Operations Manager and all he said was, "Oh, have you met him already?"

Doubting Thomas

When I was growing up Mum and Dad tried to educate me about stuff, you know aspects of life - as most parents do. During this education process there were subjects which I just didn't agree with – after all what could these old people know which could supersede my vast knowledge and experience of the world – at 12. Looking back now all of it was basic stuff but when I stood my ground they would call me a 'DT' or *doubting Thomas*. So for this reason our next Special Case for the following stories is named Thomas and you will see why he is so aptly named.

Emergencies

You work at a nuclear power plant. It goes without saying it is a professional operation after all the world's fate is conceivably in your hands, yes, it's obviously not in Russia. There are procedures to follow, which include all kinds of checks and safety strategies, and there are steps to adhere to should an emergency occur. All of these procedures have been fully tested by people with much more knowledge than you and they are set out in the Plant's operational Bible. Rest assured you can implement these procedures should that nuclear rainy day ever arrive.

In this respect aviation is a lot like nuclear power and we have our own Bible in the form of the Aircraft Flight Manual or POH (Pilots' Operating Handbook). This book explains the aircraft in its entirety and not only must it be carried on board when flying but *thepilot must understand it*. Ladies this is the one instruction manual men actually have to read before they start tinkering with anything.

The POH has the usual information (speeds, procedures, installed equipment, etc.) as well as whole section on Emergencies. These procedures have been demonstrated by the aircraft manufacturer to the aviation authority of the country of manufacture, in this case the FAA in the U.S. The demonstration is carried out by an experienced test pilot while the aircraft is being 'type certified' and so the procedures are pretty bullet-proof; not perfect - as nothing is – but as close as possible. Still not convinced, funnily enough neither was Thomas the pilot in this story.

Now our Thomas had a nagging, uneasy feeling regarding Section3 of the POH which contains all manner of Emergency procedures. His doubt was, what if someone had not thought through all the variables, *what if* the procedure didn't work when the awful day came about? Thomas decided he needed to double-check, maybe test the procedure, just to make sure it worked - after all lives were on the line. This decision seemed only reasonable – to him, anyway. Now so you understand, in aviation we do encourage pilots to *practice* certain emergencies but in doing so there are boundaries to where this self-testing can take you – you know common sense – apparently not for the day in question!

A few weeks later and the phone rings in the house of a very old and experienced ex-South Africa Air Force pilot who used to work with Thomas, or shall we address him as DT. Apparently the cat was out of the bag and Thomas had been called to account for his actions. He was in a panic, was babbling, and from the description not making much sense. Finally the old guy got a word in.

"Calm the fuck down," said the old guy. "Start at the beginning."

Thomas explained his obsession with the emergencies section of the manual, and one procedure in particular – the Air Restart. This is the procedure for starting an engine that has shut down mid-flight, or the pilot has had to shut down mid-flight. So you understand the odds of a pilot having this particular emergency in their entire career would be *just short* of NEVER. But, obviously the Federal Aviation Administration needs to have a procedure in place for the aircraft *if it happened.*

Thomas, who still works in *somewhere in Africa*, went on to tell his old boss he had been flying his Cessna Caravan to a town with a small airport last week and, as he had no one on board, he saw his opportunity for the test. He circled high above the runway, to about 15,000 feet, pulled the aircraft prop into feather, moved the fuel condition lever (selector) to low idle and then waited one minute for the turbine blades to cool down. This is how this particular engine is cooled down before it is shut off – never the less this simple procedure is always undertaken *on the ground.*

After the minute had passed Thomas then shut the engine down by closing the fuel condition lever. He was now in control of a US$1.6 million glider. He then went through the entire emergency restart procedure to ensure *it did actually work* and low and behold the manufacturer was right – it did! No surprises there Thomas, when was the last time you saw an approved emergency procedure which doesn't work? Okay, 1986 at Chernobyl, my mistake.

So now, with the engine going again, and only three thousand feet above the runway Thomas circles to land under full power. The whole thing a perfectly acceptable procedure undertaken by test pilots everywhere. *Except Thomas wasn't, and still is not, a test pilot;* add to this he had no permission to undertake such a procedure. Obviously the aircraft is a considerable investment to the company and if he had made an error it could very well have been an expensive exercise. If a company wants to undertake this sort of procedure they need to inform certain official parties beforehand. Failure to do so could reflect very badly on everyone and I am pretty sure the insurance company would not be over the moon about the whole situation.

The old pilot then asked Thomas if he had reported it. "No," was the answer, and it was late in the day with no one around. "So, how did the company find out?" asked the old pilot.

It turned out this was one of the aircraft operated by the company which had a system which monitors critical engine parameters throughout all phases of flight. Basically it is a box which can tell the engineers how the engine has been treated and if any components have exceeded their maximum parameters. In order to view the data from the unit an aircraft engineer has to download the information from the aircraft and upload it to the engine manufacturer's website, which is a secure network with a pin number. When Thomas had shut the engine down the unit had recorded it as an in-flight event, so even before the local engineers could look at the data the manufacturer had flagged it as a full-blown engine failure and telephoned the maintenance provider.

The immediate answer – 'No, the Charter Company had no knowledge of an engine failure in their fleet'. It was then date and time tracked to see who was flying and this had been when Thomas got his summons to the office. He was getting in a quick call to his former boss to see if he had any useful advice for a man about to be beheaded. In the end Thomas got a severe reprimand but he managed to keep his job – this time!

Chickening out

Here we have our friend Thomas again, this time flying a twin-engine aircraft and doing the most profitable run the company has - the chicken run. It's not a pleasant duty to fly roughly one thousand or so baby chicks crammed into oversized plastic trays to various points around a Central African country. The cabin is sealed and even chicks tend to smell a bit; but these chicks will turn into chickens and are highly profitable creatures, reproducing at vast rates and providing a stable diet to the countryside of either the meat itself or eggs.

Thomas has reported a problem with the over wing emergency door; it keeps popping open in flight. Normally it is just ajar but occasionally it can result in the door lying on the floor of the cabin. Although the company was endeavouring to fix the problem, waiting for a spare part, they were taking too long for Thomas' liking. One evening, Thomas is loaded up with baby chicks, on the taxi for take-off, when the door pops open, not on the floor, but essentially the same problem again. He is annoyed, assesses the situation and decides to continue the flight. Just so you understand these aircraft are not pressurized so it's not like a movie, when a person gets sucked out the hole.

Having said this a baby chick weighs a whole lot less than a human being. As the flight progresses, the door opens a bit further and the poor little things start to get sucked out of their cages and whisked off into airspace above the countryside – essentially, it's raining chicks.

About half the cargo, which is 500 chicks, 'stepped out' of his flight. This decision making did not endear Thomas to his boss and shortly after this he moved on to look for other employment.

The Little Engine that could

Once again Thomas has found employment: this time he is flying a small but robust twin-engine aircraft called the BN-2 Islander, formally manufactured by Britton-Norman.

The BN-2 Islander

The Islander is a heavy duty Bush aircraft which has had a number of unflattering descriptions as to how it actually flies. One tough-in-cheek story goes like this:

Design documents clandestinely recovered from the Britten-Norman shredder have solved a question that has puzzled aerodynamicists and pilots for many years, disclosing that it is actually noise which causes the BN-2 to fly. The vibration set up by the engines and amplified by the airframe, in turn causes the air molecules above the wing to oscillate at atomic frequency, reducing their density and causing lift. This can be demonstrated by sudden closure of the throttles, which causes the aircraft to fall from the sky. As a result, lift is proportional to noise rather than speed, explaining amongst other things the aircraft's remarkable take-off performance. Back to the story.

Anyone who's been flying for a while knows no two aircraft behave exactly the same way. To compare an aircraft to people – many of us leave the factory pretty much alike but it is how we handle and maintain ourselves which eventually makes us the way we are: unique. Aircraft often fall into this type-set after a while, especially aircraft engines.

Every aircraft engine has gauges installed to tell us what is going on in critical areas - for piston engines, the Cylinder Head Temperatures (CHT's) are an important part of this information. The Cylinder is the place the fuel/air mixture is ignited to release the energy thus driving the piston thereby turning the crankshaft and onwards to the propeller to provide thrust; the engine is much like your car except no propeller. So monitoring the CHT's to ensure they do not overheat forms an important part of a pilot's engine checks while flying.

When a pilot flies a single engine piston aircraft and the CHT's temperatures run hot it could be a cause for concern, but after a while and maintenance inspections you realise this can be synonymous for a particular engine. When you fly a multi-engine aircraft (aircraft with more than one engine) the same thought process exists but remember you have at least one other engine therefore one other CHT gauge to compare it to – differences can get you thinking.

On this particular day Thomas has been assigned to a BN2 Islander which has this very idiosyncrasy: one engine runs hotter than the other. This particular engine's CHT always ran hot. All the pilots knew about this and so they did not worry – in other words it was common knowledge and accepted, and more importantly maintenance approved and released.

Thomas knew this too, but a nagging feeling, the same one which got him into trouble last time, started again and so he decided he was going to do the company *a favour* – he was going to fix the issue once and for all. On a flight back to his home base with five people on board, he reduced the throttle (power) to this engine and then feathered the propeller, eventually shutting the engine down (off).

If you feather a propeller it means you turn the blades so they are producing no thrust for the aircraft, as well as a minimal amount of drag. By doing this Peter had effectively removed 50% of the power of the aircraft to fly - two engines have become one – but he has also removed at least 75% of the aircraft's performance when you factor in Drag and several other variables. Now this is normally a procedure undertaken when there is a serious problem, like a fire. Today, of course, there was no such problem – except maybe Thomas' thought processes.

But Thomas had a plan; he would just restart the engine, any of this sound familiar. Unfortunately, today's engine was not cooperating and in the end it took him seven attempts before the engine finally started. Starter motors on these engines are not designed for this type of punishment. If they are used even two or three times they can get very hot and easily burn out. Once burnt out you will never get the engine started, at least not until it is replaced which is difficult to do if you are flying the thing.

If you are having trouble starting on the ground you just wait a while for the starter to cool down. Time for cooling is not a luxury which Thomas has; he is flying around on one engine, was probably losing height, and needs to get the second engine running again and thus is cranking the shit out of his starter. Thomas maybe next time just leave it running and let the engineers decide if it is fit to fly – oh, hang on they did.

Luckily this starter didn't burn out, he eventually got it running and managed to get the propeller out of feather, which is another big ask, especially on an Islander. His five passengers had been watching with baited breath and a little more than a professional interest. Once he returned to 'ops normal' he turned, smiled, and suggested they keep the whole matter between themselves. This was unlikely to happen as the flight was a staff run and all five of them were company pilots, yes he knew they were pilots – WOW! Each of them felt the entire event was unnecessary. They reported him and once again Thomas was looking for employment.

As an aside to the above stories I would like to say something about Thomas. I can honestly say that I have met so few people who have a zest and love of life like this guy has. Thomas is committed to people and dives in to all situations to help. He is someone you could truly believe and see working as a humanitarian but he chose aviation as his profession. In this respect he knows his work, strives constantly to make himself a better pilot and is one of those who I previously mentioned suffers personally when he lets people down. Some of you out there know him as well and I can assure you your life has been bettered for it. Thomas definitely meets the requirements for a person who is "the salt of the earth", and it was my pleasure to have met him, however brief a period it was.

I'm not good with faces

As we discussed in the bigotry section of this book idiots come in all shapes and sizes. One such moron is this pilot who doesn't see the sentence in his head before it is blurted outward. In 2004, our pilot Charlie, to give him a name, touched his Cessna 206 aircraft down at a very small Botswana bush strip and, having parked he jumped out and yelled his cheerful greeting as usual. But wait a minute...he spun around and took in his surroundings.

"Ah, this doesn't look like Ntswi airstrip!"

At the airstrip there were three local gentlemen in the parking area who confirmed his suspicions: he was actually at Delta airstrip, two miles from Ntswi. Charlie had landed at the wrong place.

"Oh dear! How embarrassing," says Charlie grinning from ear to ear. "I'd better be off then."

With this he jumps back into his aircraft, starts up the engine with his seat belt still hanging out the door, applies full power in order to turn (thereby blasting dirt over these three men), shoots off down the airstrip, gets airborne to maybe forty feet above the ground, makes a sharp left turn, about 80 degrees angle of bank between a couple of trees, and disappears from sight.

Now, for the uninitiated in flight procedures, this is not what we would call a normal departure or indeed the safest way to operate an aircraft. An aircraft is not a car which you jump in, shoot through the carpark across all the parking spaces and out of the Mall across three lanes of traffic so you can make the light before they change. There are certain procedures you should undertake and rushing these can quickly bite you in the ass. What Charlie just pulled off had worked but it was less than ideal. Luckily Charlie's aircraft was empty (no passengers) but that is not the point.

On Charlie's return Steve, Charlie's boss, tells him officialdom would like to see him in their office. Charlie asks Steve what they want to see him about but Steve feigns ignorance. Charlie marches up to the Department of Civil Aviation (DCA) Flight Operations office to find out what all the fuss is about and on walking through the door he spots a familiar face.

"Hey, don't I know you?"
"Yes," came the reply. "We met briefly this morning when you landed at the wrong airstrip, immediately took off without your seat belt on and then carried out an illegal manoeuvre in your aircraft."

Charlie ignores the fact he is obviously in trouble and focuses on the social graces of the situation. "Sorry! I wasn't sure - *all you black fellas look the same to me!*" Charlie's licence was immediately suspended for two weeks for dangerous flying but his racial insensitivity was put down to pure stupidity.

Terry the Miser

Let me introduce you to a pilot we will call Terry, who is about five foot nine is a bit older than most of his peers – mid forties – is challenged when it comes to combing his hair, and in a town where pretty much everyone drinks Terry does not.

Long ago he decided alcohol was not for him and he was happy with that – good for you buddy. Terry could also be a bit tight – you know long pockets and short hands. He had one vice, he loved food and the larger the portions, the happier Terry was. A buffet was like Christmas to him, each dish cover symbolic of the unwrapping of a new present. Where am I going with this?

Budgeting for food

One day Terry meets a young lady, one thing leads to another and she decides to spend the night. They enjoy their evening but with morning comes the craving of the stomach. Terry, being a good host, cooks breakfast and his lady-guest eats. But when she asks for one more piece of toast Terry goes very quiet. She repeats her request and again gets no response. Eventually Terry says; "I think it is time you left as we really have nothing else to say to each other." The lady is obviously bewildered but without any explanation gets up and leaves. Nope I wasn't there – Terry told us the whole story later in the day of her somewhat shocking behaviour.

"Can you believe how rude she was, asking for more toast?" I can assure you his indignation was genuine. "Does she not know the price of bread?"

When we had all finished howling with laughter at his miserliness we calculated her request would have cost him all of US$00.02. Yes, two cents! Never-the-less he stood his ground; food was food and people should respect his perspective. Unfortunately this was not an isolated incident – let us move on!

It's mine!

Just like all pilots, Terry loved staying in the camps on an overnight. Terry's passion for the bush had nothing to do with wildlife and everything to do with the fact the food is included on these stopovers. Free food, and as much as he wanted suited him perfectly.

When Terry was in camp there would, from time to time, be complaints from guests to the camp's management that there had been insufficient fare at dinner. This was principally because as the dinner chime sounded Terry was straight out of the starting blocks and would be the first in the queue. After he had piled up his plate up the remaining guests were afforded something akin to a nouvellecuisine (small) portion. This is also principally because the chef cannot cook enough food for Patton's 3rd Army or indeed Terry which is essentially the same thing. Management jumped on the situation and mentioned this to the middle-aged pilot but to no avail; nothing was going to stop

Terry stuffing his face at the company's expense.

One sunny afternoon Terry was due to overnight but at the last minute the office instructed him to fly to the camp, drop the guests and return to Maun as there was more flying to be done. When Terry realized his overnight had been cancelled he lost his rag and started shouting, "That's not fair, that was my overnight. What am I going to do for dinner?"

Yes behaviour just like a six-year-old does. Try to remember he is in his 40's, yet this still didn't stop him stomping through the airport before finally getting in his aircraft and taking off to deposit the four guests at the camp. However, Terry had decided the return trip would not be done immediately. He rushed from his aircraft to the Lodge's kitchen, politely inquired what was on the menu for the evening meal, that night it was steak and potatoes, waited until no one was looking, filched some steak and grabbed two unwashed potatoes, which he then exchanged for some peeled, washed ones when they caught his eye, and quickly ran back to the aircraft with it all.

Not finished, he then trotted off to the bar to get a six-pack of his favourite fizzy apple drink. Meanwhile, the chef had been alerted to the missing meat and hot-footed it to the airstrip to reclaim the uncooked food from Terry's personal bag. Terry returned with the drink, started up and flew back to Maun, oblivious to the chef's visit. By the time he got to Maun the whole office had been informed by radio of the attempted theft.

Terry was adamant: "What's the problem, '*if*' I had stayed in the camp I would have been eating that steak and potatoes, so they're really mine anyway."

Yes I know, on what plane of existence does this form a balanced thought process? This time none of us were laughing. Skipping the obvious theft angle, this was so irrational and so far outside the box it entered the realms of a psychological issue more than anything else.

Terry actually believed what he had just done constituted *normal behaviour*! Moving on – oh no we're not finished with Terry just yet!

That's not your ring finger

The culmination to Terry's stay in Maun came in the form of an inopportune moment involving a military helicopter and Terry's right hand. Said helicopter hovered a little too close to Terry's parked aircraft for his liking so with all the dust and dirt flying around he let his emotions get the better of him. Terry used a gesture which is universally understood although considered poor manners in most civilized situations. Terry held up his middle finger and started shouting obscenities at the little craft. Of course whatever he was shouting was lost in the noise of the helicopter's rotor but the message the gesture sent obviously got through. Once the helicopter was on the ground a gentleman in a suit and tie emerged and marched straight towards Terry.

Now people, it doesn't take a rocket scientist to work out if someone dressed in civilian clothes, let alone a suit and tie exits a military aircraft then he is probably what we might term '*a somebody*'. This somebody was unused to this sort of sign language being bestowed upon him. He marched up to Terry and asked him his name.

"Nope I'm not giving it to you" was the somewhat brusque reply!

There was another pilot there and according to him the man did not raise his voice, but the request was repeated and again rudely denied. In fact Terry countered, *he* needed to know the gentleman's name, as he was going to report him for not wearing his reflective vest, an airport safety and security requirement, yes I know, what a moron. There was a long silence as the gentleman just stood there looking Terry straight in the eye before he finally said, "You'll be hearing from me very soon." When the other pilot recounted this last statement to me a small shiver went down my back. I then asked him to describe Mr. Suit and Tie's return trip across the apron. Did he rush, or was it casual, was he marching? In the end he described/mimicked someone strolling.

Some of us pay attention to these little happenings and it did not take much detective work to figure out who this guy was. It was a very senior member of the country's security services, sort of like director of the FBI or the deputy head of MI5 – something like this!

Terry never thought about the matter again but was in for a nasty shock when he went to renew his work and residence permits a couple of months later; they were rejected on security grounds. Once rejected for this reason you will not get them back.

Being an intelligent man I suppose he reckoned if Terry, essentially a guest in his country, was the kind of person to make these sort of gestures to a military aircraft then he might conceivably do the same or worse to the average citizen. Bearing in mind this country has very strict rules about offensive behaviour – yes Terry is fully aware of these niceties, although obviously he felt they didn't apply to him. Possibly in the end it was all for the best he should be on his way as he had another hand and who knows what this would be used for.

Not only did Terry leave the country but also gave up aviation and went to work for a popular worldwide burger franchise (you could say he was lovingit). We heard some months later he was dismissed for misappropriation of food before moving on to the competition.Some people will never change and I guess this is food for thought.

Burn the sheets and brush your teeth

One pilot in Botswana, call him Freddy, who fled his job here, enters the Special Case category merely for the *way* in which he did it: the *why* will probably never be known.

He seemed to be happy with his job, showing up for work each day, getting on with everyone, which is just what you would expect. One evening there was to be a small gathering so Freddy asked Frank, if he would be going and the reply was in the affirmative? 'Right, so I'll see you there,' said Freddy, and this was the last anyone saw of him.

The following day was his day off and this was when he texted the Operations Manager, saying he *couldn't do it anymore* and needed to leave; something had obviously upset him. To add to the mystery his room-mate had come home from her overnight to find his room cleaned out, his bed sheets burned in the braai pit (BBQ area) and his hammock gone. He had taken the trouble of filling in the holes in the wall used to hold up the hammock with, of all things, toothpaste.

Unfortunately his consideration did not extend to leaving his share of the previous month's rent money; his flat-mate had to fork out for that plus pay full whack until she found someone else to take over the vacated room.

Five months later Freddy contacted us by email requesting a reference for the next job! Some people's cheek is truly amazing!

ALCOHOL

People drink, regrettably things don't always work out the way they would like.

One more for the road

Some people come on Safari around the Christmas – New Year period. Makes sense, it's a nice trip and its summer. This American family of four recently had a big New Year's Eve and Vumbura Camp, Okavango Delta, Botswana; well their twenty year old boy did, let's call him Party Boy; was I there, no not at all.

It was the following day when I was flying and chatting to another pilot who was flying them (yes was, past tense). Seems he collected them at Vumbura to take them to Kasane, and was due to take them on to Livingstone, a trip of roughly one hour twenty minutes flight time. The pilot, Dusty had to make one stop ten minutes after he collected the family. Party Boy apparently was not well and needed to leave the aircraft during the stop; he did so and made it as far as a bush before *passing out*. The family attended to him and he managed to regain consciousness. They were on the ground for 30 minutes before the pilot indicated he needed to leave.

Nope Party Boy said he couldn't do it; he needed to stay. There was a short conversation with the camp and the family got off the aircraft. The camp organized them a room for Party Boy to lie down in. The family then had to Charter another aircraft later in the day to continue their journey. That's an expensive night out, anyway Cheers!

The beers on you, or at least the bottle is

There is a mentality among some young women I have watched develop over the past ten or so years. Now ladies I am not trying to be sexist here and it would be unlikely I would as my mother is still breathing and would come and kick my ass for doing so. I believe in gender equality and extend this to much of my life; in fact whether it is work or personal my thinking is just be straight with me; no bullshit or games, which to me seems fair.

One of the games *some* women like to play is – a woman can say and behave as she pleases but when it suits hershe hides behind her femininity; nowhere is this more prevalent than with a woman being violent. No, not violence against women, a woman striking a man and then stating 'you can't hit me because I'm a woman'. Yes, let us explore this rather warped and fundamentally incorrect mentality.

Enter someone we will call Kg a young local lady of about thirty who is highly intelligent. You could have a very deep conversation with her regarding most issues and come away feeling suitably challenged on your views. Give Kg a beer and she loosens up a little but as soon as she hits the second beer Kg is an argumentative and aggressive drunk you may not recognize and certainly do not want to interact with; in short she gets ugly. Still a cheap date if you don't mind all the shouting.

Enter Frank who is driving home one evening and spots Kg and Steve having a chat at Bon Arriv'e so Frank pulls in to join them. He's too late as Kg has already had five or so beers, the situation is immediately assessed and Frank says goodnight.

About ten minutes after this Kg is being so loud a local gentleman sitting nearby asks if she can keep it down. Kg doesn't like being told what to do and goes over and tells this man her views, with a few Fuck Yous to add to the class of the conversation. The man says he just wants to have his drink and is not looking for a fight. Steve is trying to calm Kg down and gets her to return to her table; upon her arrival she collects an empty beer bottle and throws it at this poor guy hitting him. Regrettably for Kg she has now crossed a line which all women should take note of.

The man is up from his seat and there is a little blood coming from where the bottle struck his forehead. He asks "what the fuck is your issue"? She replies "what are you going to do now, you can't hit a woman"? Therein lies Kg's problem; if you are going to go down this path you need to understand with behaviour like this some men no longer see you as a woman; and you may get any number of different reactions. Kg wasn't expecting to be punched but if you are going to assault someone then you ladies are taking this chance.

Everyone is always waxing on about female equality. Equality is about being equal; so don't dispense violence unless you are content it may be returned to you in kind. I fully agree it should never be initiated on a lady; but I for one, am not going to stand there and be physically hammered on while you exercise your definition of gender equality and hide behind Victorian ideals.

Kg had a very large bruise around her eye the next time I saw her and decided she would give up drinking for a while; probably a smart move. Look not many of us want it to come to this but you can't have your cake and eat it too. Remember most Laws deal in being equal; Equity is fairness for all parties, so let's call everyone equal and keep the violence in check, fair?

Just a few more

It is pushing 11PM at a Lodge in the Delta where a Local Guide, call him Gift, is bored. He has consumed his alcohol allocation for the week in one evening and has been unfairly cut off. He is not happy as he considers himself a responsible drunk and feels he should be allowed to continue; no, this will not happen, please go to bed. Gift wanders through the camp before he finally locates one of the Lodge boats which is used to take guests out on the river. Gift's thinking is if he can't drink he might as well drive; besides Gift has a cunning plan. About twenty or so minutes down the river there is another camp which is much more liberal about their drinking policy, Gift will just pilot the boat there and have a few more drinks before returning to turn in. Unfortunately Gift misses the concept of a few more.

The following morning Gift also misses the mandatory staff meeting for the day's activities. He does manage to show up at about ten o'clock after all he is a responsible employee and knows he has guests arriving in the afternoon. The manager attempts to speak to Gift about the unauthorized use of the boat, his absence from the staff meeting, and his generally poor condition; Gift refuses to discuss it as his time is precious. He must prepare for his guests arrival, the problem being he is still drunk! He is told to go to his room, he will shortly be returning to Maun for a disciplinary hearing.

Gift appears at the head office two days later for his hearing. Upper management listens to his explanation regarding the lack of fairness concerning his alcohol consumption. Yes he agrees, he did take the boat, he also missed the morning meeting, was rude and insubordinate to the Lodge Manager, and was drunk during the conversation; but if the original system regarding the alcohol had not been flawed, none of this would have happened. Therefore the whole thing is not his fault. A senior Manager looks him in the eye:

"We understand your side but you need to understand ours; we're going to have to let you go".

Gift's mood brightened "Oh, good where am I going?"

"No, you don't understand, we are firing you".

Gift's face gets very serious "You can't fire me, I need this job".

Yes another moron who just doesn't get it. You don't *own the job*, it's on loan to you – treat it well and you usually get to keep it; in this case no, another job opening created.

COMPLAINTS

In any service industry at one time or another you have complaints; I get it, you are paying for something and it should be as you would like not as the service provider wants or attempts to deliver it. In some cases it is the service provider who is at fault, in other cases it is the middle man, you know the Agent, the one you dealt with, paid the money to, the person you sought out and trusted with your hard earned cash for the family vacation. In other cases the responsibility is actually yours – yes I know it is hard to hear and this is why most people won't listen regarding the possibility they may be at fault. I will never say as an Industry we are perfect, no one is but this leaves us all with a little quandary.

More often than not it is the Agent who gets a pass, it can't be his fault, he is trustworthy, besides you picked him and blaming him might reflect on you; which moves us to the unwillingness to blame yourself, so back to the service provider, it must be him who is at fault. But people should remember some complaints can't be rationalized, so let's not be stupid about it, okay?

It's too noisy

In 2015 a couple was unhappy and could not wait to return and speak to their agent to complain so they contacted their Agent's ground service in Zimbabwe to address the issue. The hotel they were staying in was more than satisfactory, they were actually having a great time, the food was great, the activities were wonderful, the people lovely, friendly. No, this wasn't the problem; they were on their Honeymoon and they weren't getting any sleep. From my view I thought this was the idea, but hey I wasn't involved and these people were serious, they were not happy.

It seems their beautiful hotel was right next to Victoria Falls and the sound of the water going over the Falls constantly – for otherwise it would be a Dam not a water fall – was too loud!The complaint was "could the water falls sound not be turned down, make less noise especially in the evening."

Yes I know, what do you say to this? It is a natural water feature and therefore it functions twenty-four hours a day. Now many of us would understand this, but these clients still wanted a written response to their complaint. I'll leave it to you; how would you start this letter........?

This is when there was less water flowing – therefore less noise and, I guess less complaints?

Goldilocks

When I was a kid, I used to think this bedtime story was great. Looking back now and with all the poverty I have witnessed, well, I'm sorry I think the little lady was a little entitled. First of all it wasn't even her house (home invasion), she ate all of their food (theft), and then went to sleep at the scene of the crime (stupid). Maybe she should have just been happy she had a meal and shut up about the temperature of the thing.

Anyway, in Botswana we have regular complaints regarding our weather, specifically how hot or cold it is - but the number of complaints increases during our summer; principally because normal temperatures reach anywhere from 35-45 degrees centigrade (100 – 120 F). I enjoy the heat but apparently there are people who have trouble with it. Summer for us is also rainy season and of course with the rain and storms the temperature can drop a bit. But if there is no rain, the heat stays and with this so do the complaints. Some of these encompass: Why is it so hot; is it normally this hot; and my favourite: but it isn't this hot where we are from.

Why is it so hot? It is a desert, you may have noted this when you did your research for your trip – or maybe you skipped this part. It may be located at 3000 feet above sea level and have water in it but this is due to previous seismic activity which has created avenues and allows water to be present, all of this does not significantly change the weather patterns of the area – or the fact that IT IS A DESERT!

Is it normally this hot? Yes, it's summer, you booked to come in summer (Off season, you know when it is less expensive – sometimes called cheaper) not in the winter (busy season – more expensive). Winter for us is very cold after sundown and until about 9AM after which it is a beautiful 28-30 degrees, much more agreeable; summer is what is known as - fucking hot!

But it's not this hot where we are from. That's because most of you are from the Northern Hemisphere where it is now winter, you know, our summer. Also you are sounding a bit privileged if you expect *your weather* can actually follow you around the globe. If you like the weather where you are, maybe just stay there, nobody forced you to come.

Be my guest

My fellow pilots and I have flown in a lot of countries in Africa supporting Lodge operations and it would really stagger the average Guest regarding the co-ordination and communication which is required to make these operations as seamless as possible.

Having said this there are mistakes; remember the scheduling of Mrs. Smith and her late husband. With so many staff and guests coming and going there has to be a system. Companies often list staff in a **darkerfont** on their paperwork to single out who is who. This was never a complaint that I know of but it deserved to be.

247

In 2015 the Smith x4, Jones x2 and **Marie.1** arrived on a flight and they were all driven to this nameless Lodge. One of the several assistant Managers at this Camp looked at her paperwork for the day, greeted the guests and told Marie to wait for her near the Kitchen. Another Manager appeared and showed Marie to her staff accommodation. Marie asked if she could go on a Game Drive and the Manager said maybe she could organize the camp utility vehicle later. Lunch was behind the kitchen, basically 'help yourself'.

Two days later Marie left on another flight and to yet another Lodge. It was during dinner Marie commented on how much nicer the rooms were in this Lodge than the last one she had stayed in. There were a few rather probing questions by the Management regarding her accommodation and then some enquiries were made the following day. Yes, someone had mistakenly put Marie down as a staff member when she was in fact a guest. Marie had spent the previous two days in staff accommodation, been served staff food, and had spent much of her time in her room. It was her first safari and she hadn't really known what to expect so was unsure if this was it for the Lodge she had stayed in. It was only when arriving at the next Lodge did she start to question her first one.

In ten years this is the first occasion I have ever heard of something like this happening and of course the Lodge operator was hugely apologetic. Marie was offered four nights at any of their Lodges in Botswana for the following year as well as all of her flights free to get her back here again. Really, the only fair way to go for poor Marie!

GEOGRAPHICAL PROBLEMS

Getting lost is embarrassing for anyone; getting lost in an aircraft with fare paying passengers when it is your profession is a little more than this. But it does happen and will continue to happen; what is important is what we learn from these embarrassing moments which make us better aviators and help build a stronger flying ethos. I was always taught no matter how much you believe in a particular aviation decision never adopt a mentality you cannot question or change it. In other words decide - but keep checking, keep an open mind.

In addition, as many of us older folks did, I grew up without the services of a GPS in any aspect of mylife. I know it was difficult for me but it was the way it was back then; I mean you really had to look for the movie theatre, no machine to tell you "in 100 meters you have reached your destination." In those golden days you looked at the yellow pages for the street address, then consulted a map or several of them depending on how far you were going and occasionally you got lost. Getting lost also made for adventures and allowed you to find new, faster and more interesting routes to where you needed to get to.

Getting where you are going on the road can be a challenge

If you weren't in a hurry it could be a lot of fun – plus petrol was cheaper back then. Even the temporary advent of misplacing yourself taught you *self-reliance* and more importantly an awareness of where you were (yes I know, lost – but you get it). Never the less you at least had some idea where you were geographically, maybe not down to minutes and seconds like GPS units do as a measurement, but you knew.

You could say a sizable portion of the people who come here have a limited geographical perspective of their travels; this is the polite way of saying *they don't have a fucking clue where they are.* It is a shame but it may surprise you there are a few of these geographically challenged people around, pilots included; on that note.

Pre-flight at Selinda, Botswana 2007, it's always good to be aware of your surroundings

Taken for a ride

Our work is sometimes referred to as a taxi service which I believe is crude but accurate. It is described this way because most of the flights in Botswana are between 15 and 25 minutes from takeoff to landing, some as little as four minute's flight time.

250

It is a high workload environment when you consider eight kilometres in an aircraft is not a big distance. Depending on the weather, a pilot would normally be able to see their destination at this distance at pretty much any altitude. Today's pilot, who we will call Walter, is a bit new, and he is also a bit overwhelmed by the whole operational flying thing.

Other than being a legal requirement *flight training* is done to teach and establish a good mindset, proper airmanship and a thorough understanding of procedures along with everything else. *Operational flying* is where you apply all of the flight training knowledge to the real world and start thinking outside the box. Why, because any air operation can, at some point, put you under some form of pressure – it's up to you to safely manage this pressure?

Walter is having trouble making this transition; he has taken off from Vumbura airstrip with four passengers, all Agents, and he has a simple task, to fly them to their next camp which is at Omdop airstrip, about 4nm (8km) away. He has a functioning GPS in the aircraft, Omdop correctly entered in the unit, therefore seemingly not a problem.

Keep in mind, even though he has all of this equipment, Walter has already been trained to fly these routes without any navigation equipment using visual navigation techniques. Unfortunately Walter gets lost and a flight which should have taken four minutes takes twenty, but eventually he lands. Now he has a new problem, there is no one there to meet the aircraft, principally because he is at the wrong airstrip.

Walter has his map out and is studying where he might be when one of the Agents in the aircraft who lives in Botswana assists him by pointing to Seronga airstrip. Walter's not convinced, she challenges him to get his heading card out and reset the GPS. Heading cards are quick reference cards to show the heading and distance from one airstrip to another. Walter re-enters Omdop in the GPS and checks it against the card and they match, seems she is right. Five minutes later the group is off again; approximately ten minutes after they are finally at their destination.

Don't worry too much Walter didn't last, he got lost a few more times before he was pointed toward the Departure counter for his International flight home; he did manage to find that.

My last pee in Africa

There were two families totalling 9 people traveling together, (they sounded like New Yorkers so we have labelled them this). On this particular day they were being collected by a Cessna Caravan to fly from Lebala airstrip up to Kasane in Botswana (for Immigration & Customs), and on to Victoria Falls in Zimbabwe. Today the aircraft has two pilots as one of them (we'll call him Peter) was undertaking conversion training – no, one of the pilots was not black so I cannot use this analogy.

Our Training Captain, Frank is overseeing Peter's conversion and is busy counting passengers, always important lest we misplace a few and upset the office. One of the ladies asked Frank:

"What are you doing?"
"Counting to make sure everyone is here."
"But we're all here."
"Then why is it I only count eight."
"That's because someone isn't here".

I know, you might ask how we pilots get through the day having to deal with some of these rather idiotic conversations but we have fun as well. Frank skipped any smart responses for fear of damaging the woman's onward cognitive function and continued with:

"Okay while we're waiting can we start putting our seatbelts on?"
"No because not everyone is here."

Apparently the same lady was speaking again. Frank was sure somewhere in her tiny brain this conversation somehow made sense, but he now wanted to explore this remote but small island of knowledge.

"So just confirm you need everyone present before you start putting your seat belt on?"
"Yes"

Now what some of you may be thinking is she is a 5%er. Frank and I discussed this and my take on this one was OCD (Obsessive Compulsive Disorder); or at least she's test driving the affliction. She needs for everything to be done in a certain order, complete boarding needs to be undertaken before the seat belts go on, only then can she listen to the safety briefing, then she can complain about the heat, the last lodge or just having to be there at all. She is not alone in this semi OCD state, I have watched this for years. The next time you take a commercial flight watch the people around you, especially when it comes to seat belts.

There are the ones who sit down and wait; a bit more secure with themselves and to ensure they don't have to click in and out five times. But when they can see the cabin preparing for departure and everyone pretty much on board, or their row has filled up they 'Click In'. Then there are the passengers who arrive, sit down and immediately put their belts on; then complain or make faces each time they have to undo the belt to allow movement to the other seats, it's an aisle seat for a reason Bozo.

Then finally comes this woman's crowd who will wait until they have been told twice, they see everyone else has more or less got there, or the emergency briefing starts. Some of this crowd even position the belt as though it is attached but don't click it in. *Just in case there is an emergency*; then they can leap from their seat and exit the aircraft. Anyway an amateur study in human behaviour, nothing when you see it once, but when it happens over and over you could call it a case study. Back to our New Yorkers!

So finally Frank have every on board, Peter is about to close up, the safety briefing has started, but it is interrupted when one of the adults jumps from his seat and yells:

"Wait, wait I need to go have *my last pee in Africa.*"

With this the guy is gone, out the door, before running thirty meters to a tree. All Frank could think of was this person must have a really big bladder because he was at a remote airstrip in Botswana (Africa); from which we were going to fly him to Kasane (still in Africa) and then on to Zimbabwe (still in Africa) where he and the rest of the group were going to spend four more days.

Medically speaking, holding it for the next five days is probably not good for you, but the more available explanation we discussed was he didn't have a clue where he was or where he was going. So we decided to call him a *geographical moron* as Frank had no further evidence it extended beyond that.

Wrong place at the right time

The airspace of the Okavango Delta is very busy. It is also completely uncontrolled, in other words there is no Air Traffic Controller telling us what to do. This is what is sometimes called an MBZ (Mandatory Broadcast Zone), a place where you use your aircraft radio to broadcast your Position, Altitude and Intentions so other aircraft will know what you are doing.

In this respect when two or more aircraft are approaching the same airstrip we will normally go to a neutral frequency to communicate directly with one another. On this particular day, I was shortly to land at PomPom airstrip with one aircraft ahead of me piloted by Carlos who worked for a different company. We agreed I would follow him in for landing.

When I arrived overhead the airfield I was carefully looking for his aircraft but I couldn't see it. I asked my crew member to help me out and kept asking the other pilot on the radio where he was, "on final approach", still nothing. Then he finally said "look I am about to touch down". My little voice spoke to me and I glanced through the cockpit window toward Kanana airstrip (about 2 miles away from PomPom) just in time to see his aircraft touch the ground and a little dust cloud kick up as he did (landed at the wrong place). I just said: "Welcome to Kanana, you don't mind if I go number one (for landing)"?All I could hear was swearing on the radio. Fined one case of beer for getting lost!

You may have problems getting places if there are no Traffic signs left.

A Continent of nations

Recently we have had some bad business months, holiday cancellations due to the Ebola outbreak in Central/West Africa. My thoughts are yes it is a shame people do not do more research regarding such events; instead they absorb the mainstream media view.

The UK and European media services gave balanced reports regarding this tragedy, a bit over the top but not too bad. By contrast it was almost amusing the way the American media represented the whole crisis; I honestly thought it was yet another war. They really do want to scare the shit out of everyone who looks at their reporting.

Now when I speak about bad business it refers to *cancellations* and many of these were for the following year. In the current year all of the companies (in Botswana anyway) got together and basically told anyone who was coming they could cancel up to the day before their safari. There is no Ebola here but if you feel you want to change your mind you have until the day before to decide – in my view, good business sense!

There were a few present year cancellations among all groups in a very small way but visitors from the U.S. market showed the biggest drop - still a few American's managed to seep through. I spoke to three couples on separate occasions who had not cancelled their holiday but were still talking about Ebola in the same manner as the U.S. Media; like the invasion of Iraq. When I asked what their concern was they became very serious and responded with: "but there is Ebola in Africa".

Okay guys, just so we are clear for those of you who treat Africa as one country please stop doing this. Africa is a continent made up of different countries, different peoples, with vastly different cultures, successes, failures, and yes, problems.

I pointed out to this couple that Ebola had always been here and every once in a while there was a terrible outbreak. I also pointed out presently there were three Ebola cases in Pennsylvania and two in Texas and none in Botswana which made where they were standing significantly safer than their own country. For some reason the conversation finished shortly after this.

Over and Over

In some places you may do a lot of repetitive flying. In other words you fly to the same place all the time. In 2005 one pilot had been flying to the same airstrip all day long usually dropping passengers but occasionally picking some up to bring back to Maun. The airstrip is only 15 minutes away and he was on his 11th flight when he landed dropped the guests and returned to Maun. When he arrived back the Porter (Ground staff) walked up to his aircraft.

"Where are the Guests"?

"There aren't any this time it was just a drop, no collection".

The Porter stared at the pilot and then said nothing for fear of being yelled at (a select few pilots still think this is the best way of communicating). The pilot returned to the office and the Chief Pilot, who had now spoken to the Porter, also wanted to know where the passengers were.

"What's the problem I dropped them at the airstrip. They're in Camp by now".
"It wasn't a Camp Transfer it was a Scenic Flight".

The pilot just stood there a little speechless. Scenic Flights are for people who want to fly around the Delta for an hour or so, so they can see some animals and get an appreciation of the size of the place. Scenic Flights normally start and finish in Maun. The pilot had been dropping passengers at the same airstrip all day and had failed to realize this group was not going to camp. He trudged back to his aircraft and flew back to the Camp to collect his passengers who were reluctantly grateful. Reluctant because they rather liked the Lodge.

OFFICIALDOM

Yes this is what you *may* encounter when dealing with any Department, Division, and Management apparatus of different countries official structures.

A change of name is required

Having a lot of different nationalities means having a lot of different styles of names. Some are relatively simple and some are complicated; but the same can be said of accents. A woman said to a friend of mine once:

"Oh, you have an accent" to which he replied
"Madam we all have accents it just depends where we are standing on the planet as to their uniqueness".

Names are very much like accents and in Africa there are a lot of names that seem unusual to me. Seems there are some foreign names which seem unusual to Africans and in this story, unworkable to a certain African man.

Meet a man who we will call Franklin who is an African, is in a position of considerable aviation importance, a king pin, a person on the cutting edge of the industry, in a word: an aviation God – anyway this is what he keeps telling himself and anyone else under his perceived reign. Actually he does know things; he just has an affliction about how he applies and delivers the knowledge.

Today Franklin is reviewing an official document which bears the names of the people responsible for the Air Operation. One of the names on the documentation is Asian and as is some Asian people's custom this Pilot's family name is actually two names, one name originates from his grandfather and one name from his great-grandfather.

Franklin is concentrating on this name. It seems really complicated, somewhat confusing, so in true Bi-Polar fashion he makes a suggestion. Would the Pilot consider *changing his family name,* you know, something simpler, just for the documentation – it would make everyone else's life easier. Yes, no bullshit!

Asian Pilot was not happy with this suggestion to eliminate his family's linage; Bi-polar Franklin continues, digging a deeper hole for himself by saying: "I feel it is a great idea and you should really have a serious think about it."

As Bi-polar Franklin is completely serious Asian Pilot is now losing his patience. The matter is finally calmed by the third person in the room. Franklin still works within the industry and still reveres himself among the Gods – in his own little world! God is a name as well…….., Franklin don't you dare try to change it!

Stop causing static

As aircraft flying through the air certain types of electricity can build-up on the airframe of the aircraft; the faster you fly the more the chance of electricity build-up. Different manufacturers deal with this phenomenon in different ways. In General Aviation (GA) aircraft Static Wicks are a common solution to this and one Internet definition for these items is:

Static wicks are long, thin extensions that are often attached to the outboard trailing edges of wings and horizontal and vertical stabilizers to dissipate the static electricity that can accumulate in flight.

Enter the Gippsland GA-8 Airvan. In my view it's ugly, slow and uncomfortable but hey that's just me. When an aircraft Type Certification is granted it basically covers everything which is in or on the aircraft. You can't just install any part you want on an aircraft, they need to be approved once approved you need to MOD (modification to original type certification) the aircraft if you want to change anything. The GA-8 Airvan was Type Certified without Static Wicks – because Gippsland have designed the airframe to dissipate electricity in other ways so it does not need them. It doesn't fly very fast anyway, so it's great for pilots building their hours because trips take longer.

Today, Bi-polar Franklin is on the apron undertaking the regular inspection of one company and their aircraft. He proceeds past each aircraft eventually getting to one of the company's GA-8 Airvans.

"Where are the aircraft's Static Wicks?"
"It doesn't have any, it's the way it was Type Certified."
"Ridiculous, all aircraft have Static Wicks."
"Yes all of the other aircraft on the apron do but you will note all of these aircraft types (Airvans) do not"
"You can't fly without Static Wicks it's unsafe and illegal. Make sure you get them installed and until then these three aircraft are grounded"

Grounding an aircraft is making a decision not to fly it. This can be done for a number of reasons by the Operator, the Maintenance provider, and of course the Aviation Authority. Grounding an aircraft when it is operational, legal and safe is called *stupidity*. I had a quick think about today's roadblock; yes they were almost daily with Franklin.

"I will need to get something from you in writing before I can do this."
"Nonsense, I have told you, that should be enough."
"I am afraid I am going to require a letter from you, otherwise all of these aircraft will fly today; it must be official."
"When I tell you, it's official."
"I'm sorry I need the letter."

There was a strained silence before he said he was returning to his office to prepare the letter. Not a great moment if this happens during a base inspection. Luckily for him he didn't write it because I would have sent the letter straight to his bosses with a bill for the loss the company would have incurred by it being unable to use three of their very legal and airworthy aircraft.

Having the Power

Aviation Batteries are expensive. As an example a Battery for the C208 Caravan can cost a company US$2200 per unit. In order to reduce wear on batteries some companies have what is known as a Ground Power Unit or GPU. These are much more powerful than the average aircraft battery and can be used to Ground Start an aircraft through a plug on the outside of the fuselage. They are manufactured on a little wheeled trolley which Ground Staff roll up to the aircraft plug in. Once the start is complete the staff member, at command of the pilot disconnects the unit and rolls it away.

The C208 Caravan has a procedure for this in the POH (Pilots Operating Handbook). One company purchased a GPU and was immediately told they could not use it as they had '*no approved procedure*'. It was pointed out the POH had been approved by the Authority and the procedure was within this manual.

'No, that's not good enough; you need to develop a separate procedure'

I'll give you one guess who is telling the company this and it starts with an "F", no it's not a swear word.........., well to be fair it could be. The GPU sat on the ground for 5 weeks awaiting approval. The procedure was submitted within three days but the first three submissions were rejected. The final submission gathered dust for the remaining period of time.

A short time after this the same company purchased a big water tank for washing aircraft. The company put the tank in a small trailer behind a company vehicle. Yep, you guessed it they apparently now needed a procedure for the new water trailer and how it was going to be used – nobody really understood this as the unit just CARRIED WATER. The company drained the tank and moved it on to the vehicle – apparently there was no procedure required for this.

I don't feel secure

Airport Security in any country is a pain – my thanks go out to Richard Reid and Osama Bin Laden for fucking up everyone's travel experience - for life.

Anyway, when you deal with airport security you need to be patient, even obedient or - you could just arrive in a wheel chair and skip the whole process; sorry only one country fits this description.

Having said this it is difficult to keep up with all the regulations even for the average security officer. Some of these average people quickly get the taste of power and they like it – you know like the sixteen year old, just got his license and Dad gets him a high performance car, more than he can handle but hey he'll work it out...eventually, let's just see how many he takes with him while that's happening.

The biggest problem with anyone in these positions is not the regulations but the training they receive on *interpreting those regulations*. In this particular African country the conditions are a hot, dry climate and temperatures most days reach 30-35C (90-100 F). We all need to stay hydrated but pilots here apparently also have to comply with the no containers of more than 100ml, so no water. Add to this a little item called a *Leatherman* an all-purpose utility tool which many charter pilots carry. This little unit has a screwdriver, knife, saw, and a dozen other things all housed in a system which is actually the handles for a pair of pliers – very useful for securing things, tightening screws, etc.

"Sorry new regulations you can't have water or carry something with a blade".
"Okay I'm keen, I'll play, why"?
"You could attempt to hijack the aircraft or try to kill the pilot".
"But I am the pilot".
"The other pilot"
"We fly single crew; I am the only pilot; and you already know this."
"It doesn't matter this is the new regulation, newly interpreted would be more like it, to prevent someone trying to bring the aircraft down".

"If I want to bring the aircraft down I could just push the control column forward until we crash or turn off the fuel supply to the engine."

At this point the security officer just stared at the person who was speaking; it seemed he had gone too far, crossed a line. Yes, he had either spoken too quickly or the words he had used were too big for this mental giant.

"No water and no Leatherman" was repeated again. Believe it or not this was the way the pilots in this country spent most of 2010, until someone within the established official apparatus who had some common sense realized what was going on and the whole thing was amended to allow flight crew what they needed.

There is a saying about 'paying peanuts and……..' sorry I can't remember the rest!

Don't Bank on it working

It is important when opening a bank account that you prove who you are. For a foreigner they must bring their passport, seems fair. Today a pilot we will call Brian is opening a Savings account but has failed to bring his Passport with him; naughty Brian. But it should be fine, Banks hire intelligent people after all they hold on to your money.

"I need your passport"
"Why"
"I need to make a copy of your passport"
"I already have an account here; you have a copy in the file"
"No I need another copy"
"Maybe just get the file and grab the copy, make a photocopy of that"
"I can't do that"
"Why"?
"Because then it wouldn't be an *original copy*."

Now Brian is confused, first he doesn't know what the hell she means by an *Original Copy*, and it seems his current copy is no longer valid and she needs to replace this.

Let me think….. 'You pay peanuts you get…….' I know it will come to me.

Blown away by the situation

Traditionally Governments are the ones who have the most weapons in a given country. I will not go in to too much detail on the United States and its gun policy but am pretty sure the U.S. Government still has more guns than their citizens, but not sure if either group is using them properly.

East Africa is a bit of a warm climate; in fact it can be a bit more than this. It had only happened once before, no not the heat, the small fire which started in the government explosives store in the city. Now why would you put an explosives store in the middle of a densely populated African city? Because it is Africa and maybe you wake up early one morning and need to get to your weapons. This might happen for any number of reasons which could include some errant General who stayed up later than you the night before finally deciding he is not happy with the way you are running the place and he feels he could do a better job; so the idea seems to be to keep the weapons within reach.

Nevertheless in 2009 the explosives store caught fire and in the aftermath the government investigation recommended it be relocated out of a populated area; makes sense. Seemingly someone lost the report, or forgot about it, and the ammunition store was rebuilt in the same location; maybe it was done at friend rates, you know they got a good deal.

Now, Paddy has just arrived and is looking for work in this country. He is staying with another pilot he worked with previously who already has a job with the company Paddy wishes to interview with. It is his first night and before he turns in fully he is reading a book, all the while he keeps hearing a distant thump and then can see the curtains move, you know like a little breeze just went through the room. The breezes continue at roughly one every half minute.

It's now nearing 10PM and everyone has been woken up and is on their way to the roof. Seems someone closer to the noise has made a phone call. Once on the roof they can see more clearly the 21km to the airport area which funnily is right next to where the explosives store is. It also seems for yet a second time the ammunition store has caught fire. For the last two or so hours shells have been raining down around the city and yes, straight on to the International Airport.

Being pilots they all found out later when it had started an unnamed British airline on a seven mile final approach to land was told to conduct a Missed Approach Procedure, not land, and fly immediately to their alternate destination. The Captain being so close to the runway was a little confused until he received the explanation regarding the munitions and the fire, said aircraft disappeared quite quickly. It took the government most of the night to get the fire under control and move the remaining ammunition out of harm's way. Seems only then did the shelling stop; thanks guys for the all night blast!

PS: The Government Explosives store was rebuilt – yes you guessed it, in the same location. Don't worry third times a charm.

You can look up these two occurrences up on the Internet

TAXES

I pay my taxes and I hope you do as well. Everyone should pay your fair share don't you think. I mean in America and Britain you even go so far as using your tax dollars to pay for stuff in other countries; well done.

So when you pay for stuff you kind of expect it to work, this also seems fair. Like the Police, they should do their jobs, enforce the law, solve crimes, makes sense.

Extinguish the graft

Paddy is not sure this East African country has got the memo on this one. Seems interaction with their Police involve a lot of backhanders, you know bribes. On this particular day Paddy was pulled over for speeding; he was doing 37 km/hr in a 50 km/hr zone.

"We pulled you over for speeding".

"But I wasn't speeding".

"We saw you driving *veryfast*".

"From where?"

"Over there, we were parked under the tree".

"So how fast was I going"?

"*Very* fast"

"Very fast is not a speed, show me on the speed camera".

There is a short silence followed by: "We don't have a speed camera".

Now Paddy is angry, because this is the way it always starts. You get pulled over for nothing and then they start looking for something *to get you with*. Now they start dissecting his car looking for a problem: Tail lights, Head lights, Flashers (indicators) it goes on and on, Tires, ah spare tire, no all okay. Seemingly they cannot find anything wrong with Paddy's car.

"Where is your Fire Extinguisher?"

"That is a new law and is only coming into effect in two months". Paddy explains.

"So you are saying you don't have one?" The Police Officerswere apparently sparkling.

"It's not the law yet". Paddy repeats knowing where the conversation is going.

"Confirm you don't have a fire extinguisher?"

"No I don't".

"I am afraid that is an offense, we will have to write a ticket".

Now most of us would just accept the ticket and then argue it later. But these Police don't work like this; they don't want to issue you a ticket, they want some cash, now. If you are uncooperative concerning your Police Benevolent Fund donation you get a free trip to the Police station; just while they sort out all the paperwork which will be required for this most heinous of crimes. You could sit there for hours while all of this happens; it is essentially a war of attrition, see who gives in first. Just remember, enjoy your driving experience in East Africa, and when you're there I am sure you will be fine(d)!

We can't come

In another country the Police in certain more remote areas have a slightly different take on things. This is a town which will remain unnamed, where crime does happen. It happens everywhere but at least here it is pettier than other places, lots of burglary (when you are not home) and the occasional robbery (when you are home). Either way you need to call the Police:

"Hi, my house was broken in to, I need the Police to come so I can open a case."

"Are they still there?"

Yes moron, I am calming speaking to you while the Robber is having a sandwich in the corner, he hasn't noticed me using the telephone.

"No they're not."

"We don't have a vehicle so we can't come."

So why ask if they're still here – for fucks sake!

"When are you going to have a vehicle?"

"Later."

"On a scale from now until my next birthday when will 'later' be?"

"It's your Birthday, I don't understand".

Okay, a short aside on Sarcasm

I forgot to mention, sarcasm doesn't really work with most of the people in the African countries which I have visited. Picture this:

You sit in a restaurant for a long time, without any offer of service. There is a waitress who knows you are there because you have been waving at her like people from an accident do when a Search and Rescue aircraft finally arrives. At this point your waving has interrupted her call so she decides to get off her mobile phone and come over to find out what you want - *it's a restaurant; yes, can I see a Doctor;* anyway the conversation could go something like this:

"Did you want to order"?

"No I was waving because I needed the exercise and the rest of them just wanted to sit down".

Her response: "Oh, Okay" and the she'll walk away – no bullshit.

Block the Law

Roadblocks are frequent depending on what African country you are in. At every roadblock there is a Stop sign roughly thirty meters from where the Police Officer is sitting. In one country they have a unique system. As you approach the Stop sign, the Officer is immediately on their feet waving for you to come to where they are; therefore you roll forward, through the Stop sign. Upon arriving next to them the conversation will start like this:

"Good morning, Officer"

"Good morning, you just drove through a stop sign, which is an offense. Can I see your Driver's License?"

Yeah I know it's a little game the Police play to throw you off balance before you even start speaking. Most of us shot the idea around a little because it happens to everyone. There are two solutions, I recommend number one.

1) Ignore the Police Officer, come to a full stop at the Stop sign and deal with the: "didn't you see me waving at you" conversation when you get there.

2) Roll forward and when he says you have committed an offense counter with. "But you are an Officer of the Law and I need to obey your instructions, if I had not proceeded over to you when you were waving at me I would be committing an Offense".

Power trips, the whole world is on them!

Required approval

In many African countries you require Government approval for pretty much everything; for them to do this they need to sign, stamp or issue something to you. Therein lies the problem – supplies. In order to do this Head Office, the Capitol, needs to send these outposts their supplies.

"You cannot proceed without it being stamped"

"So stamp it" to this the answers include:

"Ah but I have no ink for the stamp";

"Someone has taken the stamp and will only be back tomorrow";

"I am not authorized to stamp this. The one who is, is away on a course until next month".

Or:

"You need us to issue a letter, for you to proceed".

"Okay, can I wait?"

"We are waiting for the truck to arrive with the stationary".

"How long have you been waiting?"

"Two weeks".

"So what are you doing at work each day?"

"Waiting for the truck".

You can see how some of this might slow things down a bit.

INTERVIEWS

No one can deny education has become big business; it is now about selling the idea everyone needs a Degree, Diploma, or some other piece of paper of some kind before they can obtain a job.

Some elements of society believe in the idea that once you have these credentials *you have a right to a given job, you just need to apply.* This kind of thinking is retarded! I am not saying we all don't need employment, of course we do or how could we eat and function; but if it were our *right* what about the *rights* of the other five applicants, applying for the same job?

Now those pilots out there applying for work, please try to remember Airlines do not exist to *giveout jobs*; they are in business to make money and therefore employ people to function. So you need to win or earn any job you get above the other applicants, then show up for work each day and keep earningthe job, until you decide to move on. Therefore having a Commercial Pilot's License (CPL) is not a right of employment *it is a step toward you getting employment* – for the new pilots reading this who don't understand the concept maybe re-read this paragraph and let this sink in!

Most of these initial pilot jobs you actually need to show up in person. "Hi, here I am, looking for work as a pilot" is the approach. It is expensive, time consuming, and can be frustrating. You can sit at home in your underwear and send email after email; telling your friends how you are going to be a pilot in Africa – but in the end, sorry to say, you are not.

For some the visit to Lusaka, Windhoek, Maun, Dar Es Salam, Point Noire, Brazzaville, or Nairobi, to name a few, is enough of a wakeup call. After seeing these places some pilots back away indicating this type of flying, or lifestyle, is not for them. This decision is absolutely fine with the employers, as most pilots enter into a two year contract and companies would prefer to have people who want to be here; not ones who get the job and are looking for the first emergency exit they can find.

Now, picture you are here, in some African town or city, have an interview for 9AM but you never show up, you don't call to explain why, and when you are tracked down by the company are still in bed asleep – if you're an employer here you won't need much imagination for any of what I have just described. For foreign pilots this sort of behaviour is dealt with easily - pack your bags and go home. But seemingly in many places we are still required to hire the domestic pilot regardless of how many interviews they fail to show up for or the condition they are in when they finally make it.

Regardless of the person's nationality there have been many interviews over the years which have been, well - unique!

Rainy season is always fun

Mother's Day is more than once a year

One Chief Pilot (CP) met a local lady, mid-forties in his outer office making inquiries about pilot employment. The shrewd CP immediately determined the job was not for her, she said 'no it was for her son' - the immediate question 'so, why is he not here, in person?'

'Don't worry I am just here on business and so I thought I would drop the CV off for my son'. The Chief Pilot understood but asked 'when it would be possible for the young man to get off the couch and come up to the office?' The mother said she would organize it, thanks for the time.

Ten days later Mum was back in the office: 'Hi, how is it all going, just back in town on business any progress on the job'; this sort of thing. The CP was a little confused, 'where is your son?' Seems he was still at home - probably super glued to the sofa. 'He needs to come here, is that understood?' – 'Yes.'

Two weeks later the lady stopped by again and the CP was a little more direct with mother superior. 'Absolutely no discussion of anything (including the weather) until this young man presents himself for his interview.' She was a little shocked, showed genuine surprise; 'what's the problem I am just making inquiries.' Fortuitously at that moment a young local lad popped his head through the door:

"I'm looking for the Chief Pilot; it's about a job as a pilot."
"Yes mate, come in and sit down I'll be right with you." was the response.

The CP turned to see the lady just as she went bright red and started yelling:

"NO, NO, NO, my son's CV was here first. Why are you talking to him; my son gets first chance at the job."

Seems she had already decided it was *her son's job*. The poor kid who walked through the door said he could come back later if now was a bad time. The CP told him to sit down, it was a great time, don't go anywhere he just need to deal with a <u>nagging problem</u>. All the time he was walking over to the front door which was promptly opened.

"Out, you need to leave now" was communicated to the Mother. My understanding was she actually refused to leave the office; yes, seems she was going to stay for this young lad's interview, if you can believe it. The CP pointed out he was on the verge of throwing her son's CV in the rubbish bin if she did not vacate the premises. She dragged her feet to the door saying *she would be back* to which the CP replied:

"No you won't because if you come back I will call the Police."

She looked confused; the CP went on to point out she had no business with the Charter Company; she was not booking a flight nor was she asking for employment for herself. Any further visit to the office would constitute *harassment* and could be dealt with legally. She hesitated at the door before the CP used the phrase:

"Keep going, and keep that little backside of yours moving, I am not kidding."

Apparently she was not used to such language and this moment may have constituted a new beginning judging by the facial expression which was described. Apologies were made to the young man who remained regarding the woman's outburst.

Look going for an interview can be stressful and I am sure this little scene did not help this young lad's moment, but at least he actually showed up. The lady's son did eventually get off the couch, managing to get work with another company, seemingly avoiding his Mother's preferred choice; which CP indicated he was grateful for.

Did you land the job?

Just because you actually have a Commercial License does not automatically mean you can fly safely. Yes I can see you thinking about it, what the hell is he talking about? Anyone who has recently completed their schooling or any course knows we are working on a new system, a 21st Century system. Not the system which most of us worked on twenty, thirty, or forty years ago. Students who are - well crap at what they do - are pushed through the system. You know something to say they were there but couldn't produce anything which actually appeared on the quantifiable grading scale. They can't fail them, it just wouldn't be fair; yeah but this system is only at grade school, right.

Wrong, enter the Flight School, a profit making entity; hey this is what they're in business for – funny I thought it was to train pilots. There are a few Flight schools out there which are the modern day version of the *do over* and, so we are clear I am not limiting this to African Flight schools.

A pilot fails a particular Flight exam and he is given more training so he can pass the next time. Fair, I don't have a problem with this, happened to me a couple of times. Don't worry nothing too serious, I was having an issue with landing the aircraft, nothing which might be important to continued passenger survival; I'm better now, promise.

When I say "do over" I am not speaking about the follow up training which I received I am speaking of a pilot who has consistently failed a particular exercise eight, ten, or twelve times and is still allowed to continue to try without being *independently assessed.* When eventually the pilot gets it, he moves on until, a couple of exercises down the line, the whole process repeats itself. This is great for the school as they get additional funds with all the extra training. The problem is if you give anyone enough tries at something they will eventually pass the Test, it's a numbers game. If this transpires throughout their training they will end up with a License – makes you feel confident inside doesn't it? Don't worry too much about Commercial air operations as they can spot these License holders pretty quickly.

Along comes a pilot we will call Amir a budding aviator born and bred in his country of employment. Not only is Amir an incredibly nice guy, he is not part of the group of idiots I mentioned before who think they are owed a job. He shows up for work punctually and well presented, he is polite and well spoken, and he gets along with his fellow pilots both foreign and domestic. When he is cruising around in an aircraft he operates it well, his only problem seems to be he cannot fly the thing anywhere close to the ground – yes takeoffs and landings are terror moments for Amir and his Training Captains.

Now this is a bit of a problem for the company as they fly what is known as Single Crew operations – only one pilot in the aircraft – so the company is working Amir toward the moment he will be flying on his own. No problem, he is a real catch regarding all of his other qualities; let's just do a little additional training.

All companies do what is known as Line Training; this is done to familiarize the new pilot to the company's routes, clients and other general operational requirements. Sometimes people are employed who have not flown for a while so they need to be brought up to speed – recurrence training. Every once in a while we have *an Amir type* and if the rest of the package is there the company will put a little extra training toward this to bring him up to speed. But you budding pilots out there should understand we are not Training organizations, you are a pilot with a recognized License so you should be able to operate an aircraft – basic skills at least.

Amir was all of this until he was adding power for the take-off roll or 50 feet above the runway during landings, at those two moments you could not speak to him. Normally a pilot would have their left hand on the Control column and their right on the Throttle. One day Amir's Training Captain grabbed his Throttle hand pulled it back and let go. The hand just dropped down to his side, limp, and Amir did not change expression or look around; basically he was catatonic. All of this was particularly frustrating for his three different Training Captain's. Normal Line Training is done in 30-50 hours; for Amir this figure was a distant memory. He was now starting to become a financial burden to the company; a decision needed to be made.

He was sent at company expense for external assessment to see if what the Training Captains were experiencing was reality. The report back was he was at a satisfactory PPL (Private Pilot License) level; Amir confidently reports back he was *satisfactory*, seems this is all he heard, seems he may need a hearing test as well as flying lessons. Unfortunately for Amir his standard could not be improved and he departs the company, sorry for that.

Six months later another company approaches and asks informally about Amir, they are considering employing the young man.

"He can't fly" is the direct response.

"But he seems like a nice guy."

"He is a nice guy, very passionate about flying, would make a good addition to your company. I really like him".

"So"?

"He can't fly; sorry there is no polite way to say it. If you are looking to fill a position other than a pilot, take him".

They employ young Amir; three months later, the same person approaches the previous company. "I agree you're right he can't fly".

At this point he had done an additional 35 hours of Line Training and although they said he was *better* on take-offs his landings were abysmal – train wreck territory.

All I can say is applause for the Aviation Training organizations who have practiced this sort of thinking in the past, I hope it was worth it for your bottom line.

Note: Some countries Civil Aviation Authorities have now noted this trend and insist on an Independent Assessment when a student fails exams multiple times. Having said this the respective Authority should not need to get involved – we are professionals and as such should have self Regulated this issue long ago.

I'm on the Europass(port)

One gentleman showed up and told his interviewing company he was French, no problem there, but it was noted from his CV (Resume) he was born in Germany to which, when asked he replied 'Yes'. Further digging was done regarding him being French which culminated in the question:

"Which passport do you hold?"

"An EU one."

"But what country is marked on it?"

"German"

"But you said you are French."

"Yes but I have lived in France for the last six months, so I am French."

It was pointed out this is not really the way it works; but no further explanation was offered. Okay being misleading at your initial interview has always rung *alarm bells* with me, but to each their own.

The interview continues and stops again this time concerning the aircraft the applicant is legally allowed to operate; his aircraft Types he is rated on. His CV lists a Cessna C208 Caravan unfortunately his pilot's log book does not reflect this rating or any hours on the aircraft. When asked about this he says he used to fly with another pilot who did Skydiving runs on weekends at which point the explanation stops. There are several seconds of awkward silence. The company interviewing the man then asked: "And, your Type Rating, when did you get it and where is it signed off".

Another period of silence and no explanation is offered. There is almost a full minute of silence before Captain Germany feels the need to speak. His story is he used to go along for the ride and once all the skydivers had left the aircraft, the pilot flying would let our friend have control of the aircraft during the descent; not let him land, just glide down. He said to his interviewer 'I gained valuable experience during these moments'. It was pointed out no matter how much experience he had gained as a pilot he cannot legally fly the aircraft therefore he should probably not put it on his CV. He seemed to think it was okay and said he was going to leave it there – the alarm bells had disappeared and cathedral bells were ringing!

At the time of the interview it was April and hiring season had almost finished, the interviewer suggested our friend come back in November, yes they were getting rid of him; the very next day Mr. Germany returned to enquire if anything had changed.

"You mean since yesterday?"

"Yes."

"I'm sorry, what did I speak about regarding us hiring."

"You said November."

"Well we are still in April; so as long as we understand each other and No - we are still not hiring."

Two days later he was back – "Any changes, I am available?"

"Yes thanks for the heads up, but No."

He came back the next day as well, and when he came two days after this he was told not to return again, even in November. This was the last time the company ever saw him!

Local pilots first

Always a sensitive area because, for our purposes the perception is a foreign pilot has come to another's country and is denying them the ability to have a job. For this I completely agree, if there is a suitable domestic candidate the person should be offered employment ahead of all other candidates. Everyone please focus on the word *suitable* as it is very important. As Amir unfortunately demonstrated if you cannot do the entire job – then you cannot do the job. So being available is not really the point.

For our story, our Local Pilot who we will name Kg has worked for three years within his own country – Botswana, bush flying, and is now looking to progress, larger aircraft and such. He glances around and realizes the opportunities at home are limited. Well, let's strike out and go overseas, so off to Zambia he treks – this decision now makes Kg a *foreign pilot* in another person's country; something he fails to immediately grasp.

At the interview everything looks good, his hours and experience are right, hey he's not Zambian but he is African, a good look for the company. The company is happy, and he

278

is hired - you can start as soon as your papers go through the Zambian labour process. Kg promptly submits his papers and waits; and waits, and waits, and then he says, just going to go back to his home country and wait there, less expensive.

Kg is seen in his old town of employment – waiting! He is asked how the Zambian job is going; he said it would be great if he could get the Zambian Labour Department to issue his Work & Residence permits. Kg actually states: 'I really understand what all you guys have to go through'; several pilots are now laughing at Kg – shoe on the other foot and all. But in his defence he says in Zambia it is different, as the country does not produce enough local pilots so they need to employ foreigners. To which it is pointed out his own country does not produce enough local pilots and Kg needs to wake up.

So, it's only unfair when it affects you – very mature!

Like Father, like Son

One evening a Chief Pilot who we will call Graham, was working late and just grabbed a ringing telephone as he was about to leave the office. The caller wanted to speak to the Chief Pilot about applying for a flying position with his company. As Graham started answering the caller's questions he got a funny feeling, just in the wording of what was being asked.

"Just confirm you are applying for this position, you are not calling on someone's behalf?"

"It's for my son."

"Okay, why isn't he calling me?"

"He's not very good on the telephone."

"So he has trouble operating a telephone and you would like me to consider giving him a job where he is responsible for an aircraft worth US$150,000."

"It's not really fair if you put it like that."

Yes this guy actually said this! Graham wasn't sure what other way to put it, but he continued the call answering all of the questions for the overly protective father who also offered up the two of them would be flying in to Maun in two weeks. Knowing where this might lead Graham spoke slowly so the man could understand.

"Whatever you do, if your son comes to apply for a job, you don't come. Your son shows up for the interview but not you."

The rules firmly established and everything agreed, the conversation finished. A few weeks later, the call long forgotten, a father and son entered the outer office, introductions all round. Graham noted the dynamic immediately and asked the elder of the two did he phone a few weeks before. 'Yes' was the answer and Graham opened the front office door and bid the father out, thanks for stopping by maybe go and get a coffee across the road, we will be about 30 minutes - your son and I. No, the father insisted on staying; it was strongly suggested this would not be the best course of action. The father further insisted, and in the end, Graham gave in; conducted the interview during which the boy answered <u>one question</u> on his own and managed to ask one as well. A good effort considering how much Dad talked. In the end the father asked:

"So what are my son's chances of a job with your company?"
"None..........I didn't interview him I interviewed you and you are not applying."

Graham then turned to the boy and said:

"Don't let your father do this at any of the other companies or you really will never get a job."

Then Graham turned back to the father and apologized for his mother's absence in the room. The father looked at Graham a bit bewildered and asked:

"Why would your mother need to be here?"
"I don't know for the same reason you felt it necessary to come with your son. Good bye."

Do you know they both appeared at all of the companies in Maun as Father and Son; before departing in their aircraft back to South Africa – you guessed it, no job!

Attention all applicants – maybe leave the parents at home!

Hate the world

Now those were the pilots, but have you have ever had to deal with someone in a key management position was just, well, an asshole?

Let's be clear, I am not talking about someone who is difficult, or tough on people – this is just part of life. I am also not speaking about a person who you've decided you don't like because they said NO to something you wanted. Remember 'No' is the other half of the Yes/No dynamic; if you are willing to accept a Yes then you have to take the No when it comes; it's disappointing but it is life – so grow up if you think like this.

The Asshole I am speaking of is a person who is truly angry at the world and is going to ensure they impart their anger on as many people as they can - regularly. They normally know more than everyone else, often called an opinion, and nothing they ever do is wrong. I have often wondered what it is like to live in their special little place where perfection exists.

Meet a guy we will call Dirk, aka Captain Angry, who has amassed years of flying time in addition to many hours of Flight Instruction. Dirk would best be described as tall, is solid, but not fit, or indeed fat – just a big lump of human debris. He mumbles a lot and has what would best be described as a short fuse when dealing with people.

For the uninitiated a Flight Instructor is one of the people you seek out who is legally approved to train people to fly; he is a teacher just like you would have had in University or your kids have in school. Unfortunately for his students Dirk has a slightly different teaching style than you may be used to. His style involves a lot of yelling, some swearing, and any number of lectures all while you are still operating the aircraft. Each flight sortie is usually followed with a long debrief, which is delivered as a lecture, of how disappointed he is with your flying, how he sees no promise for you even if you were to continue, and he often sends you home having asked the never ending question – 'do you think this is the correct profession for you, have a long think about it'?

I am sure he was doing this was to build the pilots resolve - or maybe not. I have always found when I am trying to learn something people yelling tends to throw me a bit; but maybe I'm just too sensitive?

We could also consider the possibility that Dirk is correct in the idea the person he is training is rubbish. Regrettably for all, this behaviour unfolds ninety percent of the time he gets in to a cockpit with a pilot. Add to this in his aircraft people of colour tend to take additional flak which is not dispensed on their white co-workers. Nothing racial is ever spoken, just a harder standard imposed; this is obviously done to ensure no riff-raff slip through, or coloured riff-raff maybe?

During one instructional moment the white pilot undertaking his type training was at an airstrip and Dirk was demonstrating a safety feature on a Cessna 210. He selected Gear Up (on the ground) to show how the Squat Switch would prevent the Gear from retracting. The Squat Switch is a device which detects the aircraft gear is resting on the ground; once in the air the switch releases allowing the gear to retract. So the idea is if Dirk selects gear up the switch will save the day.

On the day in question the switch didn't work and the aircraft promptly dropped on its nose damaging the propeller. An Aviation Authority representative came for the required inspection and found the aircraft did not have a valid Certificate of Maintenance. It had completed all the maintenance checks and been released to fly, they had just forgotten to put the piece of paper in to say it was so; seems the Dirk had forgotten to check this document. So just an unfortunate series of mistakes, they happen; it's understandable.

This was fine right up until Dirk instructed the poor guy training on the aircraft to write up the incident report – you know report it as *his* failure to check the paperwork and *him* damaging the aircraft. When this rather unfair instruction was rejected by the pilot, Dirk went on a bit of a verbal rampage. He ordered the training pilot to take full responsibility and do the required paperwork immediately; you know the bully method. Luckily the pilot involved had some balls; eventually all of the paperwork was returned to its rightful owner; but it does say a lot about a person when they do this to someone.

Fast forward eighteen months and Captain Angry is now working for another company as Chief Pilot which also means he undertakes interviews with new pilots looking for work. Seems these pilots are returning from their interviews with stories of odd behaviour. The conversation usually starts with the person being told their hours are too low for any possible employment – for most of them this would have been true, but Captain Angry then goes on to tell the candidate:

"Look with these hours you don't have a fucking chance….., you have wasted your time and money coming up here…., I don't know why you have even bothered…., not very well thought out by you, etc…….."

Now I am a big advocate of being honest, people should know the truth; don't candy coat stuff, it's really unfair to those involved to waste their time. But being direct does not mean you have to crush the person's spirit and step all over their dreams. Be direct but be professional as well.

Regrettably after a conversation like this there was also no offer from Captain Angry of any sort of advice of what the candidate could do to improve his/her job prospects. In addition the beat down was not finished for this was normally when he then would either drop their CV in the trash or tear it in half – in full view of the applicant!

Please understand this dickhead is not representative of our industry and this sort of behaviour is reprehensible to anyone looking for work. It also paints the company involved in a less than flattering manner, but this was really the Company's problem.

Captain Angry's attitude got so bad with one of his pilots he refused to train him on the next aircraft and the pilot's company had to seek approval for another company to do his Line Training. I can assure you it had nothing to do with the fact the pilot had some colour in his skin. The guys who did end up training this poor guy decided as a bit of a joke on a more positive training utensil to show when he wasn't getting it. They laminated picture of Dirk and would show it to Training guy each time he fucked up – the initial reaction was in the form of a punch - but after this it was all laughter.

On a happy note this social moron has now left us, and peace has returned to the Realms; I am sorry for the people he works with now wherever it is – good luck and thanks for taking him off our hands

Making a Connection

As a final word of attempting to get a job I would like to say the following. Some of the thinking I have witnessed over the years regarding getting a job as a pilot has been special. Aviation is a very competitive industry so getting your foot through the door anywhere can be tough. But as they say if it were easy then everyone would be doing it. It takes grit, tenacity, knowledge and if you have the right connections this doesn't hurt either.

Enter the <u>aviation moaners</u>! These are the people who are unwilling or unable to make those special connections with the people who make employment decisions at a given airline. So they sit around, complaining 'the system is rigged' and 'it's not fair', or my all-time favourite 'I am a better pilot than Fred and he only got the job because he knows someone.' So my question to these sort of people is:

If you were standing next to another pilot better qualified for the position than you but you had a connection to someone in the company *would you stand aside and let them have the job or would you use your connection*? Yeah, you wouldn't be standing aside; so maybe just try being an adult about the whole process, network a bit better and most importantly stop moaning your way through your career – it's not a good look.

EMPLOYMENT

A little about successfully getting a flying job; okay you did it, you're now employed - well done. But a job is not yours for life is it? So let's talk about employment politics as well as those employees who feel they can't be fired or now they have the job, just don't care about their work!

It's my life!

So you are 20 odd years old, are a freshly employed pilot in your country of birth obviously somewhere in Africa. It's your first aviation job, the initial hurdle, and you are now flying, and getting paid a reasonable wage; a very good wage compared to those you went to school with who do not fly.

You fly six days a week and have one day off. Why, because this is the way the contract was presented to you when you read and agreed to sign it? You know, the moment when you take responsibility for your actions and behave like an adult. So what about the other companies, no they also operate the same way so your company is no different.

Six months in the complaining starts from the pilot, well it started sooner but six months is when the company becomes aware of it. 'I don't like the terms and conditions of the document I signed' – no body forced you to sign it sunshine? 'I want more time off'; the company's response is basically No, everyone is doing the same job, if you don't like the work you can resign. This pilot elects to continue but adopts a new, more personalized working system; they aren't well, yes very sick, so sorry can't possibly come to work it would not be safe for the passengers. But maybe they are really ill; no, most of these illnesses occur the day before or after their off day – the result, a double day off. Pretty soon the company has noted this pattern and calls the pilot in for a chat. No it is just a coincidence the pilot assures them, nothing to worry.

More time goes by and more coincidences occur, the company is losing patience. But now an important event has come up for the pilot and they need to take some time off. This time off works for the company, so one month unpaid leave is arranged. Upon returning the pilot indicates they need a further one month's unpaid leave. The company says 'sorry, No, no more time off'. The pilot insists, and the company puts their foot down, you can work in accordance with your contract or you can choose to go. The pilot goes, yes, they go straight to the Labour Department and file an unfair dismissal case against the company.

I know, I agree, that terrible awful company not giving their employee the time they needed. Not allowing the employee the ability to disregard the terms and conditions of their contract and do as they please. The company who is now being taken to a Labour Court with the very same contract the pilot refuses to adhere to – it's tragic. Well it is tragic for one of these two parties if they think the world operates like this.

This pilot has since found employment elsewhere. Yes, the complaining started almost immediately for that company as well. I guess it is life as they know it!

Happy Birthday

In one country a Pilot has been working for the company for almost six months. Today he is staying in camp on an overnight. He is due to fly out four guests the following morning. He is in a great mood as he has arrived early afternoon and is unlikely to fly any more that day; add to this it's also his Birthday – Happy Birthday buddy!

On this note he immediately tucks into the bar, its celebration time. Beer, one, two, three, hell let's take some back to the room. He reappears for dinner a bit unsteady but still functional, you know on a Dudley Moore type level - look him up. The Camp Manager has noted this and has a quiet word with the Pilot, 'No', our pilot is not having any of this 'it's my Birthday' – he continues drinking.

His passengers are watching his behaviour and asking questions of the Lodge's Manager. Add to this one of the Company's senior staff is staying in the camp as well and is watching the whole show – Oops!

287

The Manager made his decision the night before to send another aircraft with a new pilot. Breakfast arrives the following morning, the birthday boy does not appear. The guests are in the vehicle to depart to the airstrip, as the vehicle is driving away from the Lodge the pilot appears still dressing and runs after the vehicle. He is then informed of the change in schedule.

Strangely this pilot became unemployed shortly after this overnight and with his new free time then made inquiries at the Labour Department regarding his dismissal – if you can believe it? The Labour officers indicated he had absolutely no case and was lucky his Commercial License was not suspended or even revoked based upon his behaviour.

Just remember once you have successfully got a job and are employed try to come to work each day and keep earning it – the job is not yours for life!

I can't make it

Kg, who was a great lad, a few teething problem in the beginning but every pilot has those. He joins the company and is off; completes his two year contract which is all the company ever asks; just fulfil the obligations of what you signed to do. At the end of two years barring serious disciplinary concerns you will be offered the option of a third year flying our biggest aircraft, the Cessna Caravan (C208B). This offers young pilots a form of progression to a larger aircraft, their initial Turbine time - Turbo Prop, and will normally give them between 600-700 additional hours in their log book.

Kg has moved on to his third year and is doing well until halfway through the season, he stumbles; he fails to show up for a flight. In addition, he doesn't call the company to let them know he can't make it – maybe no credit for his mobile? The Company calls him repeatedly, the phone rings but, no answer. Now this is a serious concern as we fly single crew operations and as such expect people to be self-reliant, dependable, and act in a manner befitting a senior pilot – you know, setting examples for the junior ones.

Kg shows up the next day; no explanation, but he is ready to go to work. Management waits all day for him to enter the office and present himself for a suitable explanation regarding his previous day's absence; nothing. Kg goes home and he is phoned to come and see Management.

"Can't we do it tomorrow as I am already home, I don't want to come back to the office?"
"No, now please, be here in twenty minutes".

He shows up forty-five minutes later (apparently Management don't run his life).

"Where were you yesterday?"
"Sick"
"So sick you couldn't pick up the telephone."
"Apparently." Is pushed out while Kg looks at his nails – maybe he's bored.

Now I can see you managers out there contemplating what you might say to someone who was behaving this way, dismissive and uninterested in the conversation. The conversation continued inquiring if everything was all right, any problems at home or something the company might help with, etc. Nope all good Kg just didn't feel up to coming to work yesterday and did not see why he needed to tell anyone; the meeting finished.

The following morning he was handed a letter to appear the next day for a disciplinary hearing and the day after this he was given a written disciplinary warning for his file; one step of a few toward unemployment. Cited was his failure to inform the company he would be unable to make the flight and gross insubordination regarding the entire matter. Kg improves and everyone is happy, seems the letter has motivated him. November arrives and his contract is coming to an end on the 31st Dec.; he indicates he might want to stay on for the following year if possible but would like to be a part time pilot. Seems Kg is starting his own business with the help of the government. The company is very interested, no problem, it can be done, but they need to discuss the details later.

December 22nd arrives and the Company is getting its Christmas rush. Kg is due to fly, he doesn't show up which essentially screws the company; another pilot is pulled in from his day off. The 23rd he does it again, the Chief Pilot talks about calling him in for a disciplinary hearing – "yeah but if we do this we lose him for the next seven days", so the company starts scheduling around him on the chance he might not show up, scheduling back up aircraft and he gets the smallest flying days.

Remarkably he shows up for the 24th through the 29th, nobody speaks about his two day disappearance - including him. He has two days left and he doesn't show up for either of them, no explanation and no phone call. He is not seen for a week, eventually one of the pilots finally comments on his absence when they see him in town, his response "I didn't feel like showing up, so what, what are they going to do fire me?" What a great attitude from anyone let alone someone who can barely grow hair on their face.

Kg is gone, but we see him again in April, he drifts into the office for a chat; the subject he had come to speak about: 'when can I start flying for the company part time, you know like we discussed.' But Kg you already did your part time flying - at the end of your contract – no thanks and good bye. You have got to be kidding.

BEHAVIOUR

Many of us strive to behave correctly; sadly not all of us succeed. We start out with the best of intentions and then somewhere down this path because of whatever variable (humour, alcohol, poor decision making) we move in a direction we should not have, it's called being human!

Being Down

So there are two pilots, Andre and Mark, who are out for a few drinks one evening. They have been to a couple of places and now decided to stop by a place called 'Star Bar'. This is a local watering hole which could be described as an off license or bottle store. Essentially you buy your alcohol and disappear home or you can sit at one of the picnic type tables outside and enjoy the sounds of African music which blare from the establishment. In short the place is very basic but still a lot of fun.

While ordering Mark receives a rather unexpected hug from behind. They both turn to find a familiar face they regularly see at their local supermarket. He doesn't work at the market officially he just shows up there every day and helps customers pack their shopping and carry it to their car. None of us have taken the time to learn the young man's name and he is a nice guy with a never ending smile, so we occasionally we give him a tip. The reason I think many of us help him is he has Down syndrome and most people have adopted the concept 'there by the grace of God, but do go I'.

Now as we do not know his name some of the pilots refer to him as 'The Down guy' or things to this effect, nothing mean just a way to identify him. For this story we will call the young man DS (sorry but he does need a name).

So it is now post hug and DS is, as usual, grinning away and asking if someone can buy him a beer. The two sort of look at each other and then at the lady behind the bar who shakes her head to show her disapproval of the idea. Mark gets the young man a Coke instead and they step outside to a table. DS shows up some minutes later and throws the now empty Coke can at Mark and Andre's table.

"I WANT BEER"! Is shouted at the two of them.

They sort of look at each other before DS finally gives up and disappears. Ten minutes later they see DS who has somehow located a beer. DS then spots one of the female patrons and convinces her he would like to dance, which request she obliges. DS dances holding the lady at a respectful distance but as time goes on, and maybe the beer sinks in, he starts to get closer. Then DS's hands start to wander and as they do the woman corrects their position. But as time passed it seemed she couldn't keep up quickly enough as like most of us DS has two hands. Shortly after this the dancing stops rather abruptly when DS progressed his hands alternately from her Ass to her very large Breasts. DS realised this was as far as he was going to get let out a high pitched giggle before running into the darkness.At least DS seemed to have fun, even though he was still a little Down. Sorry, maybe too far!

Having a shit.......flight!

The only difference between a big airliner and the kind of aircraft we fly is the queue for the toilet. We just don't have a queue simply because we don't have toilets. Passengers are warned the time to 'go' is before take-off and after landing and strictly nowhere in between, and we can't just pull over.

I was told, in early 2002-3, one intrepid pilot whose nationality is a mystery to me was flying between Livingstone Airport and Maun Airport. Basically this is an international flight which must be done between two approved entry/exit points for the customs and immigration formalities.

As the pilot flew along he could feel the pitch of the aircraft change, a sure sign that weight was moving around the aircraft. He looked around to see the big American who had chosen to sit in the back of the cabin slowly making his way forward. The following conversation ensued:

"Scuse me son, but where is the shitter (toilet) on this thing?"

"I am sorry sir, but as I mentioned when we were in Zambia there is no break for the toilet until we arrive in Botswana, 39 minutes from now."

"Well, I can tell you I don't think I am going to make it."

With this he hastened back to his seat. The next thing the pilot and three other passengers were aware of was the waft of pure, unadulterated excrement and the unmistakeable accompanying sound effects. The pilot looked around to see what the hell was going on and was greeted by the sight of this guy with his trousers around his ankles using a plastic bag as an in-flight porta-potty.

Owing to the nature of the emergency the aircraft was immediately diverted to an airstrip so his business could be completed in a little more privacy. For this his fellow travellers were very grateful. The aircraft was on the ground about 25 minutes but when the time came to board again one person was missing; who should it be but the man's wife. The mystery was short lived as the pilot located the woman who had grabbed hold of one of the propeller blades and was in the throes of squat pissing (picture it in your head) in front of the aircraft.

The nationality of these two travellers – I can't even say Americans as it would be unkind to the remainder of the country who have obviously been toilet trained; they were from Alabama. If this is the kind of thing which goes on in Alabama I think I might just give it a miss.

Save the Children

Now, I should warn you the following was not my finest hour regarding what would be considered polite behaviour. I feel no need to see someone and then immediately attack them over some perceived social infraction – unfortunately not everyone thinks this way. On this day I felt attacked and as it didn't seem it was going to stop rather than take the mature route and walk away I chose a more direct path.

The Buffet, a simple way for a large Hotel to supply food to their guests. Welcome to CSL (Chobe Safari Lodge) a very large establishment for tourism in Kasane in northern Botswana. I have noticed this evening they are serving a number of things but one of my favourites is their stir-fried noodles. As part of the buffet CSL provide raw vegetables,

293

meat, raw noodles, and any number of sauces and other spices. Basically you build your own Stir-Fry and hand it to a Chef who quick fries it on a hot plate. Now when I have this dish, I don't really have anything else as it is pretty filling and the fact that everything was raw a few moments before reminds me of the healthier aspects of Asian cooking.

So I have grabbed a dinner plate and I am standing in the queue (line) behind a lady. My turn has come and I start loading up my plate. At a certain point I become aware the lady in front of me has stopped and is staring at me. I smiled and said hello and the response she gave me was really not what I was expecting.

"Oh my God, are you kidding me"!
This was said with complete disgust as she looked directly at my dinner plate.
"Excuse me"?
"Do you think you have enough food, maybe you'd like to leave some for the rest of Africa"?

Initially, I was a bit struck for words. I looked at the plate, yes it wasn't a small portion but, in my view, it was none of her business. She then just turned and moved forward in the queue to get her meal. I stood there for about fifteen seconds and the other pilot I was with burst out laughing.

To describe the woman, she would have been mid-forties, about five foot two, had a stomach - we all have one but you get the idea, and was wearing spandex shorts which in my opinion didn't look her size. I moved up to close the gap and handed over my plate to the Chef. I was still shaking my head and was even prepared to just let it be but she was not. Roughly two minutes later she turned and gave me a really dirty look; like you would get from someone if they caught you picking your nose or had your hand down your pants. My mute behaviour sort stopped there.

"So you're just going to keep going are you"?
"Yeah, if I want. That was rather *piggish behaviour*, don't you think"?

Piggish, and with this comment something in me sort of snapped. The guy I was with said later he wasn't sure if I was going to hit her. But my feeling is words are much more powerful than any physical damage one can do. I decided to elevate my voice for this return fire moment.

"Look fatty, as if it's any of your business this is my only trip up here and this is my dinner. What are you on trip number three or four"?

She didn't react to this but I continued as if she had.

"Three is it. It's a bit hypocritical to get small plates and make multiple trips up here to give the appearance you're on some sort of Save the Children moment and then jump all over me because of my choices. American or Canadian"?

Now she was bright red and several people had stopped to gawk at our rather unusual conversation. At this point I actually didn't care anymore and was in full verbal combat mode.

"I'm Canadian"

She barely got this information out. I got the impression she was used to saying whatever she wanted and no one challenging her over it. Clearly by the expression on her face she was having an awkward moment with me.

"Originally, or did you fall over the border for the cheap Meds? Actually, it doesn't really matter where you come from because you have failed to look in the mirror recently or you might have noticed you aren't exactly tiny. What are you going with: big boned or is it an affliction? I don't buy any of that bullshit. People are fat because they eat too much, this includes you. If that's their choice good for them I don't have a problem with it. But neither you nor I are exactly thin, so don't stand here and pass judgement on me when you have skittered up here three times and its evident you didn't get your stomach overnight".

With this the Chef had finished cooking my Stir-Fry and handed the plate back to me. Obviously my fellow pilot had fled the scene. I glanced around and upwards of two dozen people were looking in our direction. As I walked away I smiled and said in my nicest voice."I really hope you enjoy your holiday".

This bed is Shit

Some clients have medical conditions and others have fetishes; at times these two subjects seem to overlap. There was a couple from Argentina; he was a grandpa of 70 and she was a stunningly beautiful woman in her mid-twenties. A case of what we cynics might call true love. What usually happens when people come to a camp is they go off early morning on a drive or other activity and this is when the housekeeping staff can get down to work. On this particular morning the staff had been cleaning this couple's room when they found something they felt might be beyond their normal responsibilities.

They sought the manager's involvement as the situation had entered the bizarre. The manager appeared and the bed sheets were pulled back to reveal a rather impressive pile of shit concealed under the covers. It was put down to the elderly gentleman, probably an accident. The instructions were to clean it up as soon as possible and no further discussion would be necessary.

The next night Captain Crap made a further deposit in his bed and then bid the camp staff goodbye. The couple moved on to the next camp, where he continued to make daily deposits – probably thought he was sleeping in a bank vault. He stayed in three camps belonging to the same operation, which makes a total of six nights with six separate deposits. There was a box for staff tips and you would have thought maybe he might have left housekeeping something, but no, he didn't. What a shitty thing to do!

Being Green

Most of the people who come here are not what one might term Environmentalists. They have come to enjoy the Wilds and the animals. In the past occasionally you would fly one of those true environmentalists, people who are often referred to as Greenie's. The ones who recycle everything, have a solar farm for their house rather than buy electricity, bike pretty much everywhere – you get the picture. If any of you are reading this it's all fine, not a problem. Then along comes the aggressive environmentalist, the one that needs to comment on every aspect of *your life* just to show *you* how much *you* are fucking up the planet.

In 2005, Steve had one of these people and the guy had just arrived off his International Flight from the UK via Johannesburg. They had made it as far as the aircraft before our Green English friend decided to let Steve know his feelings. He looked at the aircraft:"Do you know how much fuel one of these aircraft burns per hour"?

So you all understand, I would feel really uncomfortable with a pilot who didn't know how much fuel their aircraft burned. This sort of ignorance could get someone killed. Steve responded as only Steve would.

"Is this a trick question"?
"No, it's not, it is a disgrace. You pilots fly around here polluting the atmosphere when you are supposed to be supporting the environment, it's kind of hypocritical".

Most of you know this but for you people who think this way - we provide a transportation service. A pilot could hardly be considered anywhere near being an environmentalist even if he is employed to do work in a wildlife area. After all our very job involves the constant burning of petro-chemicals, so it would be unlikely we could be considered as a recruiting demographic for the Green Party. Just so we are clear, that's also not to say we pilots are here to rape the planet either.

Steve asked him where he was from and then went into a detailed description of how much pollution Mr. Greenie from the UK had created to get his Environmentalist Ass all the way to Africa. He then grabbed his company radio and contacted the office to inform them one of the guests wanted to be driven to the Lodge. This is a service which is not available – it was a bluff. The guy asked how long it would take and Steve told him.

"Four hours, and it will be uncomfortable but, so you know, it's twenty minutes in the aircraft".

Steve said there was a visible change of expression on Greenie's face and his whole indignant posture disappeared. He got in the aircraft and didn't say much more.

Lucky Boy

As has been mentioned people have varying comfort levels regarding homosexuality. In 2009 a guy who we shall call John, in another company here banged on my office window and beckoned me outside. I went out to find out what all the fuss was about and he told me he wanted my opinion on something in his office. Once there I found his Facebook page open and he was in some guys Gallery section.

"Tell me if you're seeing what I am seeing".

I glanced at the pictures which amounted to several shots in a swimming pool, several more in different bars and some shots of this guy at a beach. I told John I didn't understand, to me it's just a bunch of pictures.

"But there are no girls anywhere. Look at the pool, every shot involves this guy *frolicking* with another guy."

First, I hadn't heard the word *frolicking* ever, maybe as a line in a movie. Second I thought my time could be better spent.

"Are you kidding, this is what you brought me in here for"?

298

"You don't understand, I went to school with this guy. I have him Friended on Facebook. I never saw it until now".

As I said I am not homosexual and it is unlikely I would be considered convertible material. But I am now staring at this guy and thinking how he is not only wasting his time but more importantly he is wasting mine. I told him I needed to go and could still hear him muttering as I left the office."Went to school with him and never saw it".

My Head hurts

When you travel in an aircraft there are things you need to know. In an airliner the cabin crew normally dispense this information. Charter aircraft being much smaller vessels means the pilot is often the person who informs you about these very important things. Things like: Emergency equipment and exits, seat belts and other such items. General Aviation aircraft can be quite small so certain caution must be taken when moving around them or you may damage yourself very badly. Nowhere is this more prevalent than when a person is getting into a high wing aircraft; an aircraft whose design sees the wing mounted above its fuselage.

It is advisable when moving around the wing you duck down for fear of hitting it. Regrettably people just do not listen and no matter how many times you ask them "please mind your head on the wing" they will walk straight into it. The wearing of any form of hat contributes to these moments when the brim of the hat obscures you seeing the wing – this coupled with an inability to listen to instructions will ensure a collision. So you know, I guarantee you are not going to damage my aircraft and can say from many years of experience your head will come off second best in such a confrontation. The trailing edge of a wing is quite thin and for your head it can be very sharp.

I collected one guy in 2008 who despite me warning him to mind his head, ran into the wing twice in less than thirty seconds. I then suggested he remove his hat after the second impact and he refused. Two days later I collected him from his Lodge to fly him to another camp. He had two rather nasty red lines across his forehead, luckily for him he had not broken the skin. The only reason I could see these was because he had his cap in his hand. He then proceeded to put the hat on and walk straight into the wing for a third time. The even funnier bit to all of this was this idiot actually owned an aircraft with a similar wing design, having told me this on his first trip with me.

I have also had very mature adults, in age anyway, rush toward my aircraft; this will always be because they want a particular seat, and then run straight in to the trailing edge of the wing. The outcome is a lot of blood and a good degree of swearing usually out of embarrassment. I saw one guest knock himself cold and then get stretchered away for a doctor to examine him.

For these little impact moments, this is usually when the guest starts commenting the whole situation is dangerous and why weren't they told – Yes, the:*it's not my fault* approach which is seen so often these days. This is about the time it becomes the pilots fault and complaints are issued against the aviator. To people who think this way I say – Fuck Off - and stop causing us so much paperwork.

These little injuries technically fall under that of an Aviation Incident; they are injuries sustained by a passenger, ground staff or crew member in and around a given aircraft in connection with the aircraft's operation - in this case loading or unloading of passengers. Some Incidents can get a pilot in trouble but these sort are just filed because they meet the legal definition of the Incident portion of aviation law – hence more paperwork. They are also filed to denote trends or areas the industry might want to see an improvement in.

So in this respect and in the spirit of this text I would like to experience an improvement in the intelligence level, hearing and generally see more adult behaviour from my passengers. Stop acting like kids around an aircraft and then blaming other people for your very stupid mistakes.

My old boss who flew here for almost thirty years had long given up on these types of people so when he had excitable passengers racing around his aircraft he would just stand back and await the inevitable impact. Then he would calmly call out in a very English accent "Mind your Head"; it was always funny to watch. If you travel in one of these aircraft just move a little slower and be a little more cautious and you will be fine. To the rest who are hard of hearing – enjoy your headache.

Keep your voice down

A major aircraft for Charter operations in Southern and Central Africa is the Cessna 208B Grand Caravan. It's still the primary workhouse of the Bush, arguably worldwide for these types of operations. For many pilots, progression on to this aircraft is the summation of their goal of work in the Lodge or Tourism side of General Aviation. After flying this aircraft for a while they will move on to still bigger aircraft.

To get to the Caravan you often need to fly a piston engine aircraft for a year or two. A piston engine aircraft can be a bit on the noisy side – yes I am speaking about when you, the passenger or pilot, are sitting inside of them. I have had people say they have actually had their hearing dulled for up to thirty minutes after leaving such an aircraft. Being as noisy as they are pilots get used to shouting in the cockpit a lot when people ask you questions. In comparison the Caravan cockpit is remarkably quiet.

In 2006 there was an unnamed pilot converting on to the Caravan and he was flying with his Training Captain who obviously sat in the co-pilots seat. They were about halfway through their day when they arrived at *an airstrip* to collect two people; who turned out to be a husband and wife. The couple took the bench seat in the second row from the front and the pilots flew two more stops before dropping them off. Later in the day the pilots flew back to Maun.

The following day they were summoned to the office in regards to a very serious complaint which had been received late the previous day. It seems the two pilots while flying this couple had noted the lady was attractive. It seems their views on her body did not stop there. Phrases detailed in the complaint letter included things like: "I could really spank that ass for hours"; "I'll bet she would go all night"; and "look at the size of her tits, it's breast feeding time for me"! To add insult to injury one of the two had intimated the husband couldn't possibly attend to any of her needs as he was "too fucking old" and "wouldn't be able to get it up".

Having been a Manager it is these sort of moments you dread. It seems Conversion guy had not been briefed and Training Captain had completely forgotten just how quiet a Caravan cockpit is. I don't really subscribe to this sort of behaviour but I also know it is *a mentality* which may never disappear. You pilots progressing on to larger aircraft just test drive the cockpit regarding sound – before actually committing to these rather job shortening conversations.

I'll be watching you

I overnighted at Lebala Camp in the Linyanti area of Botswana in 2009 and arrived for pre-dinner drinks and asked for a glass of red wine. I then introduced myself to some of the other guests and enjoyed some polite conversation. One guest who I had not had the displeasure of meeting, you will see why, spotted me across the area we were standing in, stopped speaking; actually he just walked out of the conversation he was having and made a bee-line for me.

"You're the pilot" This was delivered as a statement not a question.
"Yes that's right, Hi" With this I extended my hand; he ignored it.
"I see that you are drinking".

Wow, seemed this dickhead was going to have a state the obvious competition. I knew immediately by his tone and manner where this was going so I played along.
"Well spotted, two points for you".
"I don't want to see you drinking anything else tonight; is that clear"?
Well at least he finally made it to a real question. All of this without shaking my hand, an introduction, a 'how are you', 'can I speak to you about a concern I have', etc. My answer:
"Well I'll be sure you get a seat at dinner where you can't see me *and my wine*, but it's the best I can do".
He didn't give up!

"I'm being very serious"

"Sir, what you fail to realize is, so am I. Am I making myself clear. I am afraid this conversation is finished, Good Evening?"

Then I walked away. The whole thing transpired in full view of all of the other guests and the staff. So you understand, Aviation Law regarding the consumption of alcohol is remarkably strict and all of the companies operate within this legislation. Obviously Charter Operators would be very concerned regarding any departures of the Law by a pilot concerning alcohol – I can tell you I have seen companies fall on pilots from a great height for just phoning to say they can't make it to work; while any actual transgressions will involve a loss of their pilot's license. Please remember when we are not flying this is our free time and as long as we are working within the law and the company's standards which are more harsh than the Law, then we are safe; therefore you are safe.

Just so you know this idiot then went to the Camp Manager and tried to get me cut off from the Bar. It didn't work, and I enjoyed my two glasses of wine for the evening!

Staff food

A good deal of the Management who run the Lodges are great people. Of course they have to balance the needs of the operation with their staff's needs; this is not always easy. The story I am about to tell you required no balancing of needs and was in my view done out of personal spite. Furthermore it represents one individual and in is no way reflective of the Lodge operation.

So its 2008 and I am staying in Shindi Camp run by Ker & Downey Botswana. Shindi is a great camp as are the sister camps of Kanana and Okuti. There are roughly a dozen guests in the Lodge who have just returned from a Game Drive with four more to arrive any moment from their afternoon of fishing. At some Lodges season permitting you may elect to get your guide and go fishing in the Okavango Delta.

The final four have arrived and the Manager appears to enquire how their afternoon was. Wonderful, we caught over a dozen good sized fish, drank some beer, saw the hippos and the Crocodiles; all around a great afternoon out.

The Shindi Lagoon

The Manager asks where the fish were and the guests told them they gave them to the Guides. The Guests didn't want them and were happy to hand them over to the Guides who said they will cook them up for all the back of house staff. The Manager (a woman) went quite ashen and then got very angry, told the Guests very sternly, the staff cannot have them.

"Why not"?

"Because the fish are Ker & Downey property. *You can have them*, but not the staff".

I just sat there with my mouth hanging open. She then immediately turned and marched off toward the Staff Village, presumably to retrieve the fish, and I sat there listening to the guests discussing the whole thing amongst themselves. I can tell you she was discussed in a very unflattering way.

French Fried

English is my mother tongue and regrettably I do not speak any other languages. Being able to speak another language has its distinct advantages, especially if the language is widely used around the planet. Mandarin (Chinese), German, Spanish, and French are such languages.

Out of all of the above mentioned communication methods one of them stands out – French. Why? Well, in my view, the French, generally speaking, can be a bit aloof, a bit snobby when it comes to communicating in their beautiful and very romantic sounding language. Seems if you speak French you better do so perfectly or many French speakers, predominantly the ones from France, will claim ignorance as to what you are trying to say. They also seem to be a country which shuns learning or using the English language. This creates a very real moment known as 'the Language Barrier'.

So in 2007, Steve, has just landed and finished refuelling when the company Porters bring his four clients (two couples) over to the aircraft. Steve greets them and they stare at him and do not respond. Eventually one of the men speaks:"You are.......French" is pushed out in very broken English.

As Steve is about to answer the two women have a rapid exchange which lasted about five or so seconds. Steve listens to the conversation and then responds."I am English". In answer to their question there follows another short exchange in French amongst the group and this over, Steve starts directing them into the aircraft. This process takes about five minutes and all of this time one of the men and both women are speaking amongst themselves.

Back in the old days we would give passengers a *quick* Safety Briefing when they arrived but once they were in the bush we would skip it. These days you get a Safety Briefing every time you get in an aircraft and they are pretty in-depth.

Once everyone is in Steve stands at the door and decides they all need a very lengthy and good old fashioned Safety Briefing. So he starts with the location of the First Aid kit, Emergency exits and their operation, Sick bags, Safety Cards, how long the flight was going to be etc. He said he spoke for almost four minutes before he asked if there were any questions, standing there with a silly smile on his face and staring at each of them in turn. They just stared back at him speechless, not one of them spoke; Steve even said the lady in the back looked away when he made eye contact with her. None of this was because they hadn't understood him, for he had undertaken the entire briefing in flawless French.

When originally asked if he was French, before he could answer (in French) the two women had what could only be described as an off colour conversation. Basically they pre-supposed his nationality – English - and then went on to discuss how he was probably in Africa *to fuck all the blacks he could get his hands on*. I was told this was the polite version of what was said, for not only did Steve speak the language fluently he understood many of the nuances and slang from several areas around the French country, including Paris he said "where these idiots were from".

As soon as Steve heard these comments he answered their question as accurately as he could – He was English. They had never asked if he spoke French, a decision he thought they were regretting now. During the boarding process the two women had continued their unfortunate conversation goading each other with further rather unsocial questions. "I wonder how many black girlfriends he has" to which would come back "what about the coloured babies he probably has everywhere", disease was also mentioned and this got a snort from one of the men, while the other man basically did not involve himself in the whole moment. Steve said he was the one who had originally asked if Steve was French.

As the Safety Briefing over, Steve awaited their questions but obviously under the circumstances no one was speaking. He asked for questions again and they just looked at him. He then got a kind of light bulb moment and continued in French.

"Oh that's right I completely forgot you had questions regarding, now how did you put it - how many blacks I was fucking, the number of coloured babies I have, or maybe I'll just tell you the ones I know about, after all these days it's difficult to keep track if you know what I mean (with this he said he gave them a quick wink). On the disease subject I am going to wait for your next trip as I haven't been tested for a while and will need to see the doctor. Just so you know I am an equal opportunity fucker and I like white women as well."

The man who was effectively not involved in the entire debacle was the only one to speak. 'Monsieur......nous sommesvraimentdésolés'

Something to the effect of 'Sir we are so very sorry'; Steve didn't care he just continued all smiling and jovial; still in French: "Not to worry, let's get you all off to camp so I can get back as I have a date with two ebony sisters tonight and I am feeling lucky, I might get them both."With this he jumped in the aircraft and flew them to camp. The man tried to tip Steve but he refused.

"Use it to get the other three some manners. Although I doubt if you have enough money to finish the job."

He then flew back to Maun and we had a beer together as I rolled around in tears. He got upset with me for laughing as he was still very angry himself, but eventually he saw the funny side. I am sure the Frogs didn't though.

PS. Obviously the above involves 3 and a half idiots (he's a half idiot because he married her) and I do not see it as representative of the French. Having said this all nationalities should try to remember when you are outside your own country people often don't speak your language. Get over it, make an effort, and enjoy the moment rather than complain and make faces. Also maybe watch you say as well just in case they do.

My Friends told me...

Everyone is always going on about 'Dumb Blondes' and I have met some in my time, but it is really not fair to lump them all together, that's just another form of prejudice. Having said this I am fully aware certain Americans have taken a bit of a pasting in this book so in this spirit I am prepared to......., ah fuck it, at the very least you guys deserve the pasting for the portion of the community who endorsed a bigoted, idiot to run for President – good luck with that, haha!

Anyway happily for this story the lady involved is not blonde, but sadly is an American. There are six in her group; the other five are a family, by blood or marriage. She is the brand new girlfriend of one of the sons. I meet our non-blonde friend at dinner on their second night in camp but from what I am told there have already been some fireworks at breakfast. As is some Lodges custom guests eat together and it appears during breakfast Ms. Brunette quite loudly complained about this arrangement to her boyfriend.

"Do we have to eat with *these people* at every meal?"

I can understand this as sometimes I want to be alone as well. The only problem seemed to be she wasn't speaking about the other guests she was talking about her boyfriend's family; who was sitting right there; and could hear her – oh, and her future Father-in-Law was paying for her holiday. Seems she might need some lessons in gratitude as well an understanding of manners.

Fast-forward to dinner and my small interaction. So I have assessed she is in her mid-twenties, is attractive, is currently at University but seems unsure about why she is there, and she is practicing the well-known art of verbal diarrhoea. I am not saying much of anything, nobody is, principally because no one canget a word in. It also seemed her friends held great sway over how she thought or for a more apt description her lack of thinking.

"My friends told me about this video of some Guide somewhere in Africa who was just walking along and two Lions jumped him from either side and bit both his arms off and he was just standing there in front of the camera screaming and screaming and screaming."

Many of us just looked at each other in bewilderment as something this graphic would obviously have made the rounds in our Industry but none of us could recall ever seeing such a video. Clarification was sought before she admitted she had actually never seen the video but 'her friends' had told her about it. She then, without missing a beat, blissfully continued.

"You know my friends are big environmentalists and I have decided, *like*just now, that I am passionate about the environment, and I think I *like* I could easily work in the bush. I *like*think the accommodation, and the food is great. What would be the best organisation to work for as I am really interested?"

Keep in mind this her first time in Africa (yes I asked her), this is the first Lodge she hasever stayed in, and she has been there about 30 hours. During this time she is being pampered as a guest and is seemingly equating this treatment to some perceived idea of a job somewhere in her bush future. This question could not be answered by anyone present so she moved on.

"When I told my friends that *like* I was actually going to Africa, you know *like* on a real Safari. They told me I had *like* a 90% chance of not coming back alive, yeah some animal was going to get me. 90% that's really high."

At this point I realized I didn't need to participate in the conversation as how could I possibly address statistics like this. If the risk factor was really this high I am sure someone, somewhere would have told a few people by now and our business would have dried up. Add to this with only a 10% chance of making it back – she came anyway!

This is about the time I heard her boyfriend's mother speaking with the person next to her.

"Yes, we were very attached to her and it was quite a strain when she passed away."

My immediate thinking was 'Death' was not really what one could call polite dinner time conversation either but it seems I had misunderstood. The life which had passed away was their pet dog. It's regrettable when a pet dies, but they do – THEY DIE – people Pass away, this small differentiation avoids a lot of confusion. Anyway, some people treat their pets differently, I guess.

Unfortunately Ms. Brunette continued conversations like this throughout the evening. In the end there were a few of us who were having a lot of trouble keeping a straight face; it appeared to me, even the boyfriend was starting to question why she was there.

I did think the remainder of the family (including Mom) were quite intelligent and I felt sorry for them that they would need to spend the rest of their holiday with Ms. Brunette and her _foot in mouth_ disease. As they say – choices, we all make them, but they don't always work out!

A BIT OF EVERYTHING

These stories just do not fit in to any of the previous Chapters, so......

Trying to warm up with the company

Some people are careful with money and as people essentially run companies this mind-set often extends in to this area as well. But being careful and being miserly regarding your staff is unfair. Staff have joined your operation and if there is work related problem the company should do its best to address it. Most companies provide uniforms because they want their staff to be readily identifiable and also have some control over their general presentation.

When winter started to come into its own in early May 2009 in Botswana the ground staff for this particular air Charter Company approached the Chief Pilot who we shall call Phil, and enquired about getting some winter clothing – after all they often worked very early in the morning, walked there, and the temperatures were usually in the low single digits.

Phil, being the new Chief Pilot, was a bit surprised they all didn't already have a jacket or jersey of some sort. Apparently these staff had been asking for replacements for their tattered ones for two years and the answer was always 'No'! Phil said he would look into it and later in the morning had a meeting with the *GeneralManager* who could approve the request. Needless to say the GM said 'No' – after all if you are going to go in this direction for two years, why not try for three.

Phil objected to the decision as fundamentally unfair, also pointing out not only did all the pilots have company jackets and jerseys but so did the office staff whose work was inside.
"No, and that's final. Tell them to make their own plan if they want to stay warm."

Yes, I agree, a real humanitarian, someone we can put up there with Gandhi and Mother Teresa. Phil returned to his office a bit dismayed with the whole subject but on the way back he had an idea. He called all the ground staff together and explained the official company position, which was also out of his hands. Obviously no one was really happy about it and there were a few moments where Phil thought the staff might be contemplating a bit of a mutiny. Phil told them to relax he had a solution – he explained his idea and the mutiny moment returned; but he reinforced his idea would solve the problem he just needed a few days to let it work. They were unconvinced but agreed to give it a try.

Two days later the General Manager arrived by aircraft from a Camp she had gone to see and was greeted by one of the ground staff. She immediately made her way to Phil's office, apparently she was more than a little upset.

"Do you know one of *my staff* is wearing a jacket with another company's logo on it?"
"Yes, why?"
"What do you mean - Why? That is a competing company. Tell him he can't wear it!"
"I can't do that. You told them to make a plan for warm clothes. He obviously has a friend or relative that can spare a jacket for him. He can't turn it down if it's free, he needs to stay warm."

From what Phil said the conversation got quite heated with the GM indicating she might fire the individual involved if he doesn't take the jacket off. It was pointed out by Phil pretty much all of the ground staff had a logo on their clothing from other companies. In addition, Phil was pretty sure you couldn't fire someone for solving a problem the company wouldn't address itself.Thankfully, the next day all of the ground staff were issued with a company jersey – all three of them!

Don't be so nosey

Many bigger Charter and Contract operators who work in the more remote regions (Central, West Africa, etc.) get their major maintenance done in South Africa. Some of these companies are involved in long haul freight operations which also originate from there. Maun is an airport which these aircraft can use as a refuelling stop for these flights.

The AntonovAN-26

One day a beautiful Antonov AN26B shows up in Maun heading north. This is a big twin turbo-prop (Turbine engine - propeller driven) aircraft from the Soviet Air Force days. I decided I wanted to have a look in it so I shuffled up to the starboard door where there is a ladder and see a crew member.

"How are you?"

"Gut", is all I get, then he just he stares at me. Obviously not a great conversationalist.

"Can I come in and look around"?

"Captain not here"; his English accompanies a heavy accent.

I just stand there; he looks at me for a while and then says "Okay can come"

Inside I am looking at the cockpit; this is an old school aircraft design, Cold War stuff and there are a lot of dials and gauges, many more than you would find these days. It's fascinating, as I look through the aircraft the Captain climbs the ladder, looks at me, looks at his crewman and there is a short conversation in what I take to be Russian, probably centring on why I am there. Nothing I perceive as angry, and then the Captain says 'Hello' which is about the time I spot the big lump about the size of a compact car in the cargo hold in the back. I can't see what it is because it is covered by a black tarp so I ask:

"So what's the cargo?"

The Captain looks at me then fires a verbal salvo at the crewman, this time he did seem a little upset, before turning back to me:

"You ask too many questions, time you go."

With this he points at the door and I take it as my queue to leave; so I was off. I guess one question is too many in Russia!

Cooking passengers

For the most part the camp staff's behaviour is good when they fly with us. Some of this is down to the individual person, able to take in and understand instructions, and some is down to how Management has educated them regarding the flying portion of their duties – the getting to and from the camp. In most cases it is both; smart people being briefed on what to do. If you think any of these comments remotely prejudicial try to remember all of the foreign idiots you have just been reading about who just do whatever they like regardless of what they have been instructed to do.

There is one unnamed airstrip which has more than one camp located there and when they book a staff run it is always interesting. On this day there were 11 staff to go in and 11 to come out; the going in part is straight forward; coming out is always a challenge. Upon arrival at the airstrip the customary greetings are done between those coming in to camp and those about to leave. This takes a bit of time as this is really the only time one group sees the other; you know hugs, kisses, how's the family. For this roughly 20 -25 minute period nothing gets done so the pilot normally just bides his time.

Once complete the pilot will ask to see tickets (a good indication of authorization to leave the camp) before they load luggage and the staff board the aircraft. On this day the pilot having done the tickets and loaded the people then climbed up to recount the people in his aircraft - always a good practice – don't trust anyone. This was when he encountered his problem; the aircraft was full. Not only was every seat taken, two of the staff were

314

sitting on the floor and three were sitting on the first aid kit; the head count produced seventeen passengers verse the eleven he was meant to take.

The schedule was read aloud concerning the exact names of those booked to be on the aircraft and at its end those names which were not called were to immediately disembark for the return trip to camp; unfortunately nobody moved. The pilot in question was a patient person; he read the names again, coupled with the same instruction, still no movement.

As I have said with this work you need to think outside the box. The pilot then closed up the aircraft, seemingly the staff had won, or thought they had. He finished closing everything and then sat on the aircraft's tire outside in the light summer's breeze. Summer in these parts can be a bit hot, on this particular day the temperature was a mild 39 degrees centigrade. This was outside, unfortunately for the stubborn camp staff it was a little warmer inside the aircraft.

At the nine minute mark one of the staff attempted to open the cargo door indicating it was far too hot inside the aircraft for everyone. The pilot pointed out this was exactly the atmosphere he was attempting to create and it would be much cooler once the engine was running and the air-conditioner was placed in the ON position, which was unlikely to take place until the correct six people vacated the aircraft. The pilot secured the cargo door again and a further eight minutes went by before surrender was indicated and six people vacated the aircraft.

I guess it's true; if you can't stand the heat stay out of the aircraft.

Show some depth

Runways are determined by their magnetic compass direction. So if the runway points due east it is runway 09 (for 090 degrees) the reciprocal of this being runway 27 (+180 degrees). At one airport in Africa we have runway 08/26 and traditionally we use runway 08 due to the prevailing winds.

Final Approach runway 26

When we do use runway 26 we can of course land on the end of the runway but it is a waste of time, so often we request to land deep (or further down the runway) so we don't have to taxi forever to get where we are going. To do this we normally alert the Controller when we arrive on their frequency; something to the effect of Alpha Bravo Kilo is five miles for runway 26, *request to land deep*. During the following series of radio calls there were at least five aircraft on frequency when one playful female Air Traffic Controller asked me:

"How deep do you want to go?"

To be frank I wasn't expecting this challenge, but I felt it would be rude not to accept it.

"As deep as I can possibly get" I countered.

"I'll let you know when you are finished what I think." Return fire.

Hmmm, now I was thinking.........., "Well I don't want to hear any screaming once I'm down."

This seemed to finish the duel; now there was silence, except for one pilot who said, "Really guys"?

When the Controller came back on the radio she was having a little trouble composing herself. But I was cleared: "Deep approved, cleared to land". Never-the-less the last word was not mine as once on the ground I heard her say. "Well I'm satisfied, have a good day". What do you think, does it sound like we're having fun at work?

Vegetarians

In 2008 I dropped a family of four Australians off at a camp called Shindi (Okavango Delta, Botswana). They seemed nice, Father, Mother, and two teenage kids, first time on Safari, really excited. I bid them goodbye and flew back to Maun (25 minutes). On arrival back in the office I was told I needed to do another flight, seems some Australian family at Shindi wasn't happy with the camp or something.

Shindi, Botswana (runway 09) 2007 (the black area was a recent fire)

"That's odd as I just dropped off an Australian family".
"It's the same one" my boss very dryly came back with.

So paperwork done, off I go again arriving at the airstrip and sure enough there are my same four passengers; luggage and all, ready to go.

"Hi guys, was there a problem?"

Was there a problem, yeah, it seemed this was the wrong question to ask, I had hit a nerve and the Father let loose, phrases like 'are you kidding'; 'it's barbaric'; and 'I can't believe people pay to see this' were fired in a rant most of which I couldn't understand. The Guide just stood there his eyes wide as saucers as if he had done something wrong and he was about to get fired. It was about ten minutes before I could get this guy to calm down; the other three were showing signs they had been crying. My view was I wasn't going to fly anyone anywhere until everyone calmed the fuck down.

Now as I have said people come here to see wildlife in its natural habitat, doing things which wildlife does. Apparently during their short drive from the airstrip to the camp (600 meters) they stopped to view an Impala (small Buck) when it popped on to the road in front of them. It was late in rainy season and the grass is a little dense and sat almost a meter high. So while viewing the Impala everyone failed to see the Lion moving in on the small animal at high speed; when the Lion appeared it landed on the Impala clamping on to its neck. It was not a big Impala so the neck sort of became detached from its former owner in the first thirty seconds and in a spray of blood reminiscent of a Freddy Kruger movie. The Aussies had just witnessed their first Kill.

Now to this day I have yet to see a kill, and I have been told it is not for everyone but it is the most primal thing which can happen to you out here – unless of course you get out of the vehicle and try to pet something, which would trump this; but having said this - nature is what it is. Our fourAussies didn't see it this way and were not only disgusted they were angry at pretty much everyone. This was when the Father decided I was also part of the problem and he turned on me.

"You support this barbarity, you fly people out here........." was now being fired in my direction.

Okay I understand, it was an emotional moment, but I also believe many of us are responsible for our actions. The wife and kids aside – Dad had more than likely made the decision to come here therefore Dad should have done his research; regardless of this I said nothing as I started loading the aircraft; he kept going and in a few minutes it progressed to being *entirely* my fault.

Everyone was in the aircraft, even me, and he was getting louder and louder, real children's stuff with a sharp adult edge to the content. I undid my seat belt and got out; then stood in the door; he looked at me. I had an idea.

"So you guys are Vegetarians?"
He stopped yelling and asked me to repeat what I just said; I did.
"No, of course were not Vegetarians. What the hell does that have to do with anything?"
I spoke slowly and quietly, sort of in an instructional manner.

"Look for animals this is their only way of getting meat, that is food – this is their idea of shopping. For us we go to supermarkets, but meat doesn't come from there it comes from Slaughterhouses and Abattoirs. Have you ever been to a Slaughterhouse?"

"No, I haven't so what", He was still angry but wasn't yelling which I thought was progress.
"Take the time, go down there and see the real humane way they treat the animals; the electric shock to kill them before they start cutting them up".
"So what, what does this have to do with anything?"

"Please don't speak to me about the barbarity that I contribute to when you participate in it yourself."

"How"?

"You eat the meat that comes from those places. Now please refrain from screaming as it throws off my flying; its 25 minutes back to Maun, seatbelts on please."

With this we actually never spoke again as they all said nothing; when they arrived back in Maun they just walked away from the aircraft. They stayed there one night and took the next flight back to Australia. But at least they got to see a Kill, lucky bastards!

Almost a Tag Team

I was flying the Cessna Caravan to Kwara Camp one day and looking at my schedule when I noticed a name I had flown before. Let's call the booking name Javier, and at this airstrip I was due to collect one person; but this was my problem as I had remembered flying two people in to camp.

I radioed the office and they confirmed 'only one', I challenged them about the two I had flown in, 'look follow your schedule it is one person'. Okay, okay no need to get snarky. I continued on and landed, as I pulled in to the parking there they were - two people; the issue was I only had room for one person in the aircraft. I dropped all those getting off and then collected a party of six and looked over at these two who were deep in conversation. I went over greeted them and just asked about the number difference. Apparently my schedule was correct only the lady was departing the Camp; I was hugely relieved.

She kissed her man goodbye and went off to board, this was when the guy got hold of me. He was jubilant as he told me she was off to her international flight. Yes, I said not to worry she would make her flight.

"Yes but I have another woman arriving this afternoon."

"Sorry, what?"

"As this one gets on her flight my other girlfriend is getting off."

This guy was rotating his girlfriends through the camp, which I guess says a lot for his organizational skills.

Hitchhiking is dangerous

On one overnight as I was being driven to the airstrip in Savute (the western side of the Chobe National Park); we stopped for the driver to chat to a Local guy waiting by the side of the road. This guy had three large bags with him, clearly he was going somewhere. They were chatting in Setswana (the principal language) about what, I don't know and this went on for three or four minutes. We then drove off so I could go to the airstrip; but all the time I was curious and finally asked what the guy was doing there.

"He's going to town"

"If he's going to the airstrip why didn't we take him?"

"No, I told you he is going to town, not the airstrip."

"So he's not flying, he's driving?"

"Yes."

More thinking from me

"So where's the vehicle that's going to take him?"

"He's waiting for it, it will show up *eventually*."

Okay, makes sense, things in Africa operate on a different level of urgency – commonly referred to as *Africatime*. All of the staff for the camps we fly for travel in and out in an aircraft. I knew some camps accomplished these movements by vehicle sometimes for the mere fact the camp is close to the population centre, driving made financial sense.

Savute is nowhere near any population centre – it is in the middle of nowhere. We drove on a little further and I was still having trouble rationalizing why he would be on the road with all his bags. I finally asked a direct question and was hoping not to hear a – Yes.

"Was he Hitchhiking?"

"Yes"

Damn! I immediately asked which camp operation he was working for and was told (sorry I can't possible mention it to you). Apparently whenever any of these staff need to go to and from the camp it is up to them to arrange it; the camp organizes nothing in the way of transport – ground or air. In essence, you drive yourself to work, or you hitchhike. This seems fair if you work at Costco or somewhere in town; but when you work in a national park with wild animals it seemed a bit much! A week later I was staying in another camp and brought this up with the Botswana Manager who said it was all true as he used to work for the same camp operation and quit on the basis of this and a couple of other things. He didn't feel safe wandering around in the bush trying to *thumb a ride* up to Kasane or down in to Maun with Lion, Elephants and any number of other animals which could kill him. My thoughts went to 'I wonder if everyone makes it to work' – you know staff turnover and all.

Are you bloody kidding?

I was flying two people from Limpopo Valley (south-eastern Botswana) to a Lodge in the Okavango Delta and had stopped in Francistown for fuel. About ninety minutes from our destination we were passing an area called the Makgadikgadi Salt Pans which has a big salt producing factory near-by. At the time I did not know how this process worked and could only surmise a by-product of this is an area producing a huge red stain on the ground roughly five square kilometres in size.

The lady was sitting behind me and too my right tapped me on the shoulder and asked:

"Is that blood?"
I restrained myself of my usual answer to such an idiotic question.
"No, it is a salt processing area, I am guessing it is a by-product of the process"
My response seemed to satisfy her. Five minutes later, tapped again:
"Are you sure"?
"Pretty sure."

But I suggested she could look it up when she got the chance; she seemed satisfied again. Twenty minutes later, tap, tap:

"But it really did look like blood."

I pointed out a lot of things could mimic blood, maybe it was a chemical or paint. Her response:

"Yeah maybe, but why would there be so much paint, that doesn't make any sense"? This was immediately fired back at me with some measure of disbelief. I guess for her a sea of blood does make complete sense; so I gave in:

"Okay it could be blood."

She looked at me: "So where would it have come from"?

For a moment there I felt I was still married, you know the realization you could never remotely come close to a satisfactory outcome to the conversation – this is not a male point of view as I have seen it work both directions with spouses. I immediately tapped my headset as if I had a radio call and turned around. She tried to get my attention two further times but I indicated was much too busy, I still am.

PS: The Red stain is actually Red Algae which feed on salt. The degree of redness determines the salinity of the pond. Ah, the Internet!

Salt processing area between Francistown and the Okavango Delta

Always read your schedule

When you collect people at airstrips you are trained to check the people you get are your passengers. This is done simply by reading your schedule and asking if they are the Smith party by 4 or whatever it says. Then often just as added protection, confirm they are going to the camp listed on your schedule. This eliminates booking mistakes or misunderstandings with guides at a given airstrip.

In 2007 I arrived at Selinda airstrip and shortly after this two other aircraft landed, with yet a fourth aircraft about five minutes from joining us. A guide approached me and indicated he had my 2 clients; he was dragging two suitcases behind him. I told him he was mistaken as I was due to depart empty for Lebala airstrip to pick up some people.

"But these are your clients." He repeated.
"No, they are not. Let me see the aircraft registration you were given."

All Guides are given a slip of paper with the aircraft registration and guest's name on it – this also helps avoid confusion. He withdrew a piece of paper which had the letter AGR. This was not my registration and I pointed this out to him. He replaced the paper in his pocket and without saying a word dragged the suitcases through the mud (rainy season) to another aircraft - AIV - with the clients trolling along behind; then he told the pilot:

"Here are your clients."

The pilot said he was not due to collect anyone here. The Guide then started to move toward the last aircraft AFE, I yelled out to the pilot who was new and warned him. This Guide just would not listen and this can be the problem with some people when they come to the end of their work period. For a pilot it may be the end of a flight; for the average office person it is 5 PM.

When you visit a camp a Guide meets you and he is your Guide throughout your camp stay. When he takes you to the airstrip this is the time he finishes his work and also when he traditionally gets a Tip; so the sooner he deposits you with *the pilot* the sooner this event takes place. Now if it happens to be with the wrong pilot and you end up somewhere else, not your intended destination; how does this affect his tip? It doesn't because you have already given it to him and he has departed – it then becomes the pilots fault for collecting the wrong clients.

It is a rare occurrence these days but a pilot still needs to be on the lookout because in the end they are responsible for who gets in their aircraft – we can't blame a guides regardless of the behaviour of a few!

That's just the tip

From time to time as pilots we receive tips; it's less frequent these days than it was say ten years ago. In 2015 one helicopter pilot was flying along (this requires he use both hands) and he spotted a Leopard, so he hovered down so his Chinese passengers could get a better look. He felt something in his right pocket; he looked down to find a man's hand slowly coming out. A moment later there was another hand and as he looked down he could see a folded US$ note being slid in to his pocket. The more he showed these people the more times he seemed to get felt up. At the end of three days he had received from the 21 people in the group a grand total of US$1,540 in tips. Not bad for a few hours work, almost makes you feel like a Hooker, doesn't it?

Men with guns

Most Charter Pilots work is in remote places where there is not a lot in the way of female company. For this reason a lot of pilots can only put up with these jobs for a year or two before moving on – many of us are a social lot.

Meet Ken (not real) who has been in Maun for eleven months and is about to take his annual leave. He will be jetting out of Maun to Johannesburg and spending one night there before his onward travels. Ken has decided he needs a distraction; you know a short term relationship to relieve stress before he undertakes his long international flight. He does some research on the internet before selecting a young lady to spend the evening with; she is blonde, about 25, green eyes, a pretty young woman. He makes a booking with the Agency; all very professional with a location, date, and approximate time organized.

Two weeks later Ken is in his hotel room in Joberg and calls to reconfirm with the agency; you know the 'I'm here, room 12, whenever she is ready' conversation. About 45 minutes later there is a knock at the door and Ken opens it; there in front of him is a red head with brown eyes, pushing 40 years of age. Ken asks what she wants and she says she is from the Agency can she come in? Ken leans forward and looks left and right down the hotel corridor – unfortunately it appears she is alone.

Once the Redhead is inside Ken asks about the young lady he was expecting; the Redhead spells out that she has been assigned to attend to Ken's needs before indicating 'it is just the luck of the draw darling'. Ken is dissatisfied with this explanation and tells his red headed visitor. The Redhead decides she will try to alleviate his disappointment orally; this finished she asks for R3,000 (about US$300 at the time). Ken feels this constitutes an unacceptable premium for services rendered and quickly vacates the lady from the room. There is a short tirade of abuse from the other side of the closed door before all falls silent and Ken decides the matter is resolved.

About thirty minutes later there is urgent pounding on the door; Ken approaches warily and looks through the spy hole and sees two rather large looking black men on the other side; one of them has a small shotgun. There is panicked moment before Ken decides he needs to run but he forgets his pants (a true Albert Einstein); he is only wearing a pair of tight white underwear, nothing else. There is more pounding but by now he has made it through the room and is out on his balcony. He jumps down the one floor to the grass area near the swimming pool, then he runs through the pool area and into Reception. Here there are three people checking-in but Ken is not concerned with them; he jumps behind the Reception Desk and starts yelling:

"Men with guns, men with guns."

The receptionist is asking what the hell is going on. Ken is panting.

"There are two men, one has a shotgun and they are outside my room – Room 12."

It's South Africa and gun crime is not uncommon, there are procedures for the hotel; so the lady at Reception follows them. Roughly ten minutes later something akin to SWAT (a Police Tactical Team) enters the hotel responding to the lady's distress call. Nobody is found; Ken is interviewed and has *no idea why he was targeted*, maybe because he is a foreigner. Ken asks to be moved to another room, maybe a bigger one, with no additional charges; you know we wouldn't want to have to put something up on Trip Advisor concerning the hotel, would we?

Ken spends the remainder of his evening alone, in his new and more spacious room watching Rugby – I guess Ken still wasn't finished with Hookers!

THANKS FOR READING

All good things must come to an end. Although some of you may not agree with these stories remember they happened which as people say – is Life! There is a second book in the works covering pretty much the same subject for as you can see the material seems to be self-generating, all I need to do is show up for work.

The above photo was a staff member's Mother who I flew to Guma airstrip in July 2016 to see her husband. He appeared from the Bush when we landed, collected his wife and the two wandered off down the airstrip to go home in true rural African style.

A few photos to leave you with

Very rational

I guess you could call this a non-Religious moment (please look at the named people)

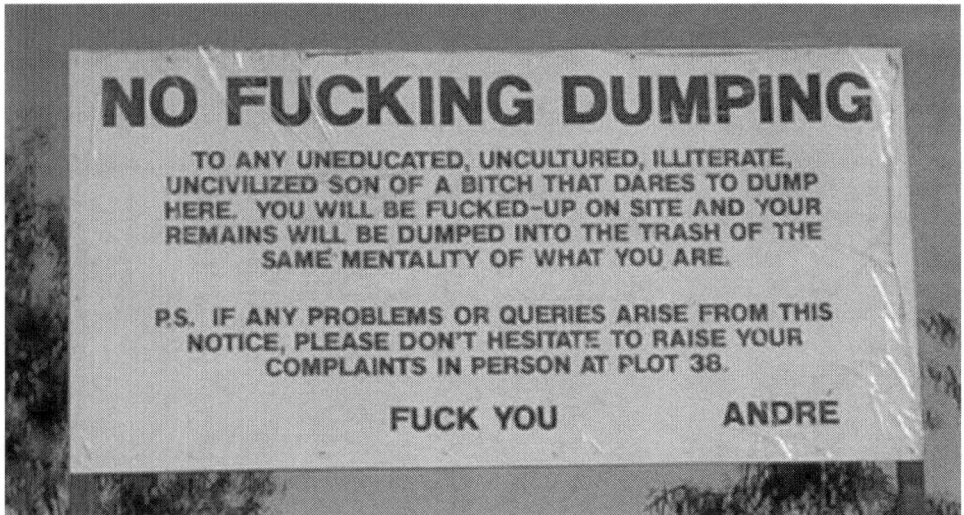

Direct Communication

Aviation a job of infinite patience; whether we are awaiting the next rating, the next job, or just our passengers we are always waiting!

Made in the USA
San Bernardino, CA
27 February 2017